The Knowledge Factory

OBSERVATIONS

A series edited by Howard S. Becker
Northwestern University

THE KNOWLEDGE FACTORY
student power
and academic politics
in America

IRVING LOUIS HOROWITZ
Rutgers — The State University

and

WILLIAM H. FRIEDLAND
University of California, Santa Cruz

ALDINE PUBLISHING COMPANY / *Chicago*

First published 1970 by
Aldine Publishing Company
529 South Wabash Avenue
Chicago, Illinois 60605

Library of Congress Catalog Card Number 77-91728
SBN 202-30151-6
Printed in the United States of America

Contents

To Thorstein Veblen —
a half century later

Acknowledgments

First and foremost we owe a debt to the department of Sociology at Stanford University, and especially to its chairman at the time, Morris Zelditch, Jr., for bringing both of us to Stanford as visiting professors during the 1968-1969 academic year. Obviously, without this fortuitous "happening" this book could not have been written, or certainly not the same way or with the same sort of intellectual cross fertilization.

Second, we must acknowledge the substantial contribution of T. Allen Lambert, whose papers on class and generational aspects of student unrest and whose independent thought and work on this subject make him in substance and effect a co-author of the chapter on "Students as a Social Class." We are also indebted to Michael Rotkin, who worked on the chapter on "Confrontation at Cornell" and provided a working outline of the book's "logic," and Harry Edwards, for his careful inspection of the chapter on "Black Experience and Campus Shock."

The criticisms and suggestions provided by series editor Howard S. Becker and Alexander J. Morin, the publisher, were of such a high order of intelligence and insight that the opportunity of having our book published under such auspices itself constitutes a huge plus for the authors at least.

The additional advantages of having the editorial assistance of Sheila M. Welch and Ruth Hein — both of whom contributed to making the manuscript more rigorous as well as more readable — are last to be acknowledged, but certainly not least in importance.

Irving Louis Horowitz
William H. Friedland

Most of the many books that deal with student unrest at American universities are either parochial reports of particular confrontations or polemics in defense of particular interests and points of view. This book, in contrast, is a serious attempt to deal with the subject objectively, on a large scale and on a comparative basis, within a broad social science framework. It attempts to provide analysis rather than description and to promote understanding rather than to provoke anger or sympathy. It is both an important contribution to social science and to the continuing discussion of the problems and prospects of American higher education and will be of great interest to many people concerned with these subjects.

he Knowledge Factory

THE KNOWLEDGE FACTORY deals briefly at the outset with the changing nature of student culture and then at somewhat greater length with the inadequacy of the many explanations of student behavior that have recently been offered. The heart of the book lies in analyses of the major aspects of contemporary student rebellion: the forms, political structures and strategies of activism, the ideologies that lie behind activism, students as a social class engaged in a class struggle to maintain and extend their rights, the response of college administrations and the professoriate to the students, and the special problems and implications of black activism of campuses. In addition, there is a discussion of the prospects for further development of student activity and a brief epilogue on students in the 1970's.

The book presents a remarkable, entirely original and illuminating perception of the nature of generation as a social class. The authors, deeply committed to writing and research on contemporary themes, were personally involved as participants and observers in the confrontations at Cornell, Stanford, and Washington University. They demonstrate an acute awareness of the intellectual traditions in which the students are embedded (quite unconsciously, for the most part) and provide an extraordinarily perceptive understanding of the students' strategic and tactical styles of life and action.

The book grew out of a series of exchanges and essays by Professors Horowitz and Friedland when both were visiting professors at Stanford University in 1968. Their continuing concern for problems in the sociology of education was increased by the fact that both of them went on to experimental programs in their respective universities.

ofessor of
Comparative
Chairman,
on College,
is author of
lt Against
e Worlds of
of Project
y: The Life
1968), and
ne, 1970). He is
Magazine.

man of the
Professor of
gy at the
z. He is author
es, among them
Underdeveloped
Vuta Kamba:

CHAPTER ONE

Student Power in Retrospect

The years between 1960 and 1970 have been marked by the conjunction of three major political struggles. Two of these rebellions against the status quo—the civil-rights revolution and the anti-Vietnam War movement—have already generated a new atmosphere in the United States. The third, distinctly the most recent product of these years, is the emergence of student rebellion. The civil-rights movement lent impetus to the politization of America's youth even as its demands were increasingly resolved by new civil rights legislation and a tougher administrative line enforcing it. At the same time the war in Vietnam began to expand alarmingly and came under increasingly severe criticism.

This study, while concerned with the interrelationship of these three revolutions, deals with the student revolt on America's university campuses. From the University of California at Berkeley in 1964 to San Francisco State and Cornell University in 1969, the years were marked by a proliferation of activities never before witnessed on American campuses. Not only were students behaving with increasing political awareness, not only were they more frequently critical of government policy and structure, but for the first time students began to question the administrative structures of universities and to make unprecedented demands upon them.

1

In many respects demands for student power that emerged during this four-year period were patterned after the Black Power slogans of Negro militants, whose revolution and its "power to the people" component have made significant contributions to the formation of tactics and orientations within the student-power movement.

Equally significant—though very differently—has been the antiwar movement. The movement has had organizational problems and has lacked the structure of the Black Power movement, but students have been major elements in it, not as directors, but as participants. When bodies have been required for mobilizations, demonstrations, and vigils, students have provided those bodies. The antiwar movement has provided organizational and tactical experience but far fewer models than has the Black Power movement. Because the antiwar movement has not been concerned with the issue of power per se for any groups within society, its essentially negative quality—against the Vietnam war and against current American foreign policy—has precluded its taking on a more coherent shape. The movement nevertheless brought students into greater contact with many elements outside the university community and provided a considerable degree of social and psychological support as students translated the war into a series of issues focused upon the campus.

For it is this issue—the war—that has been largely responsible for the creation of militant student cadres on the university campus. The movement has had its greatest success in those areas where the war and the university have come together and university administrations have become in one way or another tied to the war effort. The relationship has enabled students to generate a substantial amount of militant action on the American campus.

It is to the war that a central thesis of this book is addressed. Unlike others who have examined the student rebellion and have attributed causation to such features as the size of the university, its rate of growth, or the social origins of the student body or of sections of that body, and, unlike other explanations that center on generational conflict or oedipal explanations, we find none of these arguments compelling by themselves. Rather, we regard many—though not all—as necessary but insufficient conditions for the student rebellion. More significantly, we attribute much to the changing culture of the American student—a subject to be examined in detail in this chapter and throughout this volume. A triggering element has been civil-rights and Black Power movements—which have established a *model* for the student rebels and provided a gamut of technologies of rebellion to which student militants have added their own refinements. Had the Black Power movement not developed (with the concomitant exclusion of many of the white students who had found in it an outlet for their demands for social change), it is possible that the student rebellion might not have taken its present form.

Even more important, however, has been the Vietnam War. This has been causal to the formation of the student movement for several key reasons. First, the war created a nexus between the individual student's concern for himself, his future, and his personal self-interest, on the one hand, and his concerns for the condition of society, on the other. Confronted by a war most students consider to be morally evil, this has become, perhaps even more pragmatically, one in which all of America's might and power has been frustrated by an ostensibly third-rate underdeveloped nation. Without getting into ideological questions here of whether the war is a civil war in South Vietnam or one involving North Vietnam, what has proven significant in terms of the American character—one that demands success and is pragmatic about accomplishments—is the fact that a majority of Americans consider the war a sinkhole. The erosion of the moral basis for the war, accompanied by continual threats to students as individuals—that they can be drafted and die in a war to which so many Americans are opposed—has provided the dynamic for the formation of the student rebellion.

Even this condition would probably be inadequate for the student rebellion were it not for the fact that the university—the institution with which students are so involved—has become the articulating mechanism of the larger society (and its war) and the student. Initially this identi-

fication came about because of the university's complicity
with the government with respect to the draft, and later, it
came to encompass the entire relationship of the university,
its research, its staff commitments, and its involvements with
power structures of American society. Beginning with the
university's involvement with the war, the question of the
university's relationship to the larger society and its responsibilities to underprivileged sectors has become of increasing
concern to the students. Thus, what began as a concern with
personal self-interest and the moral state of society has been
broadened to encompass a wider range of phenomena.

This development has not meant that the goals of the
student activists have developed clearly and concisely; indeed, they remain relatively amorphous. An examination of
the various demonstrations since the first Berkeley revolt
indicates that student activists neither constitute a single
coherent whole with a definitive program nor share a consistent ideology. Even the various organizational forms they
have developed reflect this amorphousness. Despite the importance of Students for Democratic Society (SDS) and organizations such as The Resistance, most students are neither
organizationally interested nor organizationally involved. A
study by the Educational Testing Service in 1968 shows, for
example, that only about 2 per cent of the total enrollment of
America's four year college students of 6.7 million
belong to radical left organizations on college campuses. This
estimate, based on the opinions of deans of students at almost
900 colleges and universities, is probably overstated, for most
deans do not appreciate the looseness of memberships or
present structures. Even if the figure were accurate, left organizations on the American campus today are substantially
different in kind from those of the political left of the American campus thirty-five years ago. It is not the size that is
significant, but the ability of a small number of political
activists to establish moderately broad support among large
numbers of students in many elite universities.

Despite the amorphousness of goals within the student
movement, several generalizations can be made about them.
The difficulty when dealing with students is that their de-

mands are very much like those of Samuel Gompers in the original American Federation of Labor. Although to the question they do not give Gompers' crass response — "More" — all students want some kind of involvement in the decision-making processes of the American university. What is much less clear is whether they merely want access to power or are willing to make the sacrifices of time and energy necessary to exercise that power. Students continue to be relatively short-term visitors to the campus; their involvement on the campus may be logically focused on matters other than long-range decision making, for students are still at the university primarily to prepare themselves for future careers away from the university. Nevertheless, because the majority of students want to improve the nature of their existence at the university and the nature of instruction, they are coming increasingly to recognize that they must be involved in the decision-making processes of the university to achieve those goals.

Perhaps the best way to appreciate the changes that have taken place on the American campus is to place them in historical perspective. Thirty-five years ago the campus was also a place for a considerable amount of student political activism, although certainly not on a scale approaching the present situation. Nevertheless, dramatic shifts have taken place in the character of student actions in the late 1960's as compared to that of the mid-1930's. The changing character of the student movement will be examined in detail in the following chapter.

A few qualifications must be made about the nature of the analysis in this book. Though there have been a great many studies of students and student life on the American campus, many of these studies have been discontinuous and not generally available except as truncated publications. The data available for analysis are therefore extremely eclectic. On the one hand, there are fragments of quantitative data, the product of fairly well defined and rigorous studies conducted on individual campuses. On the other hand, the events of the past few years have not generated adequate research (except in the case of Berkeley), with the result that one must base analysis of events upon the plethora of writings from the many campuses in the popular media. In particular, publications aimed at the general public and alumni of universities and colleges, in attempting to explain the nature of the student rebellion, have provided the basis for some of the analysis in this study. More important, of course, has been our personal observation at Cornell University, Stanford University, and Washington University. In these cases the writers observed much of the time, but occasionally became participants in the white heat of confrontation. It has consequently been impossible to remain solely in the role of the observer on many of the issues. Both of us acknowledge our own involvement from time to time; although neither of us has initiated action, we have on occasion provided support for actions already under way. Our observations of three university situations have also been supported by less intimate visits to a great many universities, which have provided us opportunities to talk to students and faculty members about local issues and the local pattern of student rebellion. Finally, of course, we have followed events at a great many universities through the standard news media's examinations of the more dramatic confrontations of the student power rebellion.

In generalizing about a movement as large and as diffuse as the student-power movement, it is necessary to emphasize certain points that have stood out in our minds as a consequence of our direct involvement or the sheer drama of events, such as those at Columbia. Generalizing studies invariably tend to become overly broad and sweeping. A sober assessment of the student-power movement must include acknowledgment that cases may be overstated. We do, however, seek solely to delineate the main trends in an as-yet undefined social movement.

The Bases for Student Rebellion

One difficulty when dealing with the phenomenon of the student revolution in the United States occurs in placing into proper perspective two seemingly contradictory facts. The first is that the absolute numbers of students involved are small; indeed, the numbers—as a percentage of the total numbers of students in the United States or at any strife-torn campus—appear almost infinitesimal. Not only is the number of involved students small, but the numbers of campuses that have been affected, despite their growing number year by year, is also small.

Many, noting this characteristic emphasized the second fact—the insignificance of student rebellions as a social phenomenon. They point instead to the large number of inert students uninvolved to any significant degree, and those who are bystanders, whether sympathetic or hostile to demonstrators. For example, during the Stanford sit-in of April 1967, described below, only several hundred students at best actually participated in the sit-in. When a meeting was called for the entire campus, and both those favorable and those hostile to the sit-in became very highly mobilized, about 2,000 students were involved out of a total registration of over 10,000. In the Columbia actions in 1967, although the number of active demonstrators was greater than several hundred and the number of sympathizers was certainly around several thousand, while several thousand were hostile, the majority of the Columbia student body remained essentially uninvolved.

The dominant inertness, however, should not be allowed to detract from the social significance of student demonstrations. All revolutions are initiated by small numbers of people, and even at the peak of revolutionary action the bulk of the population is *not* involved. Such phenomena as the Russian Revolution mobilize the total energies of an insignificant segment of the population and very substantial energies of many, but the majority of the people are almost invariably not concerned with the revolutionary development. Activism in past periods on campuses has also never involved the bulk of the student body. In this respect the current period in the American university is no different from any other.

High mobilization, in terms of the total amount of a collectivity's or society's resources, is rare. From 1960 to 1965 the

civil-rights movement was greatly helped by a student movement of the North, but probably not more than 5,000 students—or fewer than one out of every hundred—were involved. Similarly, only a small number of southern Negroes
were active in the sit-ins, demonstrations, and marches.
Thus, the popular image of a general uprising involving the
peasants, workers, Negroes, or colonial people as a whole is
almost invariably far from accurate.

> The mass membership of the groups involved is usually only
> marginally involved; that is, its mobilization is rather low and
> limited to some economic support and generally sympathy for the
> movement. Actually, the resources mobilized—those that ener-
> gize such transformations as revolutions, decolonization, and
> wars of independence—often are only a small fraction of the total
> resources available. To put it more succinctly, *major societal
> changes are propelled by small changes in the level of mobiliza-
> tion.*[1]

A second argument about the nature of the student rebellion should perhaps be considered preliminary to serious
consideration of its bases. This is the conspiracy theory, developed by some critics of the student scene in the last few
years. In its crudest form it is voiced by the strident but no
longer influential House Un-American Activities Committee
(HUAC). To the simple-minded anti-Communists who continue to see manifestations of the "Communist conspiracy" at
work in America, the fact that student militants read the
works of Chairman Mao, Fidel Castro, or Che Guevara only
proves that Communists are still subverting American affairs.
A slightly more sophisticated—but still crude—variant of the
argument has been put forward by *Barron's Weekly*, which
has argued that SDS is conspiring to take over not only the
American campus but even the industries of America.

Even some liberals have accepted conspiracy notions, arguing that the Students for a Democratic Society (SDS) met
at the University of Maryland and formulated an overall on-
slaught on the American university. A somewhat more subtle
variant of the conspiracy explanation is held by many who

1. Amitai Etzioni, "Mobilization as a Macro-sociological Conception,"
British Journal of Sociology, 19, No. 3 (September 1968): 243; emphasis in
the original.

are uninformed about the nature of such organizations as SDS[2] but who are aware of the existence of a widespread communications network among campus radicals. The existence of this network and the obvious fact that news passes among various segments of the student militants, often resulting in common orientations toward action, has led some to believe that a generalized conspiracy exists, primarily focused in SDS.

None of these viewpoints can withstand careful examination. One of the common features that characterizes all adherents of a conspiracy theory is their tendency to continue to think in "old left" terms about the nature of student politics. Many of these critics, remembering the patterns of participation followed by the old left, project upon present-day events the type of underground organization characteristic of the old left.

The validity of this criticism is undermined by close study of the student movement. The old left is tolerated during times of crisis and confrontation, but it is otherwise unfavorably regarded by most student activists. Perhaps the best indication of the old left's minimal significance in the present political scene is its inability to recruit any significant following, to grow, or to give programmatic guidance to students, either in times of confrontation or during more quiescent periods.

Advocates of the conspiracy theory located the organizational center of the conspiracy in SDS, which was involved in the overwhelming bulk of the student confrontations and which was one of the more coherent of the organizations functioning on campus. Yet anyone aware of the organizational forms of the old left can only have been struck by the organizational aimlessness of SDS. Not only did it fail to function coherently as a national body; it did not even articulate the orientation of its various localized groupings. Although SDS held national conventions to formulate

2. SDS ceased to exist as a distinctive organization in 1969 following a split at its national convention. It remains present on many campuses only in fragmented form. This fragmentation has not changed the analysis that follows in any significant degree.

general orientations toward the world, and although it possessed national leaders who established some reputations, neither accomplishment made for organizational significance. The convention did not establish policies binding on local chapters. Most of the national leaders of the organization established their reputations as individuals involved in political action rather than as representatives of SDS as an organization. They moved throughout the United States, visiting chapters, spreading the word, encouraging and agitating, but they promulgated no organizational consistencies. Indeed, among SDS members the prevailing orientation toward organization was anarchism. The value of organizational discipline was rejected, and members were substantially hostile to any strict ideological line or set patterns of ideas. The slogan: "Do your own thing" aptly epitomized the SDS member; as a result, group standards were only vaguely defined.

In contrast to organizations whose membership requirements are clearly delineated and in which fairly definitive criteria exist by which "members" can be distinguished from "nonmembers," SDS was characterized by a few local leaders who were open, dedicated, and committed; a fairly substantial number who considered themselves members, and a good many others peripheral to the organization, participating in it for brief periods and only for specific purposes. Local chapters of SDS tolerated this definition of membership because it was characteristic of the anarchic tolerance that national SDS had toward its own local chapters.

This is not to say that SDS had no coherence and represented only a common meeting ground for a broad variety of student radicals. While the latter is true, the membership of SDS was nevertheless characterized by a common ideological orientation toward major social change. Members or adherents might change, but most held somewhat the same point of view. A second major characteristic of SDS was that its members and supporters believed, not in organizational rigidity, but rather in experimental approaches. Chairman Mao's now clichéd exhortation to "let one hundred flowers bloom" characterized the factional approach of SDS militants to their own organization and to the presentation of their point of view to the world. Thus national SDS encouraged each chapter to find its own level of activity and ideological development, and the national leadership itself revealed radically divergent views. Similarly, each local chapter tended to create organizational forms that permitted each member to participate to the degree that he desired. In 1968, for example, SDS established commissions at the local level that addressed various kinds of localized and national problems by permitting each member of SDS to join whichever commission best suited its needs.

At the same time the establishment of commissions emphasized a third orientation of SDS: the search for a mass base. In the early years SDS activits were far less concerned with finding mass support for their points of view, either among students or among other groups. SDS activists felt it to be more necessary to "do their own thing" than to find significant social support. Indeed, in this sense, the Weatherman faction typified majority rather than minority sentiments within the organization. Between 1964 and 1967 SDS began to develop a mass base capable of mobilization on specific issues. SDS began to function as a prerevolutionary mobilizing organization, although without a clearcut ideological position. The commissions established in September 1968 reflected the search for a mass base, since they were intended not only to permit individual members to "do their thing," but to let many approaches develop, some of which might be more capable than others of mobilizing large numbers of university students. It was at this point that the Weathermen began to reassert the local, neo-anarchist approach based on select vanguards rather than mass movements.

Among members of SDS, however, there never was much agreement on specific ideological forms. Though the combination of Maoism and Trotskyism formulated by some of the more ideologically oriented members would make the old left cringe, SDS experienced little difficulty in harmonizing Trotsky's permanent revolution and Mao's cultural revolution. Similarly, SDS activists concerned with broadening their ideological base read with equanimity such diverse figures as Ho Chi-minh on nationalism; Fidel Castro,

General Giap, and Che Guevara on guerilla warfare; and
Régis Debray on revolution, while at the same time ground-
ing themselves, as have radicals since time immemorial, in
Das Kapital. A few even read Herbert Marcuse, the
all-but-forgotten *bête noire* of the news media, whose influence among the German student rebels has been quite
significant, but whom many Americans find unappealing.

Intensive discussion of intellectual theories did not pre-
empt the time of the SDS activists, however. If one matter
can be said to have occupied the bulk of their attention, it
was the discussion of tactics; how to deal with specific problems in specific circumstances absorbed hours of time and
generated polemics whether in the midst of a confrontation
or during the long periods of quiescence between actions.
But even these questions of tactics were different from those
of the old left, whose tactical formulations invariably had to
be related to the fundamental ideological precepts laid down
by the founding fathers, Marx, Engels, and Lenin. For most
militants, tactics were, of course, related to ultimate goals,
but these goals remained general and vague and were rarely
specified concretely.

If there was or is a conspiracy, then, it is of unparalleled
ingenuity, for it is a conspiracy of anarchists without a coherent ideology, with no membership delineation, and with a
violent antipathy to organizational discipline.

The weakness of any conspiracy theory always lies in the
simplistic manner in which events are explained. Instead of
analyzing the social milieux that generate radicals, conspiracy theorists attribute the changes in the social milieu to
a small conspiratorial elite. Fears of conspiracy represent
escape mechanisms for elements supportive of the status quo
in society; they avoid defending the status quo intellectually
against criticism by explaining all problems as generated by a
heinous and subversive group bent on destroying society.

Social-Structural Analyses of the Student Rebellion

The largest, and for the moment the most significant, body
of explanations of the current student rebellion consists of
those that explain developments in terms of some existing
features of American social structure, the structure and organ-

ization of the university, or the social origins of the students—most particularly of the student activists. These explanations represent necessary but not sufficient conditions for understanding current developments. We contend that, while many of these "class" features have created conditions favorable to the development of student radicalism, none can explain the rapid shift in student activism immediately after the Berkeley revolt. Other factors are at work of more decisive significance than the social-structural, for most of these factors have remained relatively constant since the mid-1950's.

Social-structural explanations may be divided into three categories: general explanations about society and change; explanations accounting for differential involvement and participation; and explanations related to mobilization and crystallization of dissatisfaction.

THE CHANGING UNIVERSITY SOCIETY

Size. The influence of size upon social structures has always fascinated social scientists. The rapid growth of the American university to the enormity of Clark Kerr's multiversity has been one argument frequently used to explain the nature of student revolt. Anonymity and alienation have been identified as ostensible products of the sprawling modern university.

A variant of the argument stressing size claims that rapid social change occurred at the university in a forced expansion to accommodate the population pressures generated in the aftermath of the Second World War. This argument holds that size alone is not responsible for alienation and disorientation, but that the rapidity of the rate of growth is the causative factor.

The "Permanent" Student. Still another argument rests upon the observation that students are now remaining longer at the university, because a graduate degree has increasingly become a *sine qua non* for professional advancement. In part, of course, students' decisions to remain in graduate schools reflect their reluctance to cast themselves out of the academic world and to submit themselves to the draft. As long as graduate students remained exempt from the draft (until September 1968), inducements for males to remain in school and to extend their studies as long as possible were extremely persuasive. The burgeoning number of graduate schools and the desperate competition among universities for graduate students encouraged toleration of students' slower progress through the graduate process at a pace unknown in previous times. One consequence, of course, is that students have developed a vested stake in the university as an institution. Unlike their predecessors, who left the university after four years, those who committed a considerable portion of their life to the university were forced to confront the conditions that made life within the university unpleasant. This reasoning has been used to explain the disproportionate number of graduate students in the leadership of many of the demonstrations of the past few years.

The Disorientation and Anomie of University Life

 ... young people, particularly students, join organizations or integrated collectivities because they have just left their families, their home town, or friends and are anxious, disoriented, and lonely. They find in organizational life—particularly in movements that have a sense of commitment, purpose, and high intimacy—a kind of replacement for the collectivity they have just left. This factor, which would apply more to the new than to older students, would also vary by country and university system. It would depend, in part, on what proportion of students live at home or close to home.[3]

The utilization of any of these explanations is limited because most have existed in university life for some years; at least one—that of the disorienting quality of college life—has been in existence ever since universities were founded. The growth in size of universities began immediately after the Second World War, when substantial demands were made upon university facilities by the influx of veterans of the war. Throughout the early 1950's universities continued to grow, reaching a peak in the latter part of the decade, as "war babies" entered the university. By 1964 the adjustments necessitated by growth had already been met in most univer-

---

3. Seymour Martin Lipset, "Students and Politics in Comparative Perspective," *Daedalus*, 97, No. 1 (Winter 1968): 7.

sities, even though the size continued to increase. An examination of admissions rates at many universities shows that neither size nor rate of increase have changed significantly during the period in which most student activism has occurred. Though the rate of growth of public universities has been much higher than that of private institutions, all have grown. Moreover, little distinction exists between the rate of growth and the centers of student activism. Instead, the key distinction seems to be whether the school is in the intellectual elite of American universities or is devoted to serving training or individual mobility functions.

What does appear to be more significant than growth and size is the "ownership" of the university. On the whole this phenomenon is reflected in the fact that student rebellions take place with greater significance in private institutions than in public ones (e.g. Cornell, Columbia, Stanford, rather than the Universities of Iowa or Oklahoma). This is not to say that there have not been centers of student resistance at such public institutions as the University of Wisconsin, the University of Michigan, and San Francisco State College; but even such establishment private schools as Princeton and Harvard have become notable for the intensity of their activism. We shall have occasion at a later stage to consider the type of clientele the university recruits, since it would appear that student activism tends to be concentrated in "mainstream" universities but not at the low quality mass institutions.

The multiplication of graduate programs has also been under way for some time, although there is a little indication that these have been lengthening significantly. The period of graduate study required to obtain a doctoral degree beyond the bachelor's is even now only approximately seven years. As far as the disorientation of college life and the need to find collectivities to join, this has been present in university life since the first universities were created and students left their families to join other students. The problem remains the choice of political action as a collectivity with which to identify *at this time*, and it cannot be explained by the kinds of arguments cited.

EXPLANATIONS ACCOUNTING FOR DIFFERENTIAL IN-
VOLVEMENT AND PARTICIPATION

The bulk of these arguments have been developed by Seymour Martin Lipset in several analyses of student activism.
They are set forth most cogently and directly in the following
emphatic terms.

> The major conclusion to be drawn from a large number of studies
> in the United States and other countries is that *left wing students
> are largely the children of left wing or liberal parents. . . . On the
> whole, those involved in the humanities and softer social sci-
> ences or in the more pure theoretical fields of science, are more
> likely to be on the left than those in the more practical, applied,
> or experimental fields. Such variations, however, would appear
> to be more a product of selective entrance into different dis-
> ciplines than as the effect of the content of the fields on those
> pursuing them as students or practitioners. . . . The left wingers
> come from somewhat more affluent backgrounds than the right-
> ists.*

Lipset also argues that student protest is more likely to be
focused at high-level liberal-arts colleges and "the best state
universities."[4]

A somewhat different point of view is developed by Samuel Lubell in the same issue of *The Public Interest*. Lubell's
article is based on survey data accumulated at thirty-six college campuses in the fall of 1965 and spring of 1966. He finds
five types of students entering the new left. These are: "1)
sizable numbers of draft protesters; 2) career rebels who
reject money-making pursuits and who are often the children
of businessmen; 3) the children of former radicals, 'perhaps
the largest and certainly the most influential single new left
element'; 4) a relatively small number of drug-using beat-
niks; and 5) Christian radicals, also a small number, who
have a religious determination to accomplish via government
what God has failed to do."[5]

The main weakness of the social origins argument is its

4. Seymour Martin Lipset, "The Activists: A Profile," *The Public Interest*,
No. 13 (Fall 1968): 45–46, 47–48.

5. Samuel Lubell, "That 'Generation Gap'," *The Public Interest*, No. 13
(Fall 1968): 52–60.

failure to adduce evidence that the social origins of students are causative of the events of the past few years. There can be little doubt, for example, that children of former radicals are active and significant in the student-power movement; but we would hesitate to designate them a majority of its leadership. It is difficult to conduct empirical research into such movements as that of student power and to sort out the student activists and those who are marginal or peripheral. Our own experience has shown children of former radicals as well as children of businessmen and others become activized during periods of confrontation. The significance of parental radicalism to the leadership remains a datum not yet empirically verified.

Moreover, if social origins are in any way responsible for the upsurge of student activities, the social origins of students must have changed relatively recently or we are now beginning to get concentrations of certain types of students on the university campuses that never existed before. If this is so, we must conclude that the radicals of the 1930's were extremely late producers of children.

EXPLANATIONS CONCERNING MOBILIZATION AND CRYSTALLI-
ZATION OF DISSATISFACTION

Other explanations deal with the kinds of conditions within the university structure that generate dissatisfaction on which student activists can concentrate. A host of dissatisfying conditions has prepared masses of students for mobilization, and when a crystallizing issue develops, student activists can quite easily move students into confrontation with university authorities.

Many conditions in universities do generate tensions, as varied as the indignities of registration or confronting a professor's secretary when seeking a short meeting to ask a question. At many universities the contract dining system, requiring students to eat in university dining facilities, has been a source of continual tension. Two issues around which student gripes have focused for decades are the question of in loco parentis and the curricular requirements of the university.

The doctrine of in loco parentis, which casts the university in the role of a surrogate parent, has long been utilized to regulate the personal conduct of students. Initially a student's personal conduct was believed to be vitally related to his general education; the university not only dispensed a specific body of knowledge but also concerned itself with inculcating correct manners and orientations toward the world. This doctrine justified the intervention of the university in a gamut of personal decisions, including parietal hours, styles of acceptable clothing, and forms and modes of address. The doctrine has also been used to regulate use and possession of automobiles, table manners, and more recently, political behavior.

In the mid-1950's increasing tension focused around the issue of sexual conduct. Students chafed at the restrictions placed upon their attempts to come together with greater freedom. Most campus newspapers reveal that the doctrine of in loco parentis has in the past decade been a major irritant to students, who have increasingly felt that the university has intervened in areas of life that should have been removed from university control. In loco parentis remains an operative principle at many universities, but few students accept its validity today. The stubborn adherence of university authorities to outmoded doctrines created a high degree of disaffection among large segments of the student body.

Curricular requirements are a second major irritant in most American universities. The regulations that guide most students in the selection of their academic programs are quite complex. Two distinct trends are found in all university curricula. On the one hand is concern with students' obtaining a broad and liberal education, a goal that requires students to take courses in a variety of areas. The contrary tendency is concerned with students' emerging from the university with some kind of marketable knowledge that gives them utility as soon as they enter the labor market and therefore consists of narrowing the student's options. The broadening orientation is frequently embodied in "distribution requirements," while narrowing tendencies are exhibited by the "major" and in the prerequisites required for advanced courses. The presence of both tendencies represents the failure of faculties to resolve the conflicting demands of an increasingly technological society. As far as students are concerned, they are confronted with demands that very often seem unreasonable. All too frequently the student body is treated as a single homogeneous mass for which distribution requirements and majors are equally desirable. Some students, anxious to specialize at an early stage, resent being required to take courses that they consider irrelevant to their career and intellectual interests. Others find themselves restricted by the requirements of the major and the prerequisites for advanced courses. Although they might wish to go into other areas, they find that they have no time. The allocation of the distribution requirements and majors and prerequisites is supposedly the result of rational decision making by faculties, but all too frequently their rationale is lost to a great many students. Like the practice of in loco parentis, curricular matters have served as irritants, although action initiated against them has been more infrequent than action in the struggle for sexual freedom.

While these varying explanations point to levels of irritation and feelings of anomie to explain why certain types emerge as leaders of the student rebels, none of them are able to account for the sharp upsurge of activism in the past few years. While there have been changes in size and rate of growth, on the whole social-structural variables have been long in existence; no sharp, dramatic changes can be adduced from the data. The curriculum has always been an irritant, but only in the last few years have students sought to change it to a significant degree. Similarly, in loco parentis regulations have not only existed for decades, but were far more oppressive in the past than in the last decade. Student reaction signifies that the orientation of students toward the curriculum, toward the university itself, has changed. This is the really significant change that has occurred on the university campus. Social-structural features constitute important—

necessary—but not sufficient conditions for the development of student rebellion. The *sufficient* conditions, we believe, are to be found in changes in student culture.

Changes in Student Culture

CHARACTERISTICS OF CHANGE

A "rah! rah!" university spirit is still characteristic of the Saturday afternoon football games carried on national television networks, and the pom-poms still wave at Fall Weekend and Homecoming, but the loss of prestige of athletics at the major universities and the consequent insignificance of the accompanying frivolity have been remarkable.[6] Students continue to participate in athletics, and university budgets for sports affairs are still generous; but the attitude toward athletics has changed substantially in the past decade.

The big man on campus today is no longer the football hero or the managerial type involved in the activities ancillary to athletics. Nor is student government concerned with athletics and its auxiliaries to the degree that it once was. Though the pep rally and the bonfire remain perennial activities at some schools, these activities no longer set the pace or the direction of university evolution.

Fall Weekends and variants of "big bashes" are still events, but the big-band sound which used to fill the campus auditorium has been replaced by semi-hip, semi-protest singers such as Judy Collins and Simon and Garfunkel. Even the managerial arrangements for such affairs have changed. Decorating the auditorium for the Fall Weekend used to absorb the energies of hundreds of students; today a few organizations work behind the scenes to prepare for events that attract as many or more students.

A parallel change has occurred in the status of fraternities

6. While our concerns and loci are different, we share many of the orientations about student culture with Howard S. Becker. See especially Howard S. Becker, Blanche Geer, and Everett C. Hughes, *Making the Grade* (New York: John Wiley, 1968); Howard S. Becker, "Student Culture as an Element in the Process of University Change," in R. J. Ingham, ed., *Institutional Backgrounds of Adult Education* (Boston: Center for the Study of Liberal Education for Adults, Boston University, 1966), pp. 59–80.

and sororities. Originally dedicated to brotherhood and sisterhood, they became bastions of social snobbery and exclusiveness shortly after their birth on the American campus. The Greeks continue to have power on some campuses, but their bases have changed dramatically in recent times. Though brotherhood and ritual exclusiveness was an original feature, housing shortages continued to make the fraternities attractive on many campuses. As was demonstrated at Berkeley years ago, the importance of the fraternities can be significantly undermined by providing adequate student housing, which eliminates competition for places to live. And within student government fraternities no longer occupy a dominant position. And though some fraternity members continue to hold significant offices in student government, they more often do so today as individuals than as representatives of associations. Finally, Greeks have attempted to make themselves more relevant at many universities by becoming socially conscious. In part this new attitude is the product of the Supreme Court decision of 1954, which justified pressures on fraternities to eliminate discriminatory procedures built into their constitutions. After initial resistance, local chapters began the attempt to legitimize themselves against the criticism of independents, faculty, and administrators by seeking out leadership more compatible with the changing times. Leaders emerged who at least understood the rhetoric of the times as fraternities became more academically oriented, more intellectually concerned, and less prone to the typical high-jinks and pledge varnishings that had once characterized them.

A concomitant phenomenon was the tarnishing of the university's image as a place of fun and study—or at least a redefinition of "fun." Fun had always been defined as panty raids, dances, pep rallies, practical jokes; increasingly, fun became involvement in politics, "doing one's thing," and turning on. The hedonism characteristic of many present student activists certainly was not significantly present in the old left, but the nature of fun has changed, and fun is now conceived in very serious terms by most student activists. Even the notion of study has changed for the more serious student militants, for whom study was always one of the crucial aspects of university life. It was also, however, considered a drag. One came to the university to learn, and in order to learn it was necessary to study, but study was not an activity that aroused students. Now, for the more serious students, the changing conception of study has opened the way to consideration of changes in the nature of the curriculum and the types of courses offered. It is not simply that study should be fun—in the sense of enjoyment—but that it should be relevant and that its relevance should automatically resolve the question of involvement and motivation for the student. Study should be fun in that it has some significant meaning for each student and that it motivates him to want to work without being coerced.

All these factors have contributed to the decline of the kind of atmosphere that once prevailed at quality universities and its replacement by a seriousness combined with hedonism. This unusual mixture represents a significant change in students' values and in their orientations toward the university and the world.

THE UNIVERSITY AS A PLACE TO LIVE

Equally significant in changing the values of students has been the dismantling of the view of the university as a tunnel in time through which one passes. Student orientations to university life were once colored by the view that the university was only a transitional and brief phase of each student's existence. If one waited a short time, problems would be left behind. This conception of the university—or indeed of any kind of organization that demands social involvement—helps to make a great many sins bearable. However, many students now plan to enter graduate study and, even though the graduate work may be contemplated in a different institution from undergraduate study, students still recognize that they will be spending many more years at the university than they once did.

But the time dimension alone is probably not all that is involved. The corporate nature of the university involving the energies of students has brought about a change in orientations toward the university. The process of confrontation and activism have helped to contribute to these changes. A major direction has been to prove that the university can function as a "society" within which many elements participate for extended periods of time and which constitutes an environment worthy of manipulating and improving. Faculty members and administrators have always had this orientation, but now students are beginning to appreciate the point and insist on being involved in redefinition of the university environment.

THE DECLINE OF THE OLD MORALITY

Student enthusiasm for sex has probably not increased or diminished in the past decade. However, the way students talk about and treat the subject has changed, as have the kinds of demands they make upon the university, which all too frequently continues to adhere to old canons of morality. We are witnessing not so much a change in sexual values as a change in the values surrounding treatment and communication about sex. It is not that students insist upon flaunting four-letter words—although there are some that do—but rather that they regard mediation of relations between the sexes as none of the business of the university, of society, or indeed of anyone except the parties involved.

Partially this attitude has resulted from the role models provided by the mature and older students of the GI Bill Period. The wholehearted acceptance of the contraceptive pill has also had significant consequences. Whatever the causes, the university has since the mid-1950's been engaged in a constant erosion of the control mechanisms once accepted by students. Year by year battles have been fought over extension of curfew hours, elimination of curfews, loosening of controls on students living off campus, as well as struggles to obtain the rights of visitors of the other sex within dormitories and the accompanying warfare as to whether room doors shall be left open, the width of the aperture, the formal delineation of whether lights must be showing in such rooms, and so forth. The proliferation of regulations specifying formally what each student can do has led to increasing experimentation by students as they seek to erode the boundaries of such definitions. The continual internecine war over these definitions has led to almost permanent sessions of student conduct committees. Student radicals have rarely been involved in these disputes, for they resolved the problems many years ago by avoiding them. Dispute about regulation of personal conduct has mainly been the concern of the unpolitical, and indeed antipolitical, elements of the university.

The struggle over sex has exemplified the vastly changed attitudes of students toward relations to the university on questions of personal conduct. Here student values have been expressed with increasing clarity on campus after campus, as they increasingly insist that the university deal with them solely in an academic capacity. The traditions of segments of the administration and faculty have not permitted a gentle transition, and a great deal of strain has resulted.

THE CHANGING STUDENT WELTANSCHAUUNG

The discussed changes in student culture are difficult to document empirically, but the changing world view of students is even more inaccessible. Students have always felt a certain seriousness toward the world, manifested in high school valedictory addresses since time immemorial, but recent changes in student culture reflect a more serious and more widespread attitude toward the world. Current demands on the campus for relevance are representative of this changed attitude. "Relevance," of course, has different meanings for different students, but one of its prime meanings is that the university and educational processes should be concerned and involved with the major social problems of our time. Students no longer want the university to be an ivory tower, and not simply because the university has become the handmaiden of power centers and has established the precedent for involvement in the external world. It is, rather, that students see major social change taking place in the United States and feel that in one way or another they and the university should be involved with this change.

One indicator of the character of value change as manifested in many conversations of students is their attitude toward suburbia and their own personal occupational roles, which have been projected toward middle management. A decade ago students looked forward to graduation from the university, marriage, the home in the suburb, and 2.2 children; present similar prospects are much less highly regarded by many students. In the past these were goals to be enthusiastic about; the suburb was the symbol of "having made it." Now it has become something to be tolerated. A future which is inexorable but tolerable is hardly one for which many students can work up much enthusiasm. Perhaps the difference lies in the social origins of the student of a decade or so ago and those of the present. Many students in the past were climbing out of the upper working class or the lower middle class into higher echelons; there was enthusiasm for movement. Many of today's students, however, come from the middle-middle classes and upper-middle classes; suburbia represents no significant change in their life-style. The upper echelon of American society remains small in size and comparatively crowded. Not many of today's students will make it there; instead, they will follow their parents into the same stratum and style of life.

Thus, suburbia represents tedium rather than a challenge; few students look forward to repeating with exactitude the lives of their parents. It is interesting to speculate on the causes of disenchantment with suburbia. Not only has extensive literature decried its uniformity and conformity, but much of the literature has been used by university teachers to provide the culture shock necessary to encourage students to think about their society more critically. Students who have read William H. Whyte's *The Organization Man* have found little that is desirable in suburbia, and few of their social science teachers have encouraged enthusiasm. Except for students who come from lower classes and who therefore are upwardly mobile, the bulk of students do not look forward to a return to the familiar suburban dwellings.

Among the more politized militants the rejection of suburbia has been even more complete. Although the bulk of students may be prepared to unenthusiastically accept it as a tolerable environment, the militants have developed more positive aversions for suburbia. These few students are attempting social experiments, in particular those involving communal living. The communes formed by The Resistance in Palo Alto are prototypes of such experiments. In them students seek to develop a new way of life markedly different from suburbia and the kinds of communes occasionally developed by the old left. Unlike the old left communes, for example, a fetish is not made about communal property and contributions to the food supply. In the new communes each contributes as he chooses by placing food in the refrigerator. Once deposited, such food is regarded as common property. If someone feels that he has been contributing too much, he simply stops, and normative pressures begin to operate to make others contribute. Student communes on this order have been springing up slowly, and with the exception of The Resistance communes, they have not had high longevity. Nevertheless, they continue to grow, and it is possible that a significant new social form is emerging. How the social form will be translated as students leave the university and begin to earn their own livings remains to be seen. Ultimately the student radicals may find communal living too demanding and return to suburbia. For the moment, however, that prospect is too hard to contemplate for most student militants.

THE UNDERGROUND COMMUNICATIONS NETWORK

The establishment of a new student subculture has been accompanied by the growth of an informal network of communication by which militants keep abreast of events elsewhere and which serves as a general communication linkage feeding information into local campuses throughout the country. This network is closer to an underground communications system than to a consistent organizational form. But the ability to tap into the latest event elsewhere, to know what is happening and to translate someone else's situation into one's own situation have contributed to the rapid evolution of a new student culture. These new linkages in communications are facilitated, of course, by the peripatetic quality of American academic life as well as by lowered telephone rates. Thus the affluence of American society has facilitated movement of students (and their teachers) physically through space carrying information as well as maintaining rapid communications.

Other significant forms of communication have also developed, particularly in the underground press, that burgeoning network of newspapers that appeals to a student clientele and from which the bulk of middle-class America is excluded. The distance from the Berkeley *Barb* to New York's *Rat* may be great, but the news of what is happening on the campus spreads by way of the national Liberation News Service, and these newspapers circulate widely among the campus militants, so that the behavior on one scene is common knowledge on another scene within a relatively short period of time. Nor is it only the local newspapers that are read. In the hippie bookstores now found on the margins of many universities, New York's *Village Voice* and Palo Alto's *Mid-Peninsula Observer* will often be found side by side along with more esoteric and ephemeral papers emanating from such unlikely places as Chico, California.

All these communication linkages serve to define the special character of the student subculture and to demarcate its normative quality with respect to the bulk of American society. Even if this represents only an ephemeral quality, which will pass with the arrival of new cohorts of freshmen, for the moment the communications network of the student activists has helped to contribute to the formation of a new orientation toward the world.

Causes of Change

Elucidating the reasons for changes in the student culture is a difficult task because it involves the examination of social phenomena that have been changing in the general society for a long period of time as well as dealing with special technological developments, such as the pill, that have contributed to reorientations to the world. There are, in other words, many general events in the society at large as well as specific conditions appropriate to the university itself that have been responsible for creating preconditions for change as well as reorientations in the value systems of college students. The two major events that we see as having accelerated rapid change in the student culture have also had significant impact upon society at large, but they have affected students most dramatically. These are the black revolution and the Vietnam war.

THE BLACK REVOLUTION

The decision of the Supreme Court in 1954, desegregating public school systems in the South, laid the basis for restructuring of the Negro position in American society, although it was not to begin to have effects for several years. One consequence on the American campus took the form of the development of pressures on fraternities and sororities to cease the discriminatory practices that had characterized them in the past. But the most significant aspect was the gradual process by which Negroes themselves became involved in social actions seeking to redefine their position in American society and ultimately to give rise to a new black consciousness.

The first phase of this revolution was concerned with civil rights, and its leaders were heads of organizations whose primary concern was to integrate the Negro as a person more fully into the existing structure. Their actions were led by the leaders of the NAACP and by such individuals as Martin Luther King. While increasingly shifting toward civil disobedience, the prevailing characteristics of the civil rights movements in the late 1950's and early 1960's was an insistence upon the repeal of local laws that serve to discriminate effectively against Negroes — and to bring state statutes into line with national legislation and the Constitution of the United States. Thus, aside from the civil disobedience component in civil-rights activities, they hinged on the belief that they were adhering to higher law already existing in the United States.

The second phase of this revolution began when Stokely Carmichael coined the phrase Black Power. While it is still not clear what Black Power means—whether the development of black pride or the creation of a black territory physically distinct from the rest of the United States—the Black Power movement has shifted away from the former concerns of the civil-rights movement. Not only is there an acceleration of the kinds of tactics initiated by the civil-rights movement, but the appeals are no longer to a higher legal system but rather to a higher morality. The notion of white guilt, for example, or the culpability of all whites in contributing to institutional racism moves far afield from the kinds of appeals that characterized the NAACP and the Southern Christian Leadership Conference (SCLC) of Dr. Martin Luther King.

Whatever its characteristics and its patterns of change, the black revolution has had significant effect on student militants and student masses (although the numbers of students that were involved in the original civil-rights movement were not great). Many students found themselves peripherally engaged in protest actions on local campuses when dramatic demonstrations such as that of Selma, Alabama, took place in the South. A relatively small number of activists forsook the university in the early 1960's to participate in various ways in the civil-rights confrontations that were occurring with Southern law enforcement officials, such as Sheriff Bull Connor. And indeed several of them died in the process, and more were beaten and jailed. But it was perhaps not this direct involvement which was significant, although it should be noted that a fair number of leaders of the student protest movement following 1964 did have personal experiences in the South—went to Mississippi, for example, to work for organizations such as the Student Nonviolent Coordinating Committee (SNCC).

But the involvement of students directly in the movement and particularly in its more militant aspect has been somewhat limited. As the center of intellectual gravity shifted from Roy Wilkins of the NAACP and Martin Luther King of SCLC to Stokely Carmichael of SNCC, the white activists found themselves less acceptable to the blacks despite their continued willingness to involve themselves. As Black Power ideology took hold, the white militants found themselves totally unwelcome in the decision-making process of the black organizations, even though their bodies might be tolerated in specific actions planned by the blacks themselves. By the time of the assassination of Martin Luther King in April 1968, even the less militant of the black organizations were attempting to phase out white involvement, while among the more ideological of the black university students, white involvement in organizational activities had become anathema.

Involvements, therefore, were not materially significant in influencing the attitudes of college students generally and college militants more specifically; rather, the black revolution served as a model of what ought to be and the tactics and strategies to bring it about. As we see it, the black revolution has contributed two major impetuses to the student movement—the first tactical and the second ideological.

Confrontation has emerged as the main technique by which students come to grips with existing power structures and seek to change the university specifically and the larger society more generally. Confrontation is not, in fact, a "new" invention, since it has its roots—as Martin Luther King was quick to emphasize—in the nonviolent approaches to social action of Mahatma Gandhi. Yet confrontation was given a new twist and made distinctly American when it became a device used not by an intellectual or religious leader but spontaneously, when a tired Negro woman, Rosa Parks, refused to trudge to the back of the bus in Montgomery, Alabama.

This example of rejection of the status quo came at a time that was psychologically and socially ripe for crystallizing the broad attitudinal change that had been slowly simmering in the Negro communities of the South. Not only did Martin Luther King seize upon the action to begin a major protest campaign, but it served to bring thousands of Negroes in the South into the streets—and more importantly, into the segregated movies, shops, markets, and other public facilities in a battle to end the legal system of segregation that had existed for so long. Confrontation was a deliberate attempt to challenge the nature of a law by violating it openly and consciously. In hundreds of Southern towns Negro students confronted the law in the segregated soda fountain of the local Woolworth's and from the nigger heaven of the local movie house. The invention and spread of the confrontation technique was not lost on student militants who participated in some of these actions, nor upon the many more students who read about them and followed events sympathetically in campus newspapers. The confrontational model was soon to emerge as the prime technology for dealing with the university in much the same way as Negroes had dealt with the oppressive forces of the law in the South.

What made confrontation so attractive as a technique at the university was the recognition that the bringing in of openly coercive forces such as the police dramatically symbolized the destruction of the normative consensus that had prevailed at the university up to that time. It was not that student militants wanted the police to be brought onto campus, but that they were signaling their total dissatisfaction with the established machinery and with the university's external involvement in such a way that the university would not be able to get on with its normal business unless there was a dramatic change in the normative consensus or unless the forces of coercion were brought onto the campus to obtain compliance with the established system. In the five academic years following the Berkeley events of 1964, hundreds of confrontations on hundreds of university campuses took place as the confrontation technique became widely used by the burgeoning militants.

The confrontation device further illustrated the ideological contribution borrowed from the civil-rights movement in the form of the appeal to a higher morality and a higher law. Students engaged in confrontation activities were on the whole willing to acknowledge the fact that their actions violated established regulations of the university but that other moralities, if not laws, justified their break with the established mechanism of the past. As is always the case in such circumstances, not all students agreed on the nature of the higher law or on their treatment for the violation of the local specific regulation. Some students, for example, adopted the

viewpoint of the traditional conscientious objectors in that
they recognized that they were violating rules and were prepared to accept any punishment forthcoming because they
considered the action of civil disobedience to take preeminence over the rule they were violating. Other students,
however, refused to accept this position and argued that local
rules and regulations had to be changed and that they no
longer recognized the legitimacy of established bodies to
regulate their existence or to pass judgment on them. This
latter position has become more prevalent with the passage
of time, since it implies a demand for active participation in
the decision-making processes on a campus, and not just
withdrawal.

The black revolution, therefore, contributed significantly
to the importation of ideas and tactics into the student movement and may continue to influence its development. Indeed, at least during the academic year 1968–1969, the black
students became the shock troops on campus for the establishment of precedents and the formation of new patterns of
involvement that have potential for affecting the whole nature of the curriculum as well as the distribution of power
within the university.

THE VIETNAM WAR

The Vietnam war has been so devastating in its effect on
American students and has contributed so much to changes
in student culture because the war has brought about a nexus
between the student in his role as a person, concerned with
his own personal situation in the world, and the student in
his role as a moral individual, concerned about the nature of
the world more generally, rather than with himself as a person within the world.

The Vietnam war is one of the few United States armed
conflicts from which a significant portion of its citizenry has
been strongly disaffected. Nor has the generalized apathetic
support that has characterized the bulk of American citizenry
helped to quash the growth of the antiwar movement. Our
only concerns here are to deal with those components that
have been most meaningful to students and therefore most

influential in forming attitudes to the war and to American society. Unlike the case of the Korean war, which manifested certain similarities, the Vietnam war has been marked by the almost total inability of the United States to find indigenous allies within Vietnam who could present a palatable political alternative acceptable to the United States itself. Even though President Syngman Rhee of South Korea was hardly the world's best democrat, he had the capability of maintaining a continuing and viable government throughout the period of the Korean war. In addition, he was able to mobilize some significant indigenous military forces to supplement the massive involvement of the United States and those nations that contributed to the ostensible effort of the United Nations to sustain the South Korean government.

The contrast in South Vietnam has been startling. Not only has it not been possible to maintain any governmental stability for any period of time, but the relationship of whatever government has existed to the countryside has continually been in doubt. Perhaps even more significantly, the inability of the South Vietnamese to maintain any measurable military effort on their own ostensible behalf has served to discourage a great many Americans—who feel qualms about their own existences—from feeling concern for a people apparently unwilling to engage in military activities on their own behalf. The continuing messages about the corrupt nature of Vietnamese society have also discouraged significant support for the war.

In contrast, the continual buildup of American manpower and involvement in the war, without any concomitant tendency for the war to be brought to an end, has been clearly visible. Each American escalation has produced nothing more than the same continuing stalemate that has characterized the war for so long. Even the dubious legitimacy of "victory" has been denied to Americans. The war has become increasingly unpopular in society at large, while among college students the antipathy to it increased concomitantly with America's escalation of that war. Thus opposition to the war has a strong moral, legal, and political connotation for a great many American students.

The war also affects these same students as individuals. As long as they were insulated to a considerable degree from involvement, many were personally indifferent to it. While most were not as crass as some of the students at the University of Washington, who indicated to Senator Robert F. Kennedy their enthusiastic support for the war but their unwillingness to participate in it, a great many students preferred this easy avoidance of action. But the demands of the war have not been sparing of the American student, and only recently has he been called on to contribute to it as have other less privileged social classes in the United States. Thus the erosion of the protected status that characterized American students served to amplify their moral objections to the war. The conjunction of these two events has provided a great deal of psychological dislocation for students, making them especially prone to involvement, either directly or peripherally, in many of the antiwar activities planned by campus militants. But it is particularly the culpability of the university as a participant in one way or another in the American war effort that has served to raise doubts in the minds of a great many of the students who were neither activists nor militants. For them the fact that the university was engaging in dubious enterprises with respect to an immoral war brought many students to observe in thrilled horror and muted sympathies the dramatic confrontations that occurred on so many campuses.

In this respect the war also served to provide a larger than ever cadre of support for student militants. This supportive group consisted of faculty members and religious leaders who were frequently to be found on the periphery of the confrontations providing a leavening influence, while at the same time offering psychological support for students engaged in a series of crises. In this way student power slowly became transformed into demands for political power. These demands could not be ignored by the young, even though they could not be met by the old.

CHAPTER TWO

Stages of Student Development

While the current student uprising does not trace its roots lineally to previous student movements, it is of considerable use to examine the history of student activism on campuses, if only because of the way this history demonstrates discontinuities. In addition, an examination of historical features provides a comparative base against which the present student movement can be examined. The present strong differences in orientation, organization, approaches, ideologies, and tactics become clearer in historical perspective.

The 1930's: Heyday of Student Radicalism

The history of the American campus in the present century—at least into the 1950's—is centered around activities featuring athletics and their many concomitants. The standard rah-rah activities and the pep rallies to generate school spirit and the traditional conflict among the scholastic classes (freshmen, sophomores, juniors, and seniors) constituted the major energy-absorbing devices on the campus. Freshmen not only had to wear beanies, but their inferior status was demarcated by an exercised sophomore class concerned with fulfilling the sociological dictum that the class closest to the bottom feels more insecurity than any other class. Student

35

government through this period and into the 1950's was largely concerned with mediating student interests in athletics and interclass conflict. During this period membership in the Greek organizations—fraternities and sororities—held great significance for undergraduates. The "big dance" with the major name band was a main event of the academic calendar. The pep rally, the jock strap, and the dance were major symbols for most American universities.

National politics during this period had relatively little significance on campus. The campus was considered a place for fun and study, rather than a place in which one prepared for political participation. Indeed, even during the 1930's political participation was not highly regarded. Politics was considered to be a somewhat nasty activity, engaged in by ethnic minorities and others, whose sticky fingers accumulated lots of green dollar bills. But for the university student the notion of play was a well-developed one. It was considered normatively right that students should indulge themselves, that they should be involved in many social activities as well as engaging in studies.

This does not mean that a handful, mainly the campus radicals, were not increasingly politically active in the 1930's. Student radicalism considerably predates the 1930's. The Intercollegiate Socialist Society—founded by Upton Sinclair, Jack London, and Harry Laidler—was organized at the turn of the century; but student radicalism did not become a significant force on the American campus until the 1930's. A general radicalization was taking place in American society during the early Roosevelt years. While its prime manifestation consisted initially of formless gropings for industrial ers' state. The shape of the new left emerged as a plethora of cies. The rise of Hitler in Germany, for example, encouraged the already isolationist orientations in the United States to take the form of a burgeoning antiwar movement centered on the Oxford pledge, taken by thousands of undergraduates who vowed that they would not participate in any war. The growth of the major political sectarian groupings off campus was accompanied by their spread to the campus. The Communist Party, the Trotskyites, the Socialists, and various other political sects were present on campus through their participation and sometimes domination of such campus student organizations as the American Student Union.

If the major syndrome of the traditional Big Men on Campus was symbolized by the pep rally, the jock, and the prom, then that of the campus radicals was symbolized by the antiwar movement and the struggles to free Tom Mooney and the Scottsboro Boys. These efforts established the prime characteristic of student radicalism until the mid-1960's: the use of the campus as a site for organization, while energies were directed off campus to change the total character of society; thus, on-campus organization served off-campus action. Student radicals could hardly be bothered by the insignificant issues that boiled up on campus from time to time. Almost invariably they were concerned with the fundamental reconstitution of society along socialist lines and focused, not upon the campus and its grievances as a site for action, but on the manifold crimes of the capitalist system in persecuting trade unionists such as Tom Mooney or in preventing the spread of industrial unionism.

The student left was preoccupied—as were the political sects of that time (and as they continue to be to this day) —with demands for ideological clarity. It was much more important to have a correct political orientation toward the world than to be involved with specific issues having only local significance. Because of their beliefs about the more significant need to change society itself, very few in the student left could be seduced into a consideration of changing the university.

As isolationist feelings spread with the rise of Hitler, and as Americans became increasingly fearful of involvement in a second European war, antiwar sentiments increasingly preoccupied the student left. Much of the left was paralyzed by demands for continual shifting of ideological position by virtue of the peculiar relationship of the American Communist Party to the Soviet Union. Until 1935, for example, antiwar activities held preeminence among the Communists and were reflected in the actions of student Communists on campuses. With the adoption of the Popular Front line in

1936, antiwar orientations were played down in favor of a "collective security" approach. With the signing of the Stalin-Hitler Pact in 1939, the campus Communists were able to unfold a very strong antiwar program that fitted in with the continual fear of a great many Americans about a second European involvement. "The Yanks Are Not Coming" became the slogan of many of the students of the left until Operation Barbarossa brought the Nazis into Soviet Russia and the Communists enthusiastically out in favor of the war effort. The continual self-contradiction of the Communist Party throughout this period undermined a large portion of the student left, since Communists were by far the most significant group on the university campus.

Whether involved with the Communists or other leftist groupings, however, the campus radicals of this period were oriented toward the outside world, dealing with issues of the larger society and of world politics rather than with events on the university campus. The basic legitimacy and authority of the university administrations and faculties remained unchallenged. The right of the university to act in loco parentis with respect to its students, to control their living and sleeping habits as well as their educational development, was unquestioned.

Occasionally an issue might arise about bad food or the discharge of a popular teacher and give rise to a flurry of localized activity. In none of these cases did students question the basic right of administrators and faculty to make the decisions. If students objected to bad food, they wanted the faculty and administration to provide them with better food; it was not that they wanted for themselves involvement in any of the issues concerned with provision of food. On-campus concerns during this period were reflections of collective behavior, in the sense that they developed spontaneously rather than manifesting a high level of organization, planning, or coordination. And while the left had a national basis and could have integrated activities nationally among the various campuses, most university issues remained localized. If the left was involved, it was more by accident than by design.

This is not to say that there was not a great deal of student activity on campus. The American Student Union developed a sizable membership, and thousands of students organized to take the Oxford pledge or to demonstrate against war. Not only was most of this activity outwardly directed, but when students began to come to grips with the concrete problems of social change, this took the form of a gradual drain of some student leaders into the nascent Committee for Industrial Organization (CIO). While not drawing substantially from the student left initially, as the CIO grew in significance, many student leftists found their way into staff positions in the new organizations that began to make up the CIO.

As the 1930's drew to a close and the war approached, leftist activities began to decline, coming to a complete halt with the beginning of the war.

The War Period (1939 to 1945)

Student anti-war struggles exhibited a curious pattern between 1939 and 1941. It was a period that saw the actual commencement of conflict between the "Allied Powers" and the "Axis Powers," and also the all-important signing of a Treaty of Non-Aggression between the Soviet Union and Nazi Germany. The effects of these two events on the American student movement were both electrifying and polarizing. "Liberal" student factions urged immediate all-out support for the cause of the Allies—England, France, and the Lowlands—in defense of democracy. "Radical" communist elements, echoing the urgings of their afflicted elders, found themselves accepting the position of the neo-Nazi America Firsters, with whom they had been in mortal combat in the years of the Spanish Civil War (1936–1939), and this meant in operational terms a policy of hands-off European struggles, and a frustration of imperialist designs by tacit support of the Soviet tactics. "Radical" Trotskyist groups, which were quite powerful on select campuses during this period, maintained a constant position that World War Two, like its predecessor, World War One, was a continuation of imperialism by military means, and made more dangerous by the enlargement of

the struggle for world domination to include the Soviet
Union. In short, the period between September 1939 and
June 1941 (and perhaps December 1941 in some instances)
was one of struggle among student groups, rather than between students and other sectors of political society.

The invasion of the Soviet Union by Hitler's legions
brought about a rapid change in the political line of the
largest single group within the student left. Literally overnight the imperialist war was converted into a people's war.
From "The Yanks Are Not Coming" to the demand for American involvement in the major events transpiring in Europe
seemed consistent to the Communists and their student representatives. Much of the remainder of the campus, however,
until December 1941, when Pearl Harbor was bombed, remained antipathetic to the war. With the formal involvement
of the United States, the left found itself removed from the
campus and entering the military forces along with the rest of
America's youth. To the extent that it maintained a political
line, the Communist Left became increasingly strident in
favor of a "second front."

Throughout the war period campus activities focused upon
the training of women and the maintenance of many
armed-forces educational programs. But the student soldiers
present in ASTP and V-12 programs were hardly concerned
with campus political action—or indeed, with any kind of
politics. The war period was one in which the campus remained quiet.

The "GI Bill" Years (1945 to 1950)

With the end of the war the campus scene came to life again,
but very differently from the 1930's. The war's end and the
passage of the GI Bill initiated an unparalleled growth of the
student body and qualitative change in its characteristics.
GI's, taking advantage of the unprecedented opportunity to
obtain an education at cut rates, flooded into the university in
large numbers. These students set the tone of the American
campus for the next few years. Far more mature than students had ever been, older both in years and through their

involvements in the military enterprise, these students brought strong career orientations and a new kind of seriousness toward national politics and student government. Because many of them felt the need to catch up for the years lost and because many were entering the university who in the past might neither have been able to afford nor been interested in higher education, the GI Bill cohorts introduced a level of dedication to study and work that had hitherto been unknown to most American campuses.

Because of their age, the GI's also set a new tone for campus activities. The traditional wearing of beanies hardly had significance for students who were older than most of their senior classmates. Much of the interclass rivalry that had characterized the campus during the 1930's began to fall by the wayside. Along with this change came a decline in the sophomoric activities that accompanied university athletics. Though GI Bill students were interested in athletics, they recognized that the *mana* involved in a pep rally was of relatively little importance compared to the long months of training required to field a team, as they had learned to appreciate through their experiences with the military. In addition, many of the GI Bill students were older and were beginning to get married at a stage in their college careers that was rare in the past. For them the degree of control which the university exercised over personal conduct of students in the past was relatively meaningless. The doctrine of in loco parentis could hardly be invoked by university administrators against students who had killed other men and were familiar with the brothels of London and Naples; or, at a more obvious level, married students who have to live off campus.

Immediately after the war elements of the left also returned to the campus, but they found little hearing. The student veterans were little concerned with ideological clarity or with the need to reconstruct a brave new world. Most of them had just engaged in a major war to attain such ends, and they were satisfied merely to have survived the war; their concern was with finding a place for themselves as individuals within the existing society. The left, therefore, was of minuscule importance, particularly compared to the 1930's.

Nor were the more mature students concerned with questioning the legitimacy of the faculty and administration. The use of higher education to acquire social mobility was sufficiently new for those entering on the GI Bill that they were more concerned with obtaining the wisdom of their elders to further their careers than in questioning whether their elders had such wisdom.

The Silent Generation: The Cold War and the First McCarthy

The students of the GI Bill presaged the generation that was to follow in their general lack of interest in political questions. But the succeeding generation was disenchanted with politics for other reasons. As the cold war took hold and the United States confronted the Soviet Union in a series of conflicts in Europe and Asia, the translation of these international events into a national concern with internal subversion began to have effects upon the left generally and upon student activists in particular. As Congressman Nixon began to establish his reputation by exposing Alger Hiss, and as Senator Joseph McCarthy developed significant power, the consequences of political involvement in leftist activities came home to most of the students on the American campus.

In many respects the students of the GI Bill served as role models for the next generation of students that entered the university in the early 1950's. Not only did they continue to display strong career orientations, but the dangers of political involvements — indeed, any kind of political involvement — became increasingly manifest. If it was possible for liberal Democrats to be tarred with the brush of Communism, then it hardly made sense for most students to become involved in national political issues, since one could never be certain where guilt might fall some time in the future.

Nor were they concerned with the symbols that had characterized the 1930's for most students: the pep rally, the jock strap, and the big dance. Facing the potential catastrophe of a nuclear war, students felt the world to be too serious and the times too dangerous for frivolous activities. What they aimed at, therefore, was study at the feet of wise men and the maintenance of a discreet silence, breaking the silence only as the national witch hunters impinged on the campus in their search for internal subversion. Aside from defenses of the academic freedom of some college professors, however, campus radicalism withered almost entirely except for a miniscule fringe of those totally politically alienated from the system. Even within this group — sizably enhanced by infiltration from agencies such as the FBI — it was hard to develop any significant political activity.

This period seems to represent a working out of Fruedian notions. As student outlets became increasingly blocked at the political level, a shift toward sexual expression developed. Perhaps alteration reflected the normative changes that resulted from the presence of the GI Bill veterans, whose personal conduct could hardly have been supervised as closely as that of normal undergraduates. Whatever the cause, the middle of the decade saw the development of localized struggles against "in loco parentis." The issues of personal conduct involving sex were to cause increasingly manifest protest; while never taking political form, they laid the basis for the challenge to the entire doctrine of surrogate parenthood that the university had accepted for itself in the past.

In Loco Parentis and Sex: The Struggle Over Personal Conduct (from 1955)

It is possible to attribute the change in student orientation toward sex and personal conduct to the role models provided by the GI veterans. It is also possible to explain the changing normative expectations with respect to sex through the technological developments of the early 1960's. The development of the contraceptive pill facilitated a whole new range of sexual contact between male and female students without the worry about consequences so often a feature of such relationships in the past. Whatever the reasons, the

period after the mid-1950's became one in which university administrations had to come to grips with the dissipation
of their controlling doctrine of *in loco parentis.* As the
rah-rah atmosphere of the university declined, student government found thrust upon it a new set of demands originating in large part from the attempts of university administrations to control levels of intimacy that were essentially
uncontrollable. Thus, while beanies were being abolished,
while the traditional battles between freshmen and sophomores were being eliminated, and as the more noisome
initiations into fraternity life were coming under control,
student government found itself resuscitated and thrust into
the center of campus events. The new tendency of student
government to delegate responsibility for personal conduct of
students to various subsidiary bodies began to increase the
significance of the Big Man on Campus.

National party politics began to develop during this period. The first Stevenson campaign of 1952 had attracted many
intellectuals and some students, and this was to be repeated
to some degree during the campaign of 1956. The campaign
of John Fitzgerald Kennedy for president in 1960, however,
was probably the first national political campaign to mobilize
substantial numbers of students and to bring them into the
arena of national politics. Not only did Kennedy present an
attractive face to youth, but he also called specifically to
involve them in the major political issues of the time. Kennedy took the civic involvement of all people in affairs of state
very much for granted, and he was able to convey this notion
to students in a new way. Even more significantly, Kennedy
was able to involve students concretely and tangibly. He not
only portrayed political involvement as a civic necessity but
made it possible for students to engage in concrete political
actions dealing with the issues of the times. The Peace Corps
was the concrete embodiment of the Kennedy idealism. And,
while it had little meaning for most student radicals, it served
genuinely to involve students in political activities and problems.

In the latter part of the 1950's the student left began to
regain its voice. As the silent generation disappeared into the

voids of suburbia, it was replaced by a new group of students primarily interested in student conduct but increasingly involved in national and world politics; a student political left began to reemerge. It was a new left, however, although it initially reflected many of the concerns of the old left. Many of its members continued to struggle over such traditional sectarian questions as the nature of the Soviet Union and whether or not the Maoist revolution in China was legitimate. With the passage of time, however, these leftist elements lost interest in contemplating such issues as whether the Soviet Union was a workers' state or a degenerated workers' state. The shape of the new left emerged as a plethora of student journals appeared on various campuses. The Students for a Democratic Society was resuscitated in 1961 from the ashes of its predecessor, the Student League for Industrial Democracy, as the Port Huron statement shed the concerns of the past for the challenge of the Kennedy years. If anything, Kennedy challenged the student radicals, although the nature of his challenge did not become significant until after he was elected to office. Kennedy presented specific challenges to the youth of the country — most particularly its collegiate segment — particularly in the kinds of involvements that his administration had with the burgeoning civil-rights movement.

The left during this period was, as it is today, organizationally amorphous. Rejecting bolshevik forms of organization, the new leftists were attracted to a combination of Marxist ideology and anarchist organizational forms. But in every respect student radicalism continued to reflect the basic patterns of student radicalism of the 1930's: on-campus organization for off-campus action and goals. While the student left was less clearly concerned with a fundamental reorganization of society than in the past, off-campus issues still dominated. As Negroes in the South began semantically to stop being "niggers" and "colored" and the civil-rights revolution took hold, student leftists saw opportunities for significant political involvements. On campus this meant a struggle against discrimination by fraternities and sororities, and more generally in living units. Student radicals concerned with on-campus issues nevertheless did not often find themselves in substantial opposition to university administrations. While the administrators normally took a conservative point of view toward the pressures to be brought on fraternities or concerning the speed with which fraternities should be desegregated, the moral position of the antidiscrimination forces became broadly accepted in the university community. Throughout this period student radicals were therefore concerned primarily with organizing on campus for energies to be directed externally, and they found little cause to confront their own administrations.

Nor were the more conservative elements oriented toward struggles with the university administrations or faculties. While the conservative elements ensconced in the fraternities were generally hostile to desegregating their membership, they were congenitally unable to organize protests against the university administrations that brought pressures on them to change.

Throughout this period, then, a growing intensification of student activism aimed primarily at issues of personal conduct was coupled with an increasing political involvement and the spread of new left political activism on the campus.

Berkeley: The Watershed (1964)

The events at Berkeley joined political, personal, and off-campus issues and focused them upon the campus itself. Berkeley and the experiences it generated have had vast consequences for the formation of the student-power movement as a social phenomenon.

Berkeley is the watershed because the experiences gained there spread throughout the United States. In this respect Berkeley is not typical of the American campus but is far in the vanguard of events. The experiences of Berkeley galvanized campus radicals throughout the United States and generated a significant following of sympathetic students as well as faculty members.

The events at Berkeley began in the tradition established by the student left in the 1930's. As the war in Vietnam

escalated, the West Coast served as a staging area for shipments of military personnel. Protests against the war became
increasingly directed at these military shipments. The Vietnam war, therefore, became the generating focus for the antiwar forces on the West Coast and particularly for the Berkeley students. As the student left had always done, the
Berkeley students organized on campus for actions directed
off the campus. In the case of Berkeley, however, the escalation of the war was responded to by the antiwar forces' own
escalation of tactics, which made the group more obnoxious
than ever to the pillars of society. Pressures emanating from
the general society—and more particularly from former Senator Knowland's *Oakland Tribune*—ultimately gave rise to the
Berkeley rebellion of 1964, in which the university began in
effect to function as a preventer of off-campus action. As long
as the student leftists were permitted to organize on campus,
there were no major conflicts with the university administration. Prodded by the *Oakland Tribune*, however, a conflict
developed over the right to use a piece of university-owned
territory that had traditionally been utilized by students to
express many points of view. As the students used this territory and the university itself to organize for civil disobedience campaigns off campus, the university administration responded to external pressure and began the prohibition movement. This action turned the student leftists in-
ward and for the first time directed them against the university administration rather than against the elements in society
at large.

A number of other issues brought almost unparalleled support to the student rebels. One, of course, was the continuing
unpopularity of the war and the hostility developing in
American society and among American students toward those
responsible for it. Although students were protected from the
draft, the continued escalation in demands for manpower
made the war more and more real to many of them.

Beyond the war, however, were several issues more
directly responsible for adding large numbers of sympathizers to the student activists. For one thing, the students'
right to the Sather Gate strip had been normatively well

established, and they were aware that the university was responding to pressures from the external society and attempting to curtail the expression of dissident views. What probably galvanized the students even more was the presence of police on the university campus. While the American campus has never been a sanctuary to which its students could flee and obtain safety from the police, as it has been in Latin America, the university does operate largely within a normative consensus and without the presence of instruments of coercion on the campus. If the Free Speech Movement served as a mobilizing device that created a sympathetic political outlook toward the anti-Vietnam war campus radicals, the physical presence of policemen on campus became the crystallizing event. From that point on, the normative consensus at the Berkeley campus was almost totally destroyed.

The Berkeley experience represented the first coherent student challenge to the entire authority system of the university. The right of university administrators as well as of the legal entities who "owned" the university—in this case the Board of Regents—were questioned. Students asked by what right decisions in which they had little or no part could be made affecting their lives. Such questions focused initially upon the use of a strip of territory, but increasingly they were asked about the character of the university as a corporate institution in society, and they destroyed the normative consensus that sustains the university as an institution. From this breakdown developed not only attacks upon university officials in their official administrative roles, but as adherents and proponents of ideologies sustaining the status quo. President Clark Kerr's Godkin lectures, *The Uses of the University*, were attacked by student activists who decried the university's failure to be an independent institution searching for truth and its submission to the centers of power and privilege in society.

When the rights of boards of regents or administrators to rule the university are brought into question, many other questions begin to be asked. It is this that characterized revolutionary situations, and revolutionary situations are rarely pleasant. The Berkeley situation was most unpleasant for its faculty, which found itself polarized between those who recognized the legitimacy of the grievances of the students and were willing to accept their tactics and those who, even while acknowledging the grievances, were repelled by the breakdown in established mechanisms for ostensibly resolving such grievances. The "third force" position soon evaporated under this dual barrage. The polarization of the Berkeley faculty had most peculiar consequences. Old radicals who had a decade earlier looked forward to the fundamental reconstruction of society found themselves repelled by callow youths seeking to revise the university system and threatening its very viability in the process.

Nor were relations between the university as a corporate group and the external world improved as a result of the rebellion. Despite calling in the police, the university administration could not be draconian enough. Unaware of the university's need for a noncoercive atmosphere in which to function, the local newspapers and the general polity were appalled by the Berkeley rebels. Nor was the situation aided by the development of the "foul speech" movement after the main political success of the "free speech" movement had transpired. The parading of a student onto campus carrying a sign simply reading "Fuck," while merely amusing to most students, could only be regarded with horror by the general community.

The major contribution of the Berkeley events was the introduction of the confrontation technique of the civil-rights movement as the primary vehicle for student activism. While the president of City College in New York had, in the 1930's, lashed out at premature anti-fascist protesters against ROTC training, the use of confrontation as a strike mechanism was new on the campus. Berkeley students as well as students throughout the United States learned that they had enormous powers as long as they focused their attention onto campus issues. At Berkeley, for example, while substantial numbers were involved in the initial sit-in at Sproul Hall on September 30, 1964, the following day saw the incredible mobilization of thousands of students when Jack Weinberg, a former student, was arrested and moved into a police car in the area. The police car was promptly surrounded by 100 students; within minutes the crowd grew to about 300 demonstrators. About forty-five minutes after the arrest several thousand students were crowding around the police car and preventing its removal. The lesson was simple. Students were capable on their own turf of confronting the police, the university administration, and the general society. It was no longer adequate to point to various mechanisms that existed ostensibly to redress grievances. Students were confronting the entire university and elements of society (e.g. the police) and refusing to accept the system as defined.

While America watched in fascinated horror, the student left on other campuses studied the Berkeley case with intensity. The immediate actions on other campuses were attempts to support the Berkeley rebels, but as the Berkeley events lost topicality, longer-range issues — such as the size of the university, the relationship of students to teachers, the nature of instruction, the character of the curriculum, and the right of the university to regulate personal conduct — began to emerge. Berkeley mobilized students in the United States, and the post-1964 period reflected in other universities the events as they had taken place in Berkeley.

The Shaping of Student Power: The Post-1964 Events

Berkeley proved to be the model for other campus protest movements, but it also revealed special characteristics that made it uniquely successful as it presaged events on other campuses. Berkeley was prepared for the Sproul Hall events by the lengthy politicalization of the antiwar agitation on the Berkeley campus. Many other campuses had not experienced this lengthy agitational phase. To a considerable degree this phase was introduced to other campuses by the teach-in movement in 1965.

TEACH-INS

After an inauspicious beginning at the University of Michigan, the teach-in soon accomplished two purposes. It became the first mass movement of the American campus since the 1930's, attracting many students and faculty members. Secondly, it communicated the nature of the war to large numbers of students who had hitherto been indifferent to or only uneasy about the war. The central mission of the teach-in—the spread of information through lengthy dialogue—accorded perfectly with the traditional role of the university as an educational institution but marked an important shift of educational concern to the burning issue of the day.

The teach-in phenomenon resulted from opposition to shipping increasing numbers of ground soldiers to Vietnam and to making increased commitments to the expenditure of funds and war material upon that country. Some of the more radical elements within faculties at some of the better universities explored the possibility of calling a one-day "strike" in teaching. The "strike" would not attempt to stop classes but would encourage devotion of one whole day in the life of the university to the consideration of the major political events confronting the United States. The "strike" proposal had not, in fact, originated with the Vietnam war but had been discussed in the past during the early sixties concerned with the uncontrolled movement toward nuclear proliferation of the United States and the Soviet Union. However, the "strike" had never taken hold as a movement, nor did it now at the time of the Vietnam escalation, since only a small number of faculty members were willing to participate in such a demonstration. Although substantial support existed among faculty members hostile to the war, many felt that it would be inauspicious to discontinue the regular pattern of instruction to introduce an issue of political concern unrelated to the academic curriculum. Opponents of the "strike" argued that the establishment of such a precedent might make the university vulnerable in the future to external pressures to raise "discussions" of concern to the established powers of society.

The Ann Arbor "invention" of the teach-in provided a useful substitute for the proposed strike. In format the teach-in was intended to be an unrestricted discussion of any and all aspects of the Vietnam war. Normally centered in

some large auditorium, its public nature and the fact that any
member of the university community could speak or listen
appealed to both students and teachers and was heartily
encouraged by university administrators, since it also represented a way of eliminating the potential threat of the
"strike." Generally the teach-in began at a normal hour for
evening lectures but continued as far into the night as participants desired—in some cases into the next day.

One of the various consequences of the teach-in was immediately apparent, while others were appreciated only with
the passage of time. The most significant aspect was the
failure of the administration of the United States government
or of supporters of government policy in Vietnam to utilize
the teach-in to defend the official American point of view.
Despite appeals and entreaties to the Department of State to
send representatives to present the point of view of the Johnson administration, in almost no case were such official representatives present. The confrontation and debates that had
taken place on a number of campuses in the months prior to
the teach-in had already taught representatives of the Johnson administration that they enjoyed little support on the
campus. They were distinctly reluctant to enter into public
debate on issues before a potentially hostile audience. At
Cornell University, despite the energetic activities of a preparatory committee, only one person willing to defend the
official policy of the American government in Vietnam could
be found.[1]

But the longer-range consequences of the teach-in were
more significant. Attendance at them became fashionable for
thousands of students on hundreds of campuses. Since the
coherent and organized arguments of the antiwar critics

1. It should be emphasized here that serious attempts were undertaken to
find defenders of American policy. Many of us who participated in the
teach-ins were concerned that they would lose their effectiveness with
proponents of government policy if they were "stacked." We also felt that
teach-ins would be much more effective as an educational device in a debate
format, since many of us believed it relatively simple to demolish the
arguments of the American government. Our search made devastatingly
clear that there was *no* significant support of government policy on most
American campuses where teach-ins were held.

reached a much broader audience than had previously been possible, the teach-ins drew into dialogue large numbers of students who had previously been relatively indifferent to political events or to the war. In this they tended to heighten criticism of American government policy. At the same time the teach-ins activated many students who had previously been critical of the war but had been relatively conservative about engaging in any kind of action. The movement was climaxed in a national conference in Washington, D.C., reaching an even larger audience through the medium of television. Whatever the effects of that nationally televised debate on the country as a whole, the appearance of a number of highly respected academicians firing a barrage of criticism at American policy before a national audience gave the final seal of approval to antiwar activity for many students.

In the milieu generated by the teach-in the incipient organizations of the new left began to recruit adherents and members much more rapidly. Organizations such as SDS spread rapidly throughout the country, as did new organizations, such as The Resistance, which began in 1967.

LEGAL ACTIVITIES AGAINST THE WAR

The teach-ins laid the basis for the next phase of activity, which involved what might be termed legal antiwar activities. While civil disobedience with respect to the war was already being attempted, the overwhelming bulk of students and faculty members were as yet unprepared to engage in "illegal" actions. Immediately after the teach-ins many campuses developed activities concerned with public demonstration of opposition to the war. Throughout this period the dominant activities were legal actions, such as peace vigils, marches, public meetings, and demonstrations. While the university antiwar forces occasionally attempted dialogue with the general community, in most cases their activity made the campus itself as the center of events. The university became a marshaling ground for many off campus actions directed against the war, but many of these actions were also limited to campus people. In this interim phase, while action took place both on and off the campus, the focus of events, of organization and planning increasingly shifted to the campus and to students.

But this phenomenon, too, presaged the changing character of campus protest, since it indicated that the strength of the student movement lay with students rather than outside the university. Continued demands of the war created a situation in which the antiwar forces inevitably began to accuse university administrations of "complicity with the war."

On the whole, university administrators and conservative faculty members did not oppose either the teach-ins or the "legal " activities that developed in 1965. Except for occasional administrative harassment, most antiwar activities were scheduled according to the bureaucratic requirements of student government and administrations without any difficulty. Only as the war came closer to the campus through the medium of the selective service system did the student radicals become pitted against the university administration.

STUDENTS AND THE DRAFT

The period of peaceful vigiling and demonstrations was short because of its lack of results. The antiwar forces' ability to mobilize thousands of students on many campuses had little effect on the national administration. Despite the high level of protest at home, the war continued to escalate in Vietnam, and no results of the antiwar movement could be discerned. The more radical of the antiwar groups began to shift from legal activities to those in direct violation of university regulations. One of the earliest manifestations was conflict over Reserve Officer Training Corps (ROTC) on campus. Since ROTC was obviously training officers who would eventually participate in the Vietnam war, the more militant student activists resuscitated the anti-ROTC sentiments that had lain dormant for many years.

But student militants were not solely concerned with ROTC actions. Changes in the selective service regulations began to discriminate among students on the basis of their intellectual capacities and attainments. Until the spring of 1966 all college students in good standing had been exempted from military service. Increased demands for military manpower led Washington to grant exemptions more selectively, by making poor students eligible for the draft. Among the proposed criteria was a written exam. Since its administration would involve hundreds of thousands of college men, a debate immediately arose about the site for such tests. The campus was the most convenient place for most students to be given such exams, but this seemed to make the university a handmaiden of the selective service system and of a highly unpopular war. On campus after campus protests began about the use of campus facilities for the administration of government exams. Again campus radicals took the initiative through demonstrations to obstruct or impede the administration of the examinations. Like the anti-ROTC demonstrations, these actions brought students into direct criticism of university administrations, questioning their conduct in their official roles.

The arguments of the university administrations at this time revealed that a fundamental polarization was beginning among faculty members as well as students. The university had always provided facilities for the administration of examinations and other services to external organizations. Acquiescence to the selective service exam was consistent with previous policy. Furthermore, by seeking to disrupt the exams or ROTC activities, the student militants were neither adhering to the canons of student conduct nor facilitating the work of an institution of higher learning, since their disruptive procedures were clearly out of keeping with the normative context existing on the campus. The militants responded that the nature of this war had changed all these relationships, and that the university should in any case question fundamental assumptions about opening facilities to private organizations to sustain a war that was clearly immoral.

Throughout 1965 and into 1966 the student activists who were working out their opposition to American government policy did not consciously and rationally search for issues that would develop large-scale support in the university community. For example, it was clear that substantial segments of the university community strongly opposed demonstrations that impeded ROTC activities. Antiwar militants were concerned with demonstrating, no matter how limited the participation, in the expectant hope that such actions might prove appealing to large numbers of sympathetic or inert students. More coherent and organized searches for issues to mobilize broader segments of the campus community occurred only later, but even then they represented less a conscious phenomenon than a reflex response to the acceptance of demonstrations and increasing support among sympathetic and inert elements of the campus community.

CAMPUS RECRUITING

During 1965 and 1966 campus activists formulated the idea that the university was related to the war mechanisms of American society in a variety of ways. The discovery that agencies actively involved in the Vietnam War—such as the Central Intelligence Agency and the Dow Chemical Corporation—recruited regularly on American campuses opened unlimited potential for student demonstrations. Within a period of weeks the university's image as an ivory tower, aloof from major events in American society, was recast to that of an agency whose culpability in the immoral Vietnam war manifested itself in hundreds of ways. The university not only welcomed recruiters from government agencies involved with the war and corporations producing napalm or other war material, but also received government funds to sustain a variety of activities, from the basic applications of physics to the development of weaponry that could discern Vietcong bodies in the dark to the question of counterinsurgency in Southeast Asia. Students became acutely aware of the degree to which the university was integrated with the centers of power and authority in American society. If the demands for military manpower had never reached the levels of 1965 and 1966, it is possible that the American campus could have remained remote from the major political issues in American society; but the increasing conviction of the immoral nature of the war, plus direct assaults upon students as individuals, threatening their existence as students (and indeed as living beings), turned the university into a center of power and domination. In this it came to seem similar to the American government and the large corporations to many of the student militants and their sympathizers.

OPEN CONFLICT

Increasingly confrontation became the central tactic for student radicals. If it was not possible to stop the war by vigiling and demonstrating on the quadrangle, the confrontation with university authorities about university involvement in the manifold activities related to the war could produce some results for the antiwar forces. The ability to impede the recruitment of personnel by Dow or CIA represented at least one tangible victory. Such demonstrations brought students into unavoidable conflict, not with the general society or with the American government, but with the university administrations themselves.

A relatively small number of student militants entered into open conflict with the established mechanisms and forces within the university. In this process the numbers of people sympathetic to the student militants probably increased significantly. Administrators and conservative faculty members were clearly rational in arguing that demonstrators were violating the normative consensus and seeking to impose their own norms on the university community. They contended that the established mechanisms of the university provided ample opportunity for internal change if student militants were willing to accept these mechanisms and if adequate support could be aroused among the student constituencies to support their point of view. While many university administrators rejected out of hand the demands of the militants, some of the more sophisticated were prepared to accept change providing the sentiments expressed by the demonstrators were processed through existing channels and represented the sentiments of the majority of students. Yet in these circumstances the position of the more militant elements served to establish models for sympathetic and inert students and raised questions about the nature of the university itself. The argument that the university went about its business and its established procedures while human beings were dying in an openly acknowledged immoral war had great power. When militants declared that they were prepared to sustain whatever penalties were directed against

them by the university for their violations of university regulations, they carried strong moral weight. But even this phase
passed fairly quickly as the student militants challenged the
legitimacy and the right of established university bodies to
regulate their actions and behavior. This turned responsibility over to faculty members who, while sympathetic
with the anti-war movement, were generally reluctant to become involved in demonstrations that actually impeded recruitment and for ROTC activities and other university actions. Faculty members feared becoming implicated if, for
example, students were expelled for participating in demonstrations but refused to leave the campus and continued to
attend their classes. What would faculty members do in such
cases? Would they recognize the right of the student to attend their classes? Or would they turn them out?

FACULTY REACTIONS

The role of the antiwar faculty members and other adults
associated with the university during this period is also worth
noting. Many hoped to keep the university relatively insulated from the major political events of the time, so that it
could serve as a haven for dissent (recalling that, despite the
persecutions of the Joseph McCarthy period, the university
had been one of the few places tolerant of dissenting viewpoints). There was an interest, therefore, in keeping the university intact as a haven for the expression of minority points
of view. On the other hand, the crises created by the militant
students increased the recognition of faculty members opposed to the war that the university was deeply implicated in
policies of the American government. With only a few ex-
ceptions the militant students provided the shock troops for
the increasingly hostile confrontations with the university,
but many professors provided social and psychological support by their physical presence on the periphery of such
demonstrations. And when students were "busted" and
charged before various university bodies with violation of
regulations, sympathy and psychological support were forthcoming from various adult members of the university community. Two major groups were involved in this kind of

support: antiwar faculty members and significant segments of the campus ministries. On many campuses religious leaders played an effective role in supporting students in their antiwar activities; as they had in an earlier period in aid to the freedom-riders.

BLACK STUDENTS

While the distinctive involvement of black students in the student movement did not begin until after the assassination of Martin Luther King in April 1968, that assassination was to serve as a crystallizing agency on many campuses. Most black students did not play an important role in antiwar activities until 1967; some were always present, but they were rarely involved as active participants. In many of the better universities the number of black students was relatively small until the 1960's. Not until the civil-rights revolution took hold in the late 1950's and early 1960's did many elite institutions undertake specialized recruiting programs to increase the proportion of black students or changed and modified entrance requirements to facilitate the entry of blacks whose high-school training might not have been adequate for admission. By 1965 the number of blacks at many of the better universities had increased, and these students were undergoing a significant ideological reorientation as a result of the growth of the black-power movement. Significantly, these students rarely considered themselves Negroes but referred to themselves as blacks or Afro-Americans. In their search for ideological identity they were less concerned with the war as an issue than with defining actions in which they could engage as a collectivity. In 1967 the revolt of the black students became significant on the American campus but remained a separate though concomitant phenomenon of the antiwar movement. Blacks remained relatively removed from participation in the antiwar confrontations and began to search out their own issues and their own concerns. They found active support among the campus militants and, very often, generalized support from sympathetic and inert students.

The assassination of Martin Luther King galvanized black

students throughout the country. On campus after campus they demonstrated, confronted, and leveled demands at university administrations for special programs oriented toward black students. On most campuses these demonstrations were actively supported by a substantial proportion of the students.

The blacks established precedents in bargaining for other student organizations. Until the black confrontations of 1968 university administrators had argued that the established mechanisms of student government provided ample opportunity for the presentation of demands and for effecting change within the normative consensus of the university. The assassination of King not only enhanced the moral position of the blacks but also undermined the university administrators' insistence on adherence to established mechanisms. At Stanford, for example, the university administration broke precedent by negotiating with the black students in public, thereby making itself vulnerable to subsequent demands from the antiwar demonstrators.

But while the blacks served as shock troops, their action was a separate phenomenon. The black students were unwilling to engage in general united fronts with white student radicals and in most cases were unwilling to participate in the kind of actions that concerned the white antiwar demonstrators. The relationship between the whites and blacks is perhaps best exemplified by the situation at Columbia in the spring of 1968, where a coalition of the white antiwar students and the black students, combining antiwar and community issues, nevertheless maintained organizational separation.

COLUMBIA

The Columbia crisis was precipitated by plans for the construction of a gymnasium that, both white and black demonstrators felt, was being built at the expense of the Harlem community. At the same time demands for cessation of construction of the gymnasium were accompanied by other demands concerning Columbia's attachment to the war machine of the United States. The significance of Columbia's demonstrations lies not only in the almost total breakdown of normative consensus in the university and the ultimate recourse to the police for the maintenance of the university establishment, but also in the dramatic way in which issues internal and external to the university became focused on the university administration itself. The question of the gymnasium was only one of many, but it brought the black students into active participation and thus provided a form of moral pressure that the white antiwar students would not have been able to sustain on their own. At the same time Columbia's involvement with the Institute for Defense Analysis and with the centers of power in the American establishment was brought to the fore by the SDS militants.

The case of the Columbia disturbance is interesting because it illustrates how a nexus of events can produce a major upheaval, surpassing the Berkeley rebellion of 1964. Columbia shows how issues of the university's involvement in the war, in race questions, and in internal university matters became conjoined to produce a new level of student activism. Prior to April 1968 there had been some student activism at Columbia but nothing of great seriousness. Several confrontations and referenda involving war-related issues had occurred, but organizations such as SDS were not overly strong. Indeed, at Columbia SDS was itself involved in internecine conflict between two factions, one advocating a relatively peaceful educational effort and the second being more concerned with activizing students through more serious confrontations. The assassination of Reverend King produced a dramatic condemnation by Mark Rudd, the newly elected chairman of SDS, of Columbia's President Grayson Kirk and Vice President David B. Truman during a memorial service on Tuesday, April 9, in Columbia's St. Paul's Chapel.[2] Rudd, stepping to the microphone in front of David Truman, accused the university's two top officers of com-

---

2. This section on the Columbia rebellion is heavily based on Jerry L. Avorn, et al., *Up Against the Ivy Wall: A History of the Columbia Crisis.* New York: Atheneum, 1969. We have also drawn in part from *Crisis At Columbia* (The Cox Commission Report). New York: Vintage Books, 1968.

mitting a moral outrage against Dr. King's memory; he then led a protest walkout of forty-odd students.

The issues underlying the Columbia events were many, and only one had its origins in the implicit racial conflict between Columbia and the Harlem community over the proposed construction of a gymnasium in Morningside Park. But the assassination served not only to move a hitherto quiescent organization of black students into action, but also to provide the kinds of linkages necessary to make Columbia's leadership, as well as that of political leaders in New York City, especially cautious in handling the demonstration that began to unfold on April 23, 1968.

The construction of the gymnasium was but one of three key issues that erupted into violence on the Columbia campus, but it was its most potent because it represented the kinds of unusual relationships that can develop between highly placed officials of a private educational institution such as Columbia and of New York City. The allocation of part of Morningside Park to the university for the construction of a gymnasium—though part of the facility was to be made available to the Harlem community—reflected the attitudes of older times, when the rights and sentiments of a black community could be ignored with impunity. By the time construction began, the whole character of the civil-rights movement had changed; the precipitating element of the King assassination only served to provide the dramatic focus for black resentment against Columbia as well as entry points for Harlem militants onto the campus.

But the gymnasium issue was only one of three major questions. The second illustrated the combination of rejection of the university's relationships to the centers of power in American society and, more concretely, its tie to the Vietnam-war activities of the nation. The issue here focused on Columbia's attachments to the Institute for Defense Analysis, an interuniversity consortium that was very much involved in many aspects of defense research, including the development of counterinsurgency warfare. The fact that the university had previously been found to have attachments to the CIA did not help to increase rapport with critical students.

Nor did the attitudes expressed publicly by university officials improve the situation. On one instance the Dean of the Graduate Faculties, Ralph S. Halford, stated that the question of the IDA affiliation was "not in the purview of faculty and students. . . . This statement was followed by one by the Vice-Dean of the Graduate Faculties, Herbert Deane, arguing against the notion of the university as a democratic institution and likening the significance of student opinion about the administration to the question of his personal tastes about strawberries.[3]

These statements by high officials of the university ex-emplified the indifference of the administration to the opinions of faculty and students concerning war-related issues. Even more, however, they embodied the "proper" relationships among students, faculty, and administration. This latter issue came to a boil over the question of disciplining six students who had earlier been involved in an obstructive demonstration on campus. The disciplining issue erupted over a lengthy background of contention over how student discipline should be handled. The decision that discipline within the campus was reserved ultimately for the president was to become the focal point of contention throughout the lengthy sit-in and strike that brought the university near to chaos.

And behind all these issues were the questions of administrative ineptness, aloofness, and indifference. The mismanagement of the Strickman filter—a situation in which the university's leadership hastened to accept a dubious invention and then had the embarrassing task of extricating the university—was indicative of ineptness. The administration's aloofness was embodied in the ritual relationships between President Kirk and the students at Columbia College, wherein they met during their first days on campus and at graduation and never between. And administrative indifference was illustrated by the refusal of President Kirk to treat a report on the reorganization of student life in any reasonable fashion—releasing it, indeed, six months after having re-

3. Avorn pp. 48–49.

ceived it only under pressure of a threat by the student council. And even at this time President Kirk refused to make any comments on the report or to begin any process of implementation.

Until that time, no other student confrontation in the United States matched that of Columbia's for sheer obduracy and savagery. Beginning with a sit-in in one building on Tuesday, April 23, students took over four additional buildings. For a week the students held these buildings while frantic attempts were undertaken by various faculty groups to obtain some compromise between the administrative leadership of the university and the students. The obduracy of President Kirk in refusing to surrender even the barest fragment of power to any group within the university provided a graphic example of the burning need for structural reform at Columbia. When the police were called to the campus on the morning of Tuesday, April 30, a total of 712 were arrested, and 149 were injured in battle scenes unprecedented on the American campus. The police raid was followed by a student strike supported by many faculty members; it culminated in the reoccupation of one university building and its clearance by police, accompanied by another battle of even greater violence. By the time of commencement the university was in a shambles, with no functioning coherent administration and with President Kirk ready to announce his resignation.

The Columbia case exemplifies the increasing tendencies of student militants to turn outward in attempting to find issues that will mobilize students, for now the militants have become increasingly conscious of the need to activate inert students and to bring sympathetic students into more active involvement in demonstrations.

The student-power movement in America shows significant discontinuities over the three decades between the 1930's and the late 1960's. The development of a significant student left in the 1930's was not accompanied by the formulation of a program or an approach to the university as an institution in society. That phenomenon occurred only in the post-Berkeley period, when students began to recognize that their source of power—their ability to mobilize students around specific events—had to derive from the campus. The significance of the student-power movement lies not in its conscious ideology and orientation toward power but in the sources of this power. For the first time in the history of the American academy students have become aware of the differences between their interests as students and those of other corporate groups resident on the American campus. Student power has attained significance because it reflects the emergence of a "class struggle" on the campus. Whether students will become increasingly self-conscious and seek to develop their interests in contradistinction to the interests of other groupings in the American university remains to be seen.

CHAPTER THREE

The Anatomy of Student Rebellion

The student rebellion, like all revolutions, has not had a clear, concise, uniform expression. As with any social process, experiments, sharp discontinuities, and contradictory tendencies have characterized it. Since 1964, when Berkeley's Free Speech Movement began its first actions, the rebellion has spread. At some universities student activists have repeated techniques and methods developed elsewhere. At others new techniques or approaches have increased the levels of escalation. Thus crucial developments in the revolution can be designated: Berkeley 1964 (the Free Speech Movement); Columbia 1968 (police-student battles on campus); San Francisco State 1967–1968 (black studies and black-white confrontations with the police); Cornell 1969 (guns on campus). At each of these universities it is not that the events that occurred there were necessarily unique (police were used to "bust" sit-in students long before Columbia at Berkeley and elsewhere, but the levels of violence were higher at Columbia) but that, at the time each occurred, the repertoire of tactics of the militants or control devices of administrators was enlarged.

Despite variations among universities during the five years since Berkeley's actions of 1964, the trends have been toward higher levels of activism and militancy by students and a

66

hardening of attitudes toward such actions by administrators. This development has tended to involve external agencies — the police — in more campus confrontations and has encouraged tendencies on the part of activists toward guerilla activities.

This chapter will examine the various forms of student activism, from the peaceful demonstrations that characterize the early stages to the embryonic guerilla activities that appear to be developing. A consideration of the structure of student activism will concern itself with the two major dilemmas of the activists: that of organization and representation and that of size. Each organizational dilemma has found a partial resolution: the dilemma of organization and representation, through the norm of spontaneity; the dilemma of size, through mobilization and polarization. In addition to these two dilemmas, the student movement has confronted major problems of continuity that are a function of the periodic character of the university. Problems of continuity have been only partially resolved by the activists; for the most political militants, it has been resolved by eliminating periodicity (that is, they remain on or near the campus throughout the year). For the bulk of students, however, the basic problems inherent in the cycle of the academic year remain, tending to concentrate overt manifestations of student activism into the latter half of the academic year.

The Forms of Student Activism

Until 1964 student activism had historically been characterized by organizing on campus for off-campus actions. Since 1964 patterns of activism have focused on on-campus issues, and university administrators have become the focus for activist action. Several basic patterns of confrontational activity have now emerged.

MORPHOLOGY OF A CONFRONTATION

The issue. Each confrontation begins with the delineation of an issue, or a set of issues, by some organized or coherent group of students. Often the delineation of the issues takes place over a long period of time—lasting up to several months—in which militants search for issues capable of mobilizing a substantial number of students.

The trigger. In addition to a set of issues, a triggering device is also needed; it is generally present in the form of action taken by a university administration. Triggering devices may be precipitated by the student militants, who may violate rules in a variety of cases to find behaviors that administrators find intolerable but with which students will sympathize. Often the triggering device develops from a disciplinary case against student militants for some experimental action.

Public disclosure. Once an issue or series of issues have been defined, the mobilization process begins. The militants usually present a series of demands to the administration, usually in the name of the student body. Demands are normally issued with a maximum of publicity. It is unusual, for example, that demands will be forwarded privately to an administration without public disclosure of their contents. Giving publicity to demands serves a number of functions. The militants hope thereby to increase the effectiveness of the demands to mobilize favorable sentiments. On many campuses, as demands are issued, militants make well-organized efforts to spread them as widely as possible. This intent often includes a descent upon the dormitories by teams of militant students eager to engender discussions among dorm residents. Such action may also be accompanied by correspondence to the campus newspaper. The militants generally expect their statements to create controversy within campus media; an editorial criticizing the demands permits them to respond extensively in the newspaper's correspondence columns.

The public nature of the demands, aside from their purposes for mobilization, flows from the ideological commitment of the activists to maximum student participation in discussion. For a handful of students to formulate demands and negotiate them privately, without the involvement of large numbers of students, would be considered undesirable elitism.

Public disclosure, however, has important tactical consequences concerning the administrative authorities. Those with power dislike being confronted by demands, especially when they may have to make public commitments of concessions. The presentation of public demands requires administrators to change their traditional modus operandi. Rather than negotiating privately with other mature men who understand the uses of power and the need for concessions, administrators are confronted by demands for public acknowledgment of the validity of radical criticism. Thus the method of presentation of demands, flowing from ideological commitments of the student radicals, serves to make concessions difficult.

Focal action. Once demands have been issued publicly and the mobilizational phase of the confrontation is under way, student militants must precipitate a focal action that will mobilize large numbers of students to take positions with respect to the demands. Most often this takes the form of a confrontation—a deliberately staged violation of university rules at a preannounced time. Confrontation is invariably scheduled to maximize student involvement: the activists prepare to violate regulations at a place and time that permits large numbers to witness the unfolding of events. Confrontations therefore tend to take place at midday rather than in the early morning or evening. (In contrast, more militant tactics—seizure of buildings—usually occur at other times and are often scheduled for the early morning hours.)

Whatever the time or form, the confrontation is intended to mobilize the student body and to bring it into the decision-making process. Thus a vital purpose of a confrontation is to involve a maximum number of students through public and semipublic meetings—both large public sessions and numerous tactical and other committee sessions. Such meetings are open, and students can express themselves regarding the actions and goals of the demonstrators.

Negotiation. In the next phase negotiations begin between representatives of the demonstrators and the administration. These negotiations are characterized by several unusual features. First, they often take place after the demonstrators have issued "nonnegotiable demands" and administrative authorities have stated that discussion is impossible because rules are being violated. Second, despite the insistence by demonstrators that administrators talk to all of them rather than with representatives, representational forms do on occasion prevail. Not only is it unusual for the students to designate representatives, but the deliberate sitting down at a table to work out settlements of disputes has been negligible. In some cases demonstrators send negotiators — who they regard as messengers rather than representatives — to deal with the authorities. In other cases unrepresentative persons communicate between students and the administration, who do not meet in the same place. Such negotiators may be individual members of the faculty, organized groups within the faculty, or individual representatives of the administration who participate on the fringes of the confrontation and conduct personal discussions with prominent demonstrators, conveying messages, attitudes, and positions of the administration. The negotiations that take place do not, therefore, follow the forms characteristic of industrial relations and collective bargaining. It would be a mistake, however, to interpret failure to reproduce the standard form of collective bargaining as an indication that negotiation does not take place. In all confrontations that we have studied, extensive negotiations have taken place between the demonstrators and the administration.

Compromise. The final stages of the confrontation occur when some compromise is obtained through either negotiation or coercion. Militants are encouraged by the fact that almost invariably demonstrations have produced concessions to students. Even if the concessions wrung from reluctant administrators or faculty do not deal with the central focus of the demonstration, it remains true that some admission is made to the grievances of students and partial redress results. It is a sad fact that the small changes that have been effected since the demonstrations began are more the product of concessions made to activists under pressure of confrontation than the product of reasoned processes initiated by university authorities.

LEVELS OF ACTIVISM

Various patterns of student demonstrations have developed in the five years since Berkeley. The levels of activism that have emerged range from peaceful demonstrations to quasi-guerrilla activities. The forms we describe are ideal—typical in that they are present in most demonstrations. But demonstrations involve the presence of several forms, not one alone. Nor do the forms occur in any necessary temporal sequence. At Berkeley in 1964, for example, a peaceful demonstration ended with confrontations and seizure of buildings, but with little civil disobedience. Thus the forms do not necessarily correlate with the increasing maturity of the student rebellion, although there is a long-range secular trend in this direction. The tendency in 1964 and 1965 was mainly toward peaceful demonstrations and civil disobedience, although some confrontations took place. Seizure of buildings and confrontations became more frequent in 1967 and 1968, while civil disobedience and peaceful demonstrations receded except as preparatory actions for higher levels of activism. Finally, guerrilla activities occurred on some campuses beginning in 1968, although they remain embryonic as a major form.

Peaceful demonstrations. The intent of any peaceful demonstration is to direct official attention toward some grievance of the students. Vigils, marches or parades, and picketing (without attempting to obstruct ingress or egress) are its main manifestations. Attempts are made to mobilize substantial numbers, so that the problem being espoused can receive maximum attention. The fact that these demonstrations do not involve deliberate attempts to violate university regulations gives both strength and weakness to this tactic. Because no rules are being broken, larger numbers of students can potentially be involved (most students hesitate to undertake deliberate violations of rules). The main weakness of the peaceful demonstration is that it makes only a moral appeal to most students, many of whom take no interest in the issues involved.

Civil disobedience. In the case of civil disobedience, deliberate efforts are made to violate rules. Student violators acknowledge their willingness to accept the penalties attached to their violation, but they argue that some higher morality supersedes the university regulations under which they will be prosecuted. Examples of civil disobedience include sitting in without seizing buildings and impeding recruitment activities on campus without actually preventing recruitment from going forward. Civil disobedience, frequently used in the early stages of the student rebellion, was an important technique associated with opposition to the Vietnam war.

Confrontation. The distinction between confrontation and civil disobedience is small but crucial. Though both may often take very similar forms, the major difference rests in students' attitudes toward the university regulations they have chosen to violate and toward the judicial systems supporting the regulations. In civil disobedience, students acknowledge the legal right of the university to discipline them for violation of regulations but hold that some higher law exists superseding university regulations. In confrontation, however, students refuse to accept the punishment ostensibly due them. Although it also involves an appeal to higher morality, confrontation directly challenges the authority of the university. By arguing and refusing to accept punishment, confronters reject the university's judicial system. Confrontation poses a serious dilemma, since it challenges the system of decision making, power, and authority within the university.

Seizure of buildings. At the next level of activism, student demonstrators undertake to disrupt the university administration. In contrast to the confrontation—in which there is a deliberate violation of rules, (as well as the argument that there should be no penalties because of higher morality)—a seizure is a deliberate attempt to impede the normal operation of the university. Students justify such action on the grounds that the university is engaged in the violation of a moral code, and thus not only violation of university rules but also impediment of the university's normal functioning become legitimate forms of student political activism.

In selecting a building for seizure, two important criteria

are considered: first, that the building be of crucial significance to the operation of the university; second, that it have
some symbolic meaning for a major constituency of the university. The seizure, for example, of a school of veterinary
medicine (in most cases a peripheral unit of the university,
with a tiny constituency) would be regarded as ludicrous by
student activists. Administration buildings, student unions,
and buildings housing administrative offices of undergraduate liberal arts colleges have therefore been primary
targets.

Guerrilla activities. Guerrilla activities take the form of
conscious and deliberate destruction of property aimed at the
heart of university operations. Guerrillas rarely seek to damage vending machines but direct their attention to such
things as administrative files at Columbia and library catalogs
at Indiana. These hit-and-run actions involve small numbers
of participants, who attempt to inflict maximum damage
quickly and to disappear before penalties can be exacted.
Student guerrilla activities, like guerrilla actions in any social
circumstance, are carried on by tiny segments of the population, although there must exist large disaffected populations
to support these activities. If the bulk of students are extremely hostile to a university administration, the prospects
for guerrilla activities are better than if the majority of students is uninterested or supports the administration. Ideologically, guerrilla activities are anathema to most student militants, who are committed to broad participation by the students in the university's political process. Guerrilla groups
by definition must be small, must be elitist, and must operate
clandestinely. While some student radicals, particularly those
with Maoist affiliations, are willing to undertake guerrilla
activities on their own, most demonstrators are unsympathetic to guerrilla actions. It is difficult to make accurate predictions about the future of guerrilla activities on campuses,
since student alienation would have to increase substantially
before guerrilla groups could operate extensively.

All these self-conscious, organized forms of student activism have not taken into consideration less organized actions.

Peaceful demonstrations, for example, occasionally turn into riots. While we have not explored manifestations of collective behavior in the student rebellion, this phenomenon should not be entirely overlooked. Often the introduction of coercive elements—the police—has precipitated riotous situations. Under the same circumstances more peaceful forms of collective behavior have also occurred: the spontaneous movement of thousands of students to Cornell's Barton Hall, for example. It is difficult in analyzing collective behavior to make predictions from the analysis. Thus, we have made no systematic attempt here to account for forms of collective student behavior. In respect to collective activity, the student activists and university administrators find themselves in close agreement. No one is comfortable in spontaneous manifestations whose patterning emerges only after the fact. Human beings—student activists and administrators—prefer to know what they are doing and to build predictability into their systems.

Political Structures of the Student Rebellion

THE POLITICS OF SPONTANEITY

One significant aspect of the student rebellion has been the operationalization of spontaneity, which has become a modus operandi of most student actions. Though it has ideological and experiential antecedents, the norm of spontaneity has in fact been put into operation without much recourse to them. This is not because students lack awareness of the historical issues; many of the more politically aware demonstrators have been thoroughly imbued with knowledge about precedents for spontaneous activity, such as events of the socialist and working-class movements. But despite their willingness to discuss the works of Lenin and Mao Tse-tung with fluency, there has been a deliberate failure to relate historical antecedents to present-day student actions.

The history of spontaneity. Spontaneity was a key question for past generations of radical politicians and provided a focus for much of the intellectual controversy of the European socialist movements. Indeed, it can be argued that the tactics of that segment of the Marxist movement that became characterized as Bolshevist represented a reaction against earlier tactics of socialist organizations dependent on the development of spontaneous reactions by the exploited segments of the population. Just as Bolshevism was a reaction to the norm of spontaneity, it engendered many opposing organizational theories as the Russian Revolution degenerated into a dictatorship. Anti-Bolshevik Marxists and other socialist thinkers continued to emphasize mass-party democracy and electoral activities as a means of channeling the energy of the masses without entirely depending upon elitist vanguards to provide guidance for working-class energies. But even the urgings toward mass party democracy proved to have limiting characteristics; before Bolshevism emerged as a viable organizational approach, Roberto Michels, the brilliant anarchist strategist and sociological theorist, had shown that in the mass-based socialist movements of Europe effective control rested with a tiny leadership stratum.

For many socialists trapped in the iron collar of Bolshevism and its elitist notions or in the fraudulent democratic character of the mass parties of Europe, there were few intellectual escapes. Some, like Roberto Michels, became embittered and ended up as crypto-fascists, while others, like Max Weber, searched endlessly for viable intellectual solutions. One such group emerged in America, arguing theoretically for spontaneity as an approach to working-class organization. Reacting against the manipulation of the working class by coherent vanguards (such as the Communists) or by leaders manipulating masses from behind the scenes (as in social democratic movements), adherents of spontaniety argued that socialists had to construct organizational forms that permitted workers to learn to develop their own modes of expression. The function of an organized movement was simply to provide the forum within which self-development could occur. This approach was embodied organizationally in a miniscule Trotskyist offshoot known as the Johnson-Forrest "tendency"; it led a peripheral existence on America's left for many years and, indeed, still conducts obscure work in several industrial centers in the United States. As an organizational force, these spontaneists have had little significant influence. Only with the current student movement did spontaneity as a theory of organization emerge at all significantly. Though the past experiences of spontaneity have been available to student militants, they have not been utilized, since students have developed theories and approaches based more on their own experience than on ideological antecedents.

The experiential basis for spontaneity emerged in the postwar period as an anti-computer syndrome, occasioned by the expansion of the economy following World War II and the generation of technologies capable of handling large quantities of data. Many people have reacted against electronic processing, even while recognizing its inevitabilities. The conversion by many corporations of billing and check systems to computer processing inevitably opened opportunities for individual spontaneous acts of sabotage — stapling, mutilating, folding, and otherwise damaging the cards that have become so ubiquitous in America during the past decade.

But the anticomputer syndrome was only one overt manifestation. More significant was the development of cultural groups that opted out of the mainstream of programmed society. One of the earliest of the antiorganization movements was the "beat generation," in which individuals sought individual escape from the society. Jack Kerouac became the intellectual progenitor of the beats, moving frantically through space to avoid human entanglements because these entanglements engendered the programming against which he was reacting.

Over time the hippies, a more socially oriented group, emerged out of the beat generation. For the hippies, human constituencies became important as they developed a common group culture that rejected the programming of the larger society. The intent of the hippies, in contrast to the beats, was to find a collective solution to the problem of programming through continuous and sustained spontaneous activity. The consequences of this approach made the hippies irresponsible in the eyes of middle-class America: though willing to work and engage in other ordinary activities, they withdrew whenever they felt a spontaneous urge (such as good vibrations at a mass turn-on) to do so. What made the hippies even more irritating to mainstream America was the fact that they were not lower-class Americans, from whom one might legitimately expect "irresponsibility" in maintaining schedules. Mainly middle class, the hippies were familiar with programmed systems yet specifically rejected them. In a more direct sense than the socialists, the hippies introduced spontaneity as an organizational value to the current student movement.

The tactics of spontaneity. Spontaneity has emerged as an organizational norm, a way of functioning as an end in itself. To be sure, as concept of organization, spontaneity has its drawbacks. One is that the militants, who have relatively little coherence on tactics, may find themselves compelled to issue statements requiring changes in tactical procedures despite their own beliefs in spontaneity. When for example, student demonstrators convene a mass constituency that repudiates their tactics, the demonstrators may find themselves compelled to take actions that violate their own beliefs.

A second organizational dilemma arises because there is no central directorate or established procedure to assure passage of the implementation decisions. The action-oriented group may thus find that previous commitments can, and often are, upset and must revise its approaches accordingly. This is one reason why the emphasis on tactics has become a key feature of student demonstrations. One fascinating aspect of all sit-ins consists of the interminable decision-making sessions focused on tactics. Tactical discussions—which are second nature to the more politicized students who have read Lenin, Guevara, Mao Tse-tung, Ho Chi-minh, and General Giap—have the further merit of drawing in large numbers of politically less-developed students: the discussion of tactics, particularly in the present-day student movement, does not require an understanding of the radical liturgy or of socialist literature.

Tactics come to mean different things to different constituencies. For the politically unsophisticated, tactics refer to specific actions such as seizing buildings. Some will say an action is a bad tactic; others, a good tactic. At the next level of sophistication are those who see in tactics the encompassing of a wide variety of approaches to problems. For example, it is a good tactic to accept a meeting with the administration, but bad to participate in a meeting on their terms. At this level tactics refer to the preconditions for negotiation and decision making. A still higher meaning of tactics is a surrogate for long-range goals: tactical discussions are concerned with political outcomes rather than immediate responses to situations. Tactics can also mean a discussion of partialities versus totalities. Tactically sound decisions are those that give only total control and total resolution; tactically unsound decisions yield outcomes that may benefit the group only in fragmentary terms. In this case "tactics" is another name for a discussion of principles.

But spontaniety provides the guarantee that discussions of tactics will become no more inviolable and sacrosanct than discussions of principles. Spontaneity creates the basis for frequently perceived inconsistent and contradictory positions taken by militants even after they perform an action. In this respect there is considerable contrast between the present generation of militant students and the older generation of leftists. Democratic centralism—where debate rages until a decision is made and discipline becomes binding upon all—is inconceivable to present-day student militants. They no more accept the decisions of a majority than they accept the decisions of their own cohort group. Only the decision that has just been taken is binding, and that *only* until the next decision. The concept of spontaneity is tailored to permit the operation of a morally centered politics, since morality demands the confrontation of personal consciousness with the decision to be taken. Nor is this an entirely naive approach, for it is implicitly based on the negative model provided by the old sectarian left—which exhibited a politically centered morality.

This emphasis on participation and spontaneity has muted, but not completely stopped, some critics of student radicals from developing conspiracy theories. Many who themselves resent "power elite" concepts of conspiracy argue that a hidden band of plotters is working out an elaborate plan. As put in *Barron's* (May 20, 1968), the Columbia siege tactics "represent the latest assault by a revolutionary movement which aims to seize first the universities and then the industries of America." Such theories are comforting; it is far less frightening to believe that a small band of conspirators is plotting social change than to think it resides in large numbers of people. While odd militants with grandiose notions of dropping LSD in the water supply and turning on an entire area for a "free trip" may actually exist, witnesses of student demonstrations who have seen the open methods of decision making realize that prospects for effective conspiracy are minimal.

An examination of leadership patterns in demonstrations underscores this fact. Leadership roles emerge during the demonstrations, and some participants become more prominent than others despite the strong ideological opposition to such crystallization. But the leadership that emerges is issue-oriented rather than charismatic or formal. Rank-and-file demonstrators never hesitate to "put down" a person toward whom they have been showing respect if they disagree with him. Thus there is little accumulation of charisma even around those militants who consistently put forward useful ideas that form the basis of consensus. If such a "leader" were to make overt and specific claims to leadership as a result of being right consistently over a period of time, most activists would react strongly and negatively. As for formal leadership, the concept is explicitly repudiated. Students recognize the need for certain roles to be more clearly delineated; thus, a tactics committee or similar body always becomes the focus of decision making during an action. The tactics committee meetings—particularly during the course of the action—are usually open to all, and many (but not all) students come, listen, and participate. In this respect membership on a key committee obligates members to attend, while others may or may not attend as a matter of individual choice.

Even the existence of crucial committees does not focus power in the hands of a few. During the execution of an action, such as a sit-in, there is usually ample time for

lengthy discussion, and the key committees report to the
entire constituency at least once daily. These sessions are
usually marked by lengthy debate. Because the constituency
is usually as well educated as the leadership, the usual
differentials of knowledge and skills between leaders and led
are not as wide among the student militants as among many
other organizations, (such as trade unions). The typical basis
for the manipulation by leaders of followers does not exist.
While graduate students are disproportionately represented—particularly on crucial committees—the usual techniques of organizational manipulation practiced in most formal organizations are absent. This is not to say that organizational manipulation is completely absent; on several occasions, to the knowledge of the writers, leadership groups
have structured meetings to ensure that action will be taken
along preconceived lines. Usually, however, unless the leadership cadres have reason to be certain that their proposals
will be implemented, they hesitate to take action that will
commit them to a particular course of events. Thus, manipulation appears to take place in circumstances where the leaders are relatively certain they will be followed; otherwise
manipulation becomes a dangerous approach that most activists will actively repudiate.

The deemphasis of leadership represents the working out
of the norm of spontaneity. However, spontaneity creates
organizational dilemmas for the student radicals. Not only
does it introduce uncertainty as to what will happen, it can
frequently be inefficient: it is no accident that formal organization has long been an important and viable social form.
Thus, the student activists have begun to divide into two
distinctive wings—those that would emphasize spontaneity
(and who are often anarchists politically) and those that emphasize organization (and who are more often socialist in
their orientations).

The gap between the spontaneists and the organiza-
tionalists is directly connected to the divisions in life
styles in the bulk of the membership of student radical movements. On one side there are the drug freaks, the drop-outs,
the hippies and yippies—in short, the advocates of politics as

style. On the other side are the Maoists, the politicos in general, and the advocates of politics as substance. The former, desirous of "liberating" themselves, are indeed unlikely to worry about organization; the latter, dedicated to "liberating" others, are deeply concerned with organizational forms of cooperative behavior. Thus the question of organization hinges on a theory of mobilization.

For some student radicals the purpose of the movement is to stimulate a variety of models leading to more intense political involvement. Everything from acid-rock music to personal manners is evaluated according to its contribution to such involvement. The process of mobilizing large clusters of political support is believed to be helped by culturalism (for example, the huge attendance at the Woodstock Music Fair in the summer of 1969 was regarded favorably by many) or is seen as hindered by it when dropping out and turning on become exigencies that make their devotees useless to the movement. The gap between yippies and politicos starts with a theory of organization; but underlying this gap is a feeling that a revolution in personal behavior and personal ambition is central (or peripheral) to the political development of the young. In either event a certain amount of formal organization has become imperative for confrontational politics. Indeed, it might be argued that confrontational politics requires an even more adept form of management than the customary forms of parliamentarianism—for the former involves constant scrutiny and self-defense.

THE POLITICS OF MOBILIZATION AND POLARIZATION

Practicing revolutionaries have long had to confront the dilemma that they can never encompass the majority of a population in their movement. Social democrats have usually dealt with the same dilemma by focusing upon electoral politics: while the majority is never encompassed within the movement organizationally, it can be included through political competition at the ballot box. Others, such as the Bolsheviks, resolved the problem by establishing a division of labor between the small, conscious directorate of the movement

and the masses, incapable of conscious organization but able
to produce enormous energies capable of being directed.

The current generation of student revolutionaries, at least
to the present time, has rejected both these approaches. Unwilling, on the one hand, to enter into the organizational
frustrations of electoral politics, with all the implicit compromises and logrolling, and, on the other hand, unwilling to
engage in conspiracies to direct the energies of the masses,
the current group of activists has sought to mobilize the
masses through politics of polarization; these depend, in
turn, on the acceleration of confrontation. Confrontation represents the development of new behaviors, calculated to
mobilize an otherwise apathetic majority by forcing it to take
positions on issues. The confrontational mechanism as it has
evolved during the past four years develops through a
means-end process in which traditionally unacceptable
means (such as building seizures) are utilized to obtain commonly acceptable ends (for example, the end of the war in
Vietnam; getting the university out of classified research and
into socially relevant concerns).

Confrontation is not, however, regarded as an end in itself.
Its function is to polarize the apathetic majority so that it will
begin to participate in the political process. Bringing the
politics of means-ends to every student, it is believed, will
draw each student into the fray and force him to take a
position. Thus, confrontation yields polarization, which in
turn produces political mobilization. In terms of its historical
roots, this belief represents the infusion of Third World experience into the present-day student movement.

Confrontation has both strategic and tactical consequences.
Strategically, it forces students to take sides and to participate in the political process. Its tactical consequences
— which have become increasingly apparent to activists and
administrators — rest on the responses made to concrete actions, such as the seizure of buildings. Despite the fact that a
majority of students initially may oppose such seizures (leaving aside the issue of how substantial are the minorities that
support such actions), the introduction of police force on the
campus serves tactically to shift opinion in favor of the activists. Not only do uncommitted students resent the failure of

the administration to use reason to work out problems, but more importantly, the release of forces that are not controlled by the administration and that utilize coercion indiscriminately against all students produces favorable sentiment toward the activists.

While confrontation can take a variety of forms, one of the most disconcerting has been a refusal to accept representation as a principle for resolving conflict among groups. It has already been seen how the reaction against representative practices flows from the norm of spontaneity; its consequences for producing confrontation, mobilization, and polarization must now be considered.

Administrative and faculty officials alike tend to conceive of all forms of confrontation as coercion. To men who are comfortable with the kind of give and take that goes on sub rosa, it must indeed seem that student sit-in demonstrators use unfair tactics to gain their ends. Administrative officials admit that they feel the real problem of the sit-in demonstrators to be their kinship with fascism rather than communism. Their perception of confrontational (or nonrepresentational) politics has been framed by the Nazi and Fascist experiences of prewar Europe, where symbolic coercion (linked to a spirit of intolerance generated by irrationalism) made the proper functioning of the university impossible. Administrators' accusations of fascism are clearly geared to discourage students from participation, since they are obviously more negatively linked toward fascism and its racist overtones than toward socialism and its humanistic heritage.

Because students must at times come to grips with decision makers, they have developed a pattern of turning representatives who have to be chosen into nonrepresentatives. This process is accomplished by reducing the time spent in choosing representational groups to a matter of seconds or minutes. Students will debate tactics, issues, or the locus of power for an indefinite length of time, but they refuse to devote long discussions to the membership of any given committee.

When committee members or temporary leaders return from their assignments and report what they have discussed or heard, the full effect of this rapid-fire leadership system becomes apparent. At Stanford, for instance, a speaker who returned from a meeting with the Stanford administration officials believed in their sincerity. This student felt that, although a proposed meeting with the provost would be held late in the evening and at a site chosen by the provost, the provost's suggestions should be honored even if the grounds seemed to be of the administration's choosing. The rebuke from the floor was clear when he was reminded, "You are not our representative. You are our messenger." Indeed, this concept of leadership as a janitorial function or as a messenger service often serves group solidarity well, especially when the demonstrators are concentrated in a single building.

Loose organization permits strange anomalies, such as the presence of the police at nearly all tactical meetings. Yet this phenomenon seems, to most participants, far less risky than the representational democracy it replaces. The key aspect of the politics of confrontation is the assumption that its student leadership can not be bought off, convinced, or simply ignored out of existence by officials.

The confrontational style, combined as it is with spontaneity, creates serious problems for administrators and academicians. Among them is the administration's need to resolve problems in terms of norms of legitimacy connected with the established judicial processes. Unable to confront masses of hostile students who become openly hostile to people who speak at great length or speak with rhetorical flourishes, and who jeer in a most unacademic way at the traditional rhetoric of administrators, university leadership obviously prefers dealing with representatives. In some measure administration appeals for the rest of the students to speak out, for the conservative counterdemonstrators to show their faith and fealty to the system are less indicative of ideological solidarity with the conservative posture than of a discomfort with the style of confrontation that the demonstrators represent.

A difficulty posed by nonrepresentative confrontational politics is that it throws into jeopardy the stability of decision making itself. Administrators and academicians are dedicated to the principle that the vote is a sacred act, binding on all parties for a specified period of time. Confrontational politics takes only the most recent decision as binding. Hence attitudes toward administration-oriented committees may shift overnight from mild support to strident attack. All decisions made by student demonstrators are subject to the review of the committee of the whole; this review process provides as much shock for the administration during the demonstration period as does the political conduct of the demonstration itself. The students not only confront one another; they above all confront the administration as a unit, as a class.

THE POLITICS OF PERIODICITY

A major characteristic of corporate student life in America is its periodicity or intermittency. That is, student life and politics go on only as long as all the normal tripartite elements of faculty, administration, and students are present on the campus. The semester system, with its attendant features of students' vacating the physical plant of the university for three or four months a year, seriously weakens the forms of social organization possible in the structuring of political opposition. Even the introduction of the trimester system to American campuses has not helped, since most students appear for only two out of the three periods. In other words, the student habitat remains bifurcated between a campus "pad" and a hometown "base," and the two may be thousands of miles apart.

The faculty, too, is involved in this system of periodic residence. In its case time is needed for travel, for research, or to follow the formal amenities of extrauniversity affiliation in the form of releases (sabbatical leaves) from the rigors of university life. One of the conventional payoffs of the faculty system is extensive time off for good behavior— whether in the form of summer vacations from June through September or sabbaticals once each seven years. Consequently the faculty, or at least a portion of it, is able to separate itself from the university premises without opposition or injury.

Only the administration is uniquely situated to run the

university on a continuing basis, whatever the reasons for denial or demurrer. It is veiled knowledge to every administrator that whatever is said, done, or voted on in a university senate, the actual day-to-day implementation is performed by the administration—and, without attributing malevolence to them, decisions will be interpreted in their light. This fact gives administrators a unique opportunity to manipulate the realities and the symbols of university power without formally infringing upon the presumed rights and prerogatives of the students who pay or the faculty that teaches.

The situation thus produced might be labeled episodic politics, in which activism becomes linked to the peculiar cycles during which students and faculty are at ebb and flood tide. Major decisions are often made during the time the university is not in session. For example, the dismissal of ten faculty members at Simon Fraser University took place in August 1969, at a time when students and most faculty members were away, well before all were scheduled to return for the late Canadian academic year. Similarly, major appointments to administrative posts often occur during summer lulls, when pressures and counterpressures are not present on a campus.

The intermittency of student and faculty strata allows for periods of the calendar year when conservative and retrenching decisions can be made without fear of instant mass opposition. Administration is perceived by all to be a continuing twelve-month chore, in contrast to teaching, which goes on for only nine months. And learning is really only a seven-months activity, spread over nine months and broken by vacations, holidays, and study and examination periods, as well as intersessions or semester breaks.

Time often works to the advantage of the conservative administrative stratum, not only through the academic calendar but also through the peculiar structural characteristic of the university, in which a new student cohort is introduced annually while the most experienced and sophisticated cohort is graduated out. The constant reshuffling of the student body imposes on those students seeking to form a coherent and organized group the obligation of establishing rapport with returning students—who have been away for substantial periods of time—as well as of involving new students, for whom the university represents a strange and esoteric environment.

Because of the need to reestablish rapport with returning students and to bring new students into active participation, the early periods of the new academic year are those in which overt activism and confrontation tend to be relatively insignificant. While organized student groupings may seek an early confrontation to establish a political tone or culture for the coming year—or to use the confrontation as a device for mobilization—the academic year usually begins quietly as students work out their relationships with each other, develop a "feel" of the climate of student opinion, and develop trust through interaction and experience.

It is difficult to organize action at the beginning of the new academic year not only because students need to develop their knowledge of each other, but also because the beginning of the academic year is broken up by holidays and vacations of greater significance and duration than those that come later. Thanksgiving, Christmas, and the New Year are more assiduously celebrated than are Easter and Memorial Day. Thus the constellation of holidays between the first and the last half of the academic year plays a role.

For this reason student demonstrations begin to increase in the latter half of the academic year and reach their peak toward its end. By that time the student militants have had ample opportunity to interact with each other, to learn a university's strengths and weaknesses, and to test the mettle of administration and faculty. The politics of periodicity flow, therefore, from the structural features of the university, the particular characteristics of its calendar, and the larger aspects of climate and geography.

There do exist some mitigating tendencies that may produce changes in intermittency in the future. The increased amount of graduate activity—which is carried on year-round and with fewer breaks and which involves large numbers of students—is providing the basis for continuing organization.

Thus, student subcultures grow up around universities having graduate students as an important stratum. Athens, Ohio, can develop in time as strong a subculture around Miami University of Ohio as Berkeley does around the University of California.

A similar development is the refusal of small numbers of student militants and activists to leave the campus during the summer. Summer has become a retrenching period, devoted to assessing the events of the past year and projecting new approaches for students as well as administrators. The rise of a new subclass of professional dropouts, i.e., former students who remain near campus, contributes a permanent revolutionary cadre. Thus, former handicaps may be used to provide militants with opportunities to consolidate their experiences and lay plans for the coming academic year. And invariably around the cadre of militants develops a group of followers who, for a variety of reasons — generally nonpolitical — have remained on the scene but who participate in summer events, if only because these represent the main intellectually meaningful activities at that time.

Despite these features the bulk of students continue to follow traditional patterns and depart from the campus for the entire summer and for various holidays. This deficiency in student politics distinguishes it from national or local politics in that student politics lack consistency over time and a stable constituency.

CHAPTER FOUR

The Ideology of Student Rebellion

Forces on the Campus

CAMPUS COMPOSITION

The explosions that have rocked American academic life — from the strike at Columbia in New York to the major confrontation at the University of California (Berkeley) and at San Francisco State College — represent high points in the multiple movements for social and educational reform that in the past have concerned rather than involved the student population. That this transformation from acquiescence to action may represent the ideology of a minority should provide small solace for those subject to student grievances, since in fact students' protest movements are conducted with the tacit consent of the silent and express a great deal for their generation.[1] The campus has become the organizational base on which the ideology of the young radicals has gained maturation, if not legitimation. Despite the fact that conservative student political organizations and traditional student government groups continue to debate and challenge the new student radicals, it is the ideology of the latter that

1. See Daniel Seligman, "A Special Kind of Rebellion", *Fortune*, 74,1 (January 1969), 67–69, 172–175.

has gained the support of those who recognize that times are changing.[2]

Students, both in lower schools and in universities have always been "political." They participate in or accept well-established student organizations patterned after adult civic organizations. But the student movements of protest and dissent that have moved leading intellectuals to lively controversy are separable from student civic activities—both in their ideological persuasion and in the personal commitment demanded of members.

Approved "student politics" consists of student organizations and elective bodies that consider or disseminate rules of the college institution or that establish means for articulating student feelings and aims concerning campus affairs. These bodies function to resolve problems of interaction among discreet student groups—fraternities, sororities, and athletic, social, and religious organizations; they enable students to practice self-direction through student assemblies; and they create a leadership to carry on these tasks. Student civics, purposefully organized for student participation in the management of those aspects of campus affairs bearing directly on student social behavior and organizational life, serves as a means of access to and communication with school administrations on these matters. It is almost exclusively concerned with the local campus and organizational life of students-in-attendance, and its final outcome is "student government."[3]

Student political movements differ in one important respect. They are composed of persons concerned with contemporary politics and determined to organize for participation in the determination of domestic issues concerning the welfare of peoples within the society and the relation of these issues to world problems. They represent an organized

2. See Seymour Martin Lipset, "Students and Politics in Comparative Perspective," *Daedalus*, 97, 1 (Winter 1968), 1–20; and by the same author, "Student Opposition in the United States", *Government and Opposition*, 1, No. 3 (April 1966), 351–374.

3. See Howard S. Becker, Blanche Geer, and Everett Hughes, *Making the Grade: The Academic Side of College Life*. New York: John Wiley & Sons, 1968, pp. 8–10, 43–62.

attempt to bridge the gap between the student's life and studies at school and the larger world and to establish an identity in that world through political articulation of discontent and criticism. Even when campus affairs are a focus of attention, they are related to questions on the nature and purposes of education.

Seven million students now attending institutions away from home remain financially dependent throughout their school careers. As a consequence, administrations, through various student deans and their assistants, often assume a parental role in student lives. They see to it that student activity does no serious or active damage to the dominant social values and practices regarding sex, religion, and politics. They establish rules for behavior that reflect what parents themselves would expect of their children, and they are informally guided by a principle commonly referred to as "in loco parentis." Thus administration, and sometimes faculty, becomes a target for those students to whom parental authority—perhaps control in general—is to be resisted in order to attain maturity. Fearing adverse publicity, administrative authorities have often shown prime concern with placating and supporting community and parental values and only secondary interest in the critical individuality of the student.

Challenges to patriotic, religious, or sexual standards from the intelligent young adult pose a threat to sacred notions in a way that "panty raids" or childish outbursts (which are in accord with stereotypical adult expectations of children) do not. Administrations guided by the doctrine of in loco parentis, who can psychologically cope with deviant outbursts, are unable to deal with radical political challenges to prevailing beliefs, values, and supervisory rights.[4]

REASONS FOR CAMPUS RADICALISM

There are complex and diverse reasons why student strike movements and campus radicalism have increasingly become part of the American university scene. With the exception of

4. See Irving Louis Horowitz and Martin Liebowitz, "Social Deviance and Political Marginality," *Social Problems*, 15 (Winter 1968), 280–296.

land-grant schools, nineteenth-century higher education was only for "gentlemen" or "clergymen". Aristocratic notions of cultivation and preparation for a life role did not involve widespread professional training. Many professions—such as schoolteaching and journalism—did not yet require college degrees. Furthermore, only the prosperous could afford the expense of college. And finally, the university's role was linked more to dispensing culture than to sharing knowledge. Not until the student body became broadly middle-class, subsidized by adequate middle-class incomes or by scholarship aid, did a mass student population intent on further upward mobility emerge.

The needs of an insatiable and expansive technological society for a stable supply of professionally trained personnel drove all who could meet the intellectual demands and financial burden to work through college requirements to respectable places in middle-class society. More recently, as a by-product of the cold war, politically inspired fear of losing the technological race to the Russians raised standards and intensified competition. Given a massive college population pragmatically created to provide a supply of professionals and badly pressured by mounting tough competition for survival in the "halls of ivy," elements of friction and anxiety developed along with entrepreneurial and government opportunities. As the college student population increasingly derived from the "popular" instead of the "upper" classes, society's framework for "growing up" gained in complexity and competitiveness. High mobility and a proliferation of intermediary income groups destroyed status boundaries of social "place." The American dream of wealth as a reward to those who make their own way established economic expectations that would not easily withstand frustration.

Twentieth-century America brought heavy immigration and increased participation of ethnic and lower-income groups in political life. These developments were reflected particularly in the composition of urban public schools and city colleges. Educators introduced "citizenship training" or student government at all levels of school life, as part of a large assimilation drive, designed to socialize and integrate the immigrant stranger into the prevailing social and economic system. These massive integration efforts were democratically motivated and part of a pragmatic revolt in American education against "uselessness" and scholasticism in educational programming and in favor of attempts to prepare students for "life." University students, no less than high-school students, emulated the councils and assemblies, found in the larger civic culture, associated with local democratic citizen participation. Fraternity and other campus organizations, under attack for snobbish, cultist, and undemocratic practices, began to soften and develop a leadership outlook that accommodated the lower middle-class style.

As one major outcome of this "Americanization" of universities, a more innovative student-oriented policy guided administrations, and the imitation of European authoritarianism was minimized. But popularization also brought university student affairs under the benevolent but pervasive scrutiny of administrative authority, which fostered the ideal of the respectable community and acted to counteract the "anarchy" thought to lurk behind radical interpretations of student independence. The liberal, practical, Americanizing intentions of citizenship training, under the supervision of administrative parent surrogates, limited student self-determination to parochial, if not outright conservative definitions.

Intercollege competition for resources and the need for "business sense" excelling at fund raising brought boards of trustees composed of rich businessmen and professional notables into leading places in college organization. Representing the values of success and competition as well as middle-class democracy and professional usefulness, the limited-citizenship standard became a sacred practice of college communities. Middle-class American college students of mixed ethnic composition found extensions of their sector's values when they entered the university. Students came to be regarded as future professional servants of an expansive and wealthy middle-class national society. Such rebellion as there is against administrative or faculty authority on campus is thus often attached to hostility toward middle-class expectations and "local citizen" political ideals. The inherited dependence on authorities—even benevolent authorities, such as parents and their campus "representatives"—came to appear stifling, offensive, infantilizing, and deadly to a search for personal expression through education. Charles Doebler, a college admissions officer, has written about this problem: "The importance of a college education to the career of any young person and the increasingly high cost of that education have been instrumental in maintaining a golden umbilical cord between parents and students that is severed far later than it should be . . . more ultimate choices of which colleges to attend are made by parents than by students. Even worse, once the period of education has begun, there is a continuation of a long distance but forceful 'interest' that permeates and affects the student's entire college career."[5]

Administrative policy that does not clearly and forcefully disengage itself from goals of middle-class status and professional expertise as the end product of a university education is likely to find itself attacked as a professionalizing and parental middle-class agent, unable to assimilate or inspire higher aims in educational programming. And an administration is likely to be amazed and offended when its democratic and practical intentions are so bitterly assaulted by the radical student critic.

The complexities of modern science, industrial life, and the vast and infinite resources of the humanities demand long periods of immersion in disinterested study apart from considerations of opportunistic career choices. Postgraduate education has become essential for professional pursuits as well as for intellectual development. An increasing number of these graduate students, who are in their late twenties or older, have generated great friction about their deprived status and dependent state. Their presence has, among other things, created pressure for recognition of students as adults and has made the "rah-rah" generations of college students a relic of less serious times. These students adopt non-familial models such as trade union or political party styles of organizing their activities.

5. Charles H. Doebler, *Who Gets into College—and Why*. New York: MacFadden Books, 1963, p. 166.

Prolonged education and renewed emphasis on high academic performance has produced great anxiety about surviving in undergraduate work and now, also, about gaining coveted entry into the graduate schools of the better universities. This increases possibilities for frustration and intensifies subjection to an already unprecedentedly competitive situation. And with prolonged periods of information ingestion, passive note taking, and subordinate status has come the need to delay adulthood beyond the levels culturally or previously defined in the society—when young people came of age not for college, but to go to work and assume family responsibilities. Manhood, womanhood—that state of social and financial self-sufficiency and community responsibility—are increasingly postponed until masters' and doctorate degrees are safely in hand, until the person approaches or passes thirty. Thus a sizable college group, in training for "citizenship" and "expertise," guided by administrations in loco parentis, has been showing the strains of balancing adult lives and serious intellectual aims in a framework set up to guide "youngsters" and "communities of Americans."

Integrating liberalism, with its citizenship models and training, in the past has succeeded in preventing severe class and ethnic strife over the struggle for material goods and political liberties. The seemingly inexhaustible wealth of the United States has eased major class contentions in the society. It made possible a so-called American genius for consensus-building and for a compromising pragmatic style. Aside from the raging "Negro question," other kinds of class and ethnic strife have, at least temporarily, lost significant dimensions. The general increase in the possession of goods and rights has gone hand in hand with a decline of doctrinaire utopian or socialist ideology (however much the latter may have inspired or caused the former). Incorporation of working classes and ethnic outgroups into the prevalent value system and rise in prosperity—with loyalties to voluntary associations, professions, and universalist categories such as nationhood overshadowing or destroying local, particularistic, class, and ethnic loyalties—was paralleled by a decline in radical politics, especially after World War II. Previously, when the century has witnessed great lower-class or racial upsurges, students had participated in organized protest. Out of the frustrations and propensities acting to reinforce student idealism, a radical tradition asserted itself among student bodies—always within a minority, but a noticeable one, commanding sympathies wider than indicated by the actual organizational membership. Thus the radical student throughout recent history became a great source of support for protesting social groups.

Conscious radical commitment no longer enjoys a small, hearty following among the "farmers and toilers" of America. The oppressed Negro and student radicals have become the current, perhaps the last, battering rams of political radicalism—a fact that may help account for the politics of desperation now pursued. Radicalism has provided a ready-made outlet for the frustration built up by academic competition, middle-class values, technological education, local citizenship ideals, and parental and administrative authority.

The decline of doctrinaire radicalism and populist movements and the rise of individual types "lost" in the great American complex had bred a fashionable pessimism, making romantic alienation an indispensable pose for the serious, thoughtful young intellectual. Faith in reason and in the eventual perfection of the lot and nature of mankind through improvements in education and the material environment, inherited from the Enlightenment, gave way to romantic introspective styles brought to heroic expression in the nineteenth century. For a long time these styles enabled the student to separate himself from the common and commercial in middle-class culture. The revival of protest among blacks, coupled with their small but impressive campaign victories, revivified an ideological optimism among radically minded persons. These could now turn from "beatness" and willed isolation to socially effective protest. The Negro civil-rights campaign encouraged attachment to other issues; protest against United States policy in Vietnam and pressures for educational reform expanded the base of the new student radicalism. Thus a slow middle-class buildup in American education and the gradual emergence of radical student minorities as a campus tradition flared up into a "new" student radicalism of the present when they were sparked by the Negro's struggle. His political successes ushered in a period of optimism about the effects and the potential of social action in the present decade.

Students from Tokyo to Paris have traditionally played the role of radical protesters. In the international context there is nothing remarkable about American student movements. The involvement of students in the Hungarian uprising; in the Soviet Union in protest against the imprisonment of two free-thinking writers; in the liberalization of Czechoslovakia; and the intense politicalization of student bodies throughout the underdeveloped world as well as the English and French "New Left"—these comparisons make the American student movement appear as a response to a general trend, rather than the cause of such trends. Insofar as all class movements exhibit some form of international solidarity, the United States student movement can be understood in class terms.

In the underdeveloped areas few except students have the education, the leisure, or the leadership role which can induce a general acceptance of values aiming at social change. That other sectors rarely attain these (and then only with student participation and leadership) together with the fact that student expectations in these nations are great because of educational preparedness for professional roles, renders these students vulnerable to radical movements and doctrines to a far greater extent than in the United States. Furthermore, in some areas (such as Latin America) the campus is a sanctuary, which the police are forbidden to enter, and thus agitation and radical student action can proceed with little official interference. This fact has functioned to hamper dictatorial regimes in their drive toward total control, but it has also limited free professional inquiry, making "academic freedom" something conceived in entirely different terms from the United States context.

Ironically, because of little political development among other popular sectors in underdeveloped countries, and because of a decline in radical protest among America's work-

ing classes, less complex and more complex societies alike
are witnessing student radicalization. Obviously there are
features of student life around the world, aside from those
especially applicable to the United States, that stimulate
"student movements."

Student Idealism and Politics

Before reaching the university, the student has found that
value-bearing agents, such as the family and religious institutions, present moral ideas in absolute and oversimplified
terms. Education, in relativizing these absolutes, offers a
basis for student rebellion against the simplified morality that
has marked his precollege background. Students are too
young or too separated from the larger society to have experienced serious responsibility for the management of their
lives. Our culture no longer values early assumptions of
financial responsibility, and generations of parents expend
themselves giving to the young more than they were able to
enjoy during their own youth. Consequently no fund of experience exists that unites the student with mate, children,
office holding and the like. In an already amorphous social
structure, students are more without a rooted "place" than is
any other group of comparable size. With no overpowering
status drives to deflect them, students' capacity for universal
identification with the "oppressed" and the "outcast" is
greater than it may be ever again in the course of their lives.
Tendencies in our technological society incorporate a taste
for innovation into education; the preoccupation with technique tends to justify attacks on past practices as conservative. Youthful demands for novel styles to meet new
situations, with a certain legitimacy in this context, readily
become fused to idealistic impulses.

The "generational struggle" can be as intense as the "class
struggle" when the former is not overwhelmed by the prevalence of the latter. Indeed, the two can shade off into each
other. In an atmosphere in which social place can only be
won by competitive struggle for the establishment of personal identity, new generations feel the need to group together.

An individualistic cultural emphasis in a youth-worshiping society has been extended to an expectation and an anticipation of the rebellion of young people as natural within family-controlled limits, though in criminal form — such as types of juvenile delinquency — it is, of course, intolerable. But in political form it also takes on a noxious cast for many adults, who cannot bear to see their stake in the status quo threatened. This polarization gives credibility to those who claim that student movements have a generational aspect. Furthermore, the commercial youth culture, created and bred by "the media," upon which many manufacturers of clothes, cosmetics, and the like depend, has capitalized upon a relatively rich youthful market. The college student who is already irritated by his dependence and disgusted by lack of seriousness, childish escapades, and commercialism does not want his inexperience to be mistaken for mindlessness. He resents shallow images of himself. He dislikes the good-guy fraternity equally as much as that of the semiliterate ignoramus appealed to or bred by the mass media at their worst. The commercial "youth industry" antagonizes serious students and compels them to dissociate themselves from the inanities peddled in the name of youth appeal. But periods are differentiated by many criteria, and generational identification is often a reaction for or against what is stressed for a time in the society; it is now an actual cause of social movements.

When intellectual disciplines are translated into the special language of institutional uses; when professional or "caste" possession of them tends toward exclusivity; when argument turns on hair-splitting disputation, formal "model building," and rephrasing of conventional wisdom — then we may expect the "antischolastic" burst from some direction (within the Christian faith or in humanistic or Renaissance reactions to such faith). So the imbalance is rectified, and fresh winds revive cloistered and formalized habits of thought. At the present time serious students have become increasingly dissatisfied by established formulas, and for many, education seems to have lost its "meaning." Dissatisfaction from many quarters, especially from the student

movement, has turned upon the professional training model
for education. "Those of us who have studied college students know that the work demanded of them cannot be fulfilled in a usual forty-hour week. Most students do not mind
hard work . . . the problem is that too often they cannot feel
that the work is leading to any worthy purpose."[6]

The humanistic tradition has emphasized education for
individual ends and the improvement of society through ag-
gregate knowledge. The medieval tradition, regardless of its
rigidly catechismic style, stressed service to a higher purpose, be it God or man. As a leisure activity of the refined,
education was traditionally considered a higher end in itself.
The gentlemanly tradition elevated education as an ideal
pursuit. The tradition of Christian service and Talmudic
adoration of "the word" has fostered an ideal aura about
higher education. The pursuit of "truth" and "goodness"
were considered greater than practical uses found for them
and from which use values derive in the good society; and in
the process, vocational training itself became suspect.

Individual careerism may be a forgivable motive for pursuit of learning, but it was expected in the "great tradition"
that such selfishness would be unlearned in the process of
education. Such traditional aims are secondary in present
university education, borne essentially by the more prin-
cipled among students and faculty. These aims are brought to
administrative attention largely through complaint—students
caught up in the "great tradition" want to learn; they do not
want to be "trained." The modern campus, with its exhaust-
ing demands for research, provides little time for learning
through the indispensable "long discussion" and heated argument. It creates situations that encourage an intense personal stake in being "right," rather than in finding "truth,"
leaving little room for experimentation with learning.

Student rebels responded by finding refuge in the living
laboratory provided by the Negro civil rights movement. The
"plight" of the Negro provided not only a rallying cry for

6. Joseph Katz and Nevitt Sanford, "The Student Revolution," in *Current*,
February 1966, pp. 6–7.

liberals and radicals; it also presented a clearcut moral issue calling for "good works." In this movement opportunities existed for the student movement to derive a model that could never be gleaned from a schoolroom. The radical or unique individual departed from established curricula in order to devote energy and time. Students who were in the movement agreed that the campus chapter or group working among the poor and the blacks was a valuable workshop in relating academic endeavors to real human problems, building up an understanding of collective, cooperative leadership, and gaining invaluable experience in politics and organizing. The rise of Black Power militancy, of demands for black separatism—rivaling in intensity, if not in character, the anti-Negro sentiment and segregationist demands of whites—caused changes in student radical tactics.

Such student organizations as Students for a Democratic Society (SDS) increasingly reached out into the lower-class white communities off the campus, rather than treating the campus as "the community." This effort began as an attempt to unite the poor with the Negro into a broad movement. In Chicago an organized effort called JOIN (Jobs or Income Now) succeeded in canvassing the city for available jobs for the unemployed or unskilled, maintaining a useful employment file, educating the poor to the sources of jobs or welfare in the city, and bringing many together for some concerted action for the first time. While it is foolhardy to make dramatic claims for this effort, the education provided for participating students was at least as great as the benefits that accrued to those poor within the city who were serviced. SDS field workers, however disastrously utopian their dreams of a labor-Negro radical alliance may have been did manage to step into a situation no one else was likely to tackle.

With the decline of ethnic benevolent-aid associations among the poor; with a trade union leadership concerned more with enriching already organized members than recruiting the unorganized; without a classic machine boss likely to dispense favors to win them, the poor have had to shift for themselves, often resulting in drift and failure. President Johnson's "War on Poverty," structured to fill a welfare void from the top, had a limited success in this capacity but no basis with which to mount an attack upon the cultural void left by lack of organization or a psychology of solidarity among the poor. But the students in the movement, unable to limit themselves to campus affairs, shared an empathetic experience with the peoples with whom they worked— something that schematized social science courses were unable to stimulate.[7]

The practiced politician, in the inevitable process of specialization, becomes adept at managing and pacifying his constituency. The representative role is inherently conservatizing, since responsibility for representing varied interests and maintaining professional prestige make it impossible to isolate "the poor." It is not the task of congressional representatives to plead the case of the poor but to represent a whole community. Such representation is clearly impossible without damage to some interest, and its lack of influence usually puts the poorest elements of a community into this position of neglect. Idealistic leadership is an art in itself and a luxury the representative finds it difficult to afford, even when he is inclined to consider it. Thus the idealistically motivated student performs a practical task for which no specialized professional leadership exists — except, perhaps, among Black protest or pressure organizations. Idealistic politics is a specialty that students can afford and that enriches their education. In this way they are weighing and writing about experiences that will contribute more than can mere academic assignments to meaningful intellectual communication. Their work becomes a record for future historians of the less common experiences of a decade.

Aims and Methods

Democratic ideology fosters a literal interpretation of individualism, of the individual as a "vital center." This view

7. Another case in point is reported by students in the "Bruns Volkswagen" strike. See C. Clark Kissinger, "The Bruns Strike: A Case Study in Student Participation in Labor," *The New Student Left*, edited by Cohen and Hale, Boston: Beacon Press, 1966.

is often at the root of rebelliousness, whether it wears "collectivist" or other garb. Much in student radicalism is a literal and intense commitment to democratic individualism as a way of life. This assumption is so common that with little evidence many interpreted the Berkeley student rebellion in terms of antibureaucratic individualism. In reviewing the Berkeley revolt, however, Robert Somers reports:

> We found sympathy for the demonstrators to be widespread and dispersed throughout the campus, even to the extent of one-third of the students approving the tactics that demonstrators had used. This support was clearly concentrated among students in certain fields—the social sciences, humanities, and physical science—but as strong among freshmen as among graduate students, and not related to the number of semesters a student has been on this campus. Nor is support particularly related to feelings of dissatisfaction with the educational functions of the university. On the contrary, we found a remarkable amount of satisfaction with courses, professors . . . and appreciation of the efforts made by the administration to provide top quality education. . . . *Thus the prevailing explanation in terms of characteristics peculiar to the "multiversity" seems to have no support.* Rather, it appears that students resent being deprived of their rights to political activity, being excluded from full political citizenship, and this sentiment is especially strong among those who are emotionally involved in the civil rights movement. Thus the material we collected suggests that the mainsprings of the rebellion are an optimistic idealism about the type of society which can be shaped by the new generation, and an unwillingness to allow the paternalism endemic to college campuses to extend its coverage to the activities necessary for the furtherance of these ideals.[8]

The disciplines from which, according to Somers, especially sympathetic students were drawn represented those that were integrated within the university and were not part of special schools (such as schools of fine arts or music), and yet with less direct lines to professional security than are provided by engineering, medicine, or law. These data reveal how dangerous and narrow it is to reduce the present

8. Robert Somers, "The Mainsprings of the Rebellion: A Survey of Berkeley Students in November, 1964," in *The Berkeley Student Rebellion: Facts and Interpretations*, edited by Lipset and Wolin. New York: Doubleday, 1965, p. 534 (italics added).

student political movement to psychodynamic terms. Student politics are not a guise for sexual freedom, an attempt to win professorial attention in an "anonymous" atmosphere, or an outcry against bureaucratic incompetence or impersonality. The student movement is a genuinely *political* one. Because it involves young people, such politics is not likely to be fully conscious of its exaggerations, inexperience, or full range of motives. Though these politics take place on campus, they are nonetheless oriented toward wider political issues. Somers continues:

> It is disconcerting but instructive to note that . . . when over half the campus apparently agreed that the demonstrations had some legitimate substantive basis, the administration never gave evidence of a desire to correct the public view of the protest movement which it had created by announcements . . . that nearly half of the leadership of the movement were Castro and Mao sympathizers. My personal observations are that the apparent unwillingness of the administration to consider the possibility of a legitimate intellectual and ideological ferment underlying the protest pressed more and more moderates into a coalition with the early activits. [Pp. 537–8]

Furthermore, the activists are often among the best students. Despite the irritants of the campus environment—the pressures of a system that does not adequately integrate self-expressive goals into educational programming— participating students were not generally those who were hampered by the routine procedures from learning enough to exhibit or strive for good grades. At Berkeley there seemed a strong correlation between high academic achievement and support for the demonstrators. While this relation might be limited to certain academic fields, the extent to which the most articulate become the most militant provides serious problems and pressures for both administrators and faculty alike. Draper, in citing the Graduate Political Scientists' Report (a fact-finding committee of graduate political scientists), notes: "In a survey of the Free Speech Movement students who were arrested in the mass sit-ins of December 3, it was found that most are earnest students of considerably better than average academic standings."[9] The thought that

9. Hal Draper, *Berkeley: The New Student Revolt*. New York: Grove Press, 1965, p. 14.

the rebellion of students against impersonality and bureaucracy are products of crippling alienation ignores the real "working conditions" of students that lead to such alienative responses.

In a tradition extending from Rousseau to Sorel, student radicals disenchanted by the corruption and isolation attending developing civilization conceive individuality in restorationist terms, as the reinstatement of an original human capacity for good through reform of the present. Absolutely essential to such reform is the restoration of the individual as the bearer of an inviolable dignity and will that, when educated to the common good, are exercised in its behalf; no substitute for this exercise is possible without violation of the common good. Thus individuality is conceived as the exercise of will for social purposes as well as the means by which selfish private man is transformed into a socially responsible creature. To prevent anyone from the exercise of that will is to take from him the means to count as a social entity. For an individual to surrender the right and obligation to unfettered volition is to surrender an essential component for genuine independence and to forfeit the right to criticize the actions of others. This tradition preaches an active relationship to a social environment in which each significantly contributes to the whole. This contribution is necessary — indeed mandatory — for the realization of a united private and public self and the basis for what is truly meant by democracy. By definition, unexercised will is nonexistent, and an individual so deprived falls into a dependence that robs him of mature status. The social self is realized politically; by extension, political choices not exerted are nonexistent.

By the same theory, individual men diminish themselves by failing to act politically. An attendant revulsion with politics as a specialized professional task stems from the belief that political rights have been usurped from individuals, who must then proceed to reshape society to restore the rightful exercise of individual will upon the environment in order that "wholeness" may be resurrected.

Radical politics turned romantic implies the restoration of "moral politics" — the involvement of all in social activity politically defined. The cure for "apathy" and "fragmentation" lies in a revival of those conditions that restore political decision making to all levels, preventing it from constituting the special preserve of a professional class. Thus "civic man" — a creature who has lost his glorious tradition and has retreated to privacy and only occasional community activity, the once proud citizen now a localized unit created by democratic professionalization, acting out of bald-faced interest or not at all — confronts "political man," the creature of individualist morality committed to action to shape a common good, a broad democracy, for the collectivity.

In comtemporary life, restriction of the concept of citizenship results in a confrontation or tension between "civic" and "political" types. Equally, student government and student movements represent two opposing outcomes of modern politics: this is the "difference in quality," mentioned at the outset. While one reflects the specialization of politics, the other, in the name of "injustice," cries out against it in moral ferver: "No! You false liberals are suffering from the failure of your youthful dreams; you are eviscerating the great optimistic tradition from the Enlightenment to the twentieth century; you are justifying disinterest in morality; you are eliminating emotion, dissent, outrage, and yes, the wellsprings of life itself." Or again: "Liberal tactics have been successful in winning office, but they have been part of the destructive force tearing the common good, the social tie to shreds."[10] Carey McWilliams represents the same view when he inveighs against the "anti-morality of the wheeler-dealer practitioners." The SDS expression of this view is clear in its Port Huron statement: "A new left must transform modern complexity into issues that can be understood and felt close-up by every human being. It must give form to the feelings of helplessness and indifference, so that people may see the political, social, and economic sources of their private troubles and organize to change society."[11] Thus radicalism seeks

10. Thomas Hayden and C. Reinier, "A Letter to the New (Young) Left," in *The New Student Left*, ed. by Cohen and Hale. Boston: Beacon Press, 1966, pp. 4, 40.
11. "Port Huron Statement (Students for a Democratic Society), *Ibid.*, p. 223.

out doctrines that promise to usher in the new day of a "new" political morality—which, it turns out, is really an ancient political right.

The contemporary student movement is strongly concerned with the dangers of total morality, total change, and demands for total commitment. The legendary "proletarian" 1930's carried their lessons through a literature of the "disenchanted" and through a politics of terror that seized revolutionary nations in the name of total doctrinal morality. The present student movement has developed something of an ideology that might be called anti-ideology. It is by no means the open pragmatism of the professional politician, to be sure, although it is pragmatic. It is rather the morality of openness, of antidoctrine, of a "way of life" and a crusading style. Segments that have embraced variants of Marxism, such as the W. E. B. DuBois Clubs or the Progressive Labor groups, represent an ideological strain in the movement, but they are more affected by the present openness of the majority in the larger movement than by their Stalinist or Maoist forbears. They are not obsessed by "democratic centralism," criticism and "self-criticism," or blueprints of revolutions after the tenets of Marxism-Leninism. There is a widespread belief that ideological purity is poisonous to moral purity, that it breeds sectionalism, dispute, disaffiliation. Thus, ironically, the disgust with wheeling and dealing has not given rise to ideological politics, except in shadow form, largely because of the failures of leftwing movements of the past. In this sense the student movement represents a new radicalism. For it is not unconscious of ideology; it quite consciously eschews it. Radicalism is morality itself; it is an attitude. "Radicalism finds no rest in conclusions, answers are seen as provisional, to be discarded in the face of new evidence."[12]

Student radicalism is open-ended, seeking to include as many sympathetic members as possible, embracing all among the "mass" with a grievance. It seeks to make an addition to personal lives. Leaving "cell" organization far

12. Thomas Hayden, *Ibid.*, p. 6.

behind, it is, rather, mobile and flexible. Coordinating committees (such as SNCC) tie up loose ends, initiate actions, guide the interaction of many groups. Programming follows from perceived needs and not from doctrinaire commandments. The radical program is simply the radical style as it attempts to change practical politics. Organization is often improvisational (as JOIN), guided by a free-style radical leadership and run on participatory democratic procedures. Tom Hayden, a founder and past president of SDS, writes: "Another essential . . . is that we visualize and then build structures to counter those we oppose. This extends from the concrete formation of a national student organization to the conceptual formation of a different society." Radicalism is dynamized by the apocalyptic temper: "Our work is guided by the sense that we may be the last generation in the experiment with living."[13]

"Participatory democracy" in the movement is an organizational method deriving from the radical mystique of mass consensus. Groups and organizations are small, manageable. There are coordinating bodies exemplified by (SNCC), local organizations improvised to meet local issues (WAGE), or chapters of national organizations (CORE). Built around issues (civil rights, peace in Vietnam, poverty, educational reform) rather than doctrines, organizations are loose and decentralized, and a literal democracy prevails, where "each counts as one" — that is, leadership cannot count more than rank-and-file members. Mass consensus is arrived at by persuasion, irrespective of slowness of decision making, and the role of leadership is minimized. The student movement aims at moral ends won by moral means.

Many problems arise. The conflict has been posed in the question: are the ideals of participatory democracy and community organizations compatible with the growth of industrialization and urbanization?[14] "Elitism" and "indigenism" are terms expressing the conflict over the role of leadership. What is more, "Today the picket sign seems to have entered the stage of diminishing returns, and more and

13. *Ibid.*, p. 9.
14. Cohen and Hale, *Ibid.*, Introduction, p. XXV.

more signs and pickets are needed to achieve the same impact on the political community."[15] Will the organizations adjust to loss of momentum and develop styles of work based on more centralized leadership or should they strive for mass participation, perhaps leading to the same need in the long run? Further, how viable an alternative is pacifism—the most durable "ideology" of the movement insofar as one may be attributed to it—unless the issue is presented and perceived as a clearcut and moral one, like that of the war in Vietnam, or black rights?

Direct action techniques, however necessary on political grounds, have a polarizing effect with respect to strictly educational goals. Further, is there such an entity as "the poor," merely awaiting organizing agents? Or is "the poor" a collection of groups and strata that must be carefully appraised for potential irritation with the ongoing system? How can these issues be resolved "pragmatically" or by mere radical "oppositionism"? Shall we join and construct, influence, win partial aims? Shall we preserve our moral purity as outsiders and risk utter loss? What good is partial reform? Without explicit ideological cohesion, can conflicts around leading personalities be contained? These questions are raised and disputed constantly. And the dangers are noted: "the very intensity of this sort of political organization, demanding wholehearted commitment and much time and emotion, makes it particularly unstable." Furthermore, it "does not combine well with freedom or with a broader sense of fraternity."[16] To drown these questions the movement depended heavily on the momentum achieved by high public interest, on relatively broad participation, and on the dramatic appeal of the "new". But the questions will not stay submerged. The "moral style," even in pragmatic form, is threatened by temporariness. But whether or not this particular style will long survive, politics in the age of mass participation will draw opposition again, for the fragmentation of "political man" into "civic man" is intolerable to the romantic moralist who is not "practical."

15. Jonathan Eisen, "Coming of Age: The Legacy of Protest," *Ibid.*
16. Bruce Payne, *New Student Left*, ed. by Cohen and Hale, *op. cit.*, p. 100.

Radical Types

Given its aims and methods, the student movement should be much larger than it is. If there are so many legitimate, understandable reasons for its existence, why has it not involved the majority of American college students? Obviously, one reason is that only small groups of individuals are politically active under any conditions except those of severe crisis, radical distaste for this notion notwithstanding. Yet the matter of minority status is complex. For the most part, the sociological backgrounds of participating and sympathetic students are not strikingly unusual. It appears that three groups are broadly discernible in the student movement.

1. Students from families with liberal backgrounds with notions of social service. Whether they manifest a high degree of "Christian compassion" or are college-educated social workers, the parents espouse a marked private and/or political morality concerned with help for the less fortunate. These students often carry the liberal implications of their home experience to greater lengths than parental approval would have encouraged—but they are not faced with active parental opposition. Many report early experiences of contact with the poor or (idealizing even to the point of romantic daydreams) a Jew, a Negro, or someone considered "outside" community, parental, or general social approval.

2. Students from small-town or suburban communities and from strictly conventional homes. These students are opposed by their parents, whose opposition may be expressed in physical action against the students for their political activities or in consistent pressure to end political affiliation. Students in this group do not clearly recall early contact with the poor, but they have always sympathized with the "underdog" and are largely inflamed by parental authority and conventionality. Humanizing contact with poverty occurred usually after they joined the movement.

3. Students with parents who adhered or adhere to some variety of Marxist radicalism. These are a small, vocal minority within the movement. The parents of these students encourage participation, and the students themselves are well versed in Marxist literature, able to take the lead in dis-

cussions, activity, and the like. They have frequent contact with small circles of radical friends of parents throughout childhood. The participation of these students has often led to "focus treatments" on the part of right-wing publications.[17]

Research on student participation in peace marches and peace activities has shown that: (1) Demonstrators, in contrast to leaders, were quite young—the median age being eighteen to nineteen. (2) They had no well-formed, comprehensive political ideology. (3) Many students (though not usually those in leadership positions) expressed moral objections to the cold war and to nuclear weapons—though little or no personal religious commitment is evident in the majority of demonstrators. In their statements and actions there seemed to be a striving after purity, a combination of idealism and protest. (4) Data suggest that the age period in which feelings for social or political "causes" are most likely to develop is twelve to fifteen. (5) The majority of students came from politically liberal families but they were "rebelling" in going far beyond parental experience in the realm of public action. About one-fourth of the students characterized their homes as politically conservative or reactionary. Some demonstrators appeared to display a quality of simultaneous rebellion against identification with parental images. (6) Older demonstrators, in their middle twenties, seemed to form a psychosocial population different and separate from the younger students. (7) Opposing counterpickets from conservative student groups differed markedly from the peace demonstrators on many parameters of belief and behavior. Particular attention is drawn to the psychosocial dimensions of trust and distrust in comparing the two groups.[18]

17. In addition to exposés from the right, a byproduct of committed Marxist participants, and like this exposé literature, is the god-that-failed disenchantment, now receiving an airing. See ex-Progressive Laborite Phillip A. Luce, *The New Left*. New York: McKay Publishers, 1966. Through them the movement is "exposed" (as for example a treatment received in the publication of the YAF, *The New Guard*, under the Heading "Red Diaper Babies," September 1965, pp. 6–12).

18. Solomon and Fishman, "Youth and Peace: A Psychosocial Study of Student Peace Demonstrators in Washington, D.C.," in *Journal of Social Issues*, 20, 4 (October 1964), p. 55. Essentially the same findings were established by Richard Flacks in "The Liberated Generation: An Exploration of the Roots of Student Protest," *Journal of Social Issues*, 23, 3, 1967, pp. 52–75.

The uniformity of most activist students' backgrounds reveals how distinctly a social movement the students are embarked upon. They are much less dependent on psychological uniqueness, deviance, and aberration, even as compared with the "beats" of the 1950's. However much personality growth and personal experiences may lead to participation, involvement is better explained by political examination of a strong reaction against conditions and policies in the United States at a time when a catalytic agent (black rights) made organization possible and optimism plausible; such a time calls forth the "political moralist."

There is no escaping the question of what breeds political moralism, especially of the left, in a society that does not easily accept or sanction it. The answer must be found in examination of some of the leading tendencies of life in the advanced, industrialized, and urbanized United States. The positive myths of American life have been undergoing gradual disintegration. New intellectual trends, ideals, styles of "collective belonging" have a discernible identity. Occupational specialization and professional autonomy permit new adaptations of competitive individualism in a rich, crowded United States in which disgruntled groups are outdistanced by new status climbers, new participants in the democratic way, and small gains are more easily threatened by newcomers.

Previously, utopian and futuristic dreaming stimulated a common and generous national feeling, an optimistic transmission of the "democratic" culture for the guidance and enrichment of other individuals. National myths about riches and achievements for "him who labored and deserved" showed faith and commitment to the nation, all its faults and absurdities granted. Competitive individuals were pitted against "forces," wrested their wealth from nature and from other men through shrewdness and daring, and were urged to test the limits. Generations were supposed to inherit and build upon parental stakes. Youthful rebellion concerned itself with new styles of acquisition. Expectations were high for self-reliance and work responsibilities. Strong as ties of locality, family, and community were, they remained fused to the greatness seen to lie in an expanding America. Accompanied by industrial work styles and rationalization, values of efficiency, scientific exploration, and innovation gradually shaped attitudes to work and achievement. The predominance of these developed new types of men who could run the system, who could survive or flourish within it. The management and survival of the society by the process of psychological natural selection called forth the types to lead and to set the pattern for others to survive and gain.

Kenneth Keniston has searched out a characterization of prevailing and opposite types of new radical opposition. His useful, if highly ideological, vocabulary for the expression of older and new styles of thought will be drawn upon for present purposes.[19] When religious and local values regulated an "inner self", aggressive conquest "outward" served to establish a stake in the American community. Acquisition was a generational building block. The "future" meant an optimistic and reassuring state. Sons would build on the gains of their fathers. Commercial pursuits and industrial skills were not yet oppressive or isolating in their effect. The world seemed fit for generational building. Religious belief, life style, and a great nation's growth implied no contradictions. Collective dreams of the better life, the material horn of plenty, utopian transformations of man did not imply revolutionary aims toward the American government. Populist movements notwithstanding, Americans have been transcendentally identified with their country. Personality was not yet fitted to the machine and management skills. Intuition, shrewdness, tall taletelling imagination had not yet become second to logic, efficiency, rationalization. Ideological predilections among the American intelligentsia had not yet undergone analytic revolutions. The mass of immigrants, coming from non-industrialized cultures, became the bearers of the intuitive romantic values that were beginning to fade among Americans. The better opportunities of the latter led them to rapid assimilation into the growing industrial-administrative styles. While the "synthetic" romatically ori-

19. Kenneth Keniston, *Young Radicals: Notes on Committed Youth.* New York: Harcourt, Brace & World, 1968.

ented styles were transferred to isolated or excluded groups, analytic styles and psychological adaptations increasingly characterized the "Yankee." Modern Yankee culture called forth types that would enhance its progress and shape new generations, not for conquest, daring, or generational inheritance, but for management, citizenship, and salable skills. Scientific rationalization and occupational specialization, once fully under way, suggested a new kind of competitiveness, based upon the advancement of self through the acquisition of technological skills and managing; manipulative genius for organization prevailed. Hero types and intellectual models reflected this circumstance in turn, with methodological and specialized concerns over "ultimate" philosophizing. Reinforced at colleges, analytic, rationalizing, scientific models prevailed as much as methods and became identified with achievement and self-advancement.

In a period of ascendant analytic models, rebellion is identified with the intellectual images of fusion, sythesis, and romantic restorationism seeking "wholeness" and an "organic" world. Quality of life becomes an uppermost concern for the rebel who cannot or will not turn his skills to rationalizing the system or emulating its problem-solving styles. These seek "fusion" with something "higher" than self to overcome the fragmentation of selfish competitiveness; they choose the synthesis of the whole "world view" over analytic middle-range problem solving. The colleges as the new bearers of the prevailing technological "Yankee" style become particularly distasteful and repressive to "learning" in the romantic imagination—for young people of this type, as well as their teachers, are herded like everyone else to the colleges in order to make something practical of their lives.

Generational emulation has little meaning in a rich society, and the educational system simply appears mean and commercial, reinforcing the destruction of the imagination. The technological environment, requiring analytic intelligence, breeds and develops it in the majority. Minority rebellion wells up among those whose way of life or personality is fused to romanticism concerned with "essential" qualities of life, individual expression, and minimal emphasis of efficiency and quantity. Thus contemporary rebellion is often romantic, ideologically as well as psychologically. This was not always the case. When religious and aristocratic values of the organic society prevailed, rationalistic-scientific doctrines were revolutionary. The French *philosophes* in response to their semifeudal environment demanded reason, writ large and glorious. This word was the rallying cry before which everything gave way. To the rebels of the present, prevailing rationalistic philosophies or styles have narrowed the domain of reason to technicism. They seek the "higher" purpose in fusion with the great idea or cause and react against realistic, skill-producing adjustment pragmatism.

Everything has now been given its rational place. The state, the law, the factory, the university are collective units constructed out of isolated individuals, fitted into niches by task and skill, mobilized by opportunity and reward. Problem-solving styles are organized, quantifying, scheme-building, systematized. Efficiency, order, and stability are values linked to scientific progress, which endlessly arranges a chaotic universe. It was Karl Mannheim who brilliantly observed that historically opposed to "bourgeois" rationalism are "essential" philosophies of life, valuing intensity, conflict, sensuality, organicism, intuition. These thought styles can be attached to conservative, revolutionary, or liberal uses, depending on circumstances.

> The great importance of the philosophies of Life consists in their constant emphasis on the limitations of bourgeois rationalism which in its expansion threatens gradually to obscure and devitalize everything that is alive in the world. The philosophy of Life is never tired of pointing out that whatever passes for "real" in our rationalized world is merely a reflection of the specific categories of Reason of which modern man has made an idol, in other words, that this world of alleged reality is merely the world of capitalist rationalization. As such it conceals behind it a world of pure "vital experience."[20]

Although Mannheim is referring to a conservative variant of "life philosophy," one which specifically became German

20. Karl Mannheim, "Conservative Thought," in *Essays on Sociology and Social Psychology*. New York: Oxford University Press, 1953, p. 162.

romanticism, its quality is broadly applicable. Like their conservative forebears, apolitical "philosophies of life" are either too helpless or too negative to be bound to social action for purposes of social change. This was largely the character of the "beatness" of the 1950's, when there was no real activity in the civil-rights movement, when the left collapsed under Joseph McCarthy's attacks, when leading leftist intellectuals were busily recanting and regretting their former associations. The declamatory "beats" represented apolitical and passive withdrawal or genuine alienation. These personalities were unable to accept or to assimilate the rationalism and the achievement pressures of the culture, turning instead to "experience," fusion fantasies with non-ego ideals, "communication." They rejected the responsibilities of our technological society and turned to unbound personal freedom, negatively conceived.

The civil rights movement gave radical romantics the initial impulse to play a new role. Those among them who did not fear battle; to whom experience meant aggressive shaping of the environment; who as maturing adults wanted—indeed, needed—and demanded responsibility for making the world they lived in and were learning about; and who were not alienated (except for peripheral hangers-on)—these came forward to create the student movement. Thus, after radicalism among students had become something of a minority tradition, under pressure of institutional irritants those susceptible to romantic intellectual styles became members of a movement and "took off" when triggered by the optimistic impact of the civil rights struggle. The prevalence of romantic styles and institutional pressures provides assurance that, despite periods of decline, student movements are potentially always with us.

The romantic is close in feeling to the heroic. Romantic heroism now has its ideological payoff in radical terms: in attacking the common middle-class bourgeois, with his conventionality, his safe, small notions of the good life. The rebel student, newly emerged from suburbia to the campus, turns upon the middle-class ideal as much for its lack of passion, for its absence of heroic conquest, as for any other failing. In the movement the "hero" is restored to an honored place, whether as martyr or leader. This opportunity to perform heroically further justifies rejection of small-minded, timid bourgeois society.[21]

Finally, aside from the real iniquities in American society that will stimulate efforts at resolution, and aside from the sociological causation and political character of the student movement, the movement involves a minority because in its ideological values and moral restoration it serves best and is best served by that minority number who cannot and will not assimilate the values and qualities upon which the present social environment thrives.

---

21. See Irving Louis Horowitz, Preface to the Second Edition of *Radicalism and the Revolt Against Reason* ("Radical Irrationalism: Then and Now"). Carbondale, Illinois: Southern Illinois University Press, 1968.

CHAPTER FIVE

Students as a Social Class

The most intensive conflict in contemporary industrial societies is not among religions, political parties, workers and
management, or even races, but between youth and adults.
To be sure, race riots in America have proved costly in terms
of lives and economics, but generational differences underlie
even participation in racial conflict: the Black Power movement is largely staffed and led by young people, and rioters
tend to be young.[1] Student revolts are taking place on hundreds of university campuses and in dozens of countries; and
they are occurring with increasing frequency, intensity, and
duration. Generational conflict is multinational and crosscul-
tural.

Generational conflict is a universal theme in history, and
student revolts have been part of higher education since its
beginnings.[2] But if these facts are well documented, they are
little attended to; acknowledging the ubiquitous occurrence
of student revolts is different from recognizing their importance. To dismiss student unrest by pointing out that it is
perennial is to miss the point. If students have almost always

1. For a description of the "typical rioter," see *Report of the National
Advisory Commission on Civil Disorders*. New York: Bantam Books, 1968.
2. Cf. Lewis Feuer, *The Conflict of Generations*. New York: Basic Books,
1969.

and everywhere revolted in or against society, it can only be because there exists a continuing objective basis for opposition. Yet in the past, society usually ignored the plight of students, failed to take them seriously, and refused to consider their collective problem as structural and political, instead treating their behavior as malicious deviance.

Society's attitude toward students is reflected in social science. Although books and articles on adolescents, youth, and students now appear in great quantity, and although many "facts" and "measurements" are gathered and displayed in tables, little systematic theory has emerged.[3] Not only has the pioneering work of Mannheim and Davis largely been ignored, but conceptual distinctions current thirty years ago have been blurred in recent scholarship.[4] Many prostigious spokesmen continue to minimize the seriousness and the potential for sociopolitical revolution or rejuvenation through student rebellions.

Since student unrest has not been treated as a social movement, as a societal and political problem, and as a driving force in history, no social theory has been developed to account for it. In light of the contemporary epidemic proportions of student revolts, this failure becomes a curious social fact in itself. Its explanation may inhere partly in ideologically induced blindness, but it rests also in distorted theoretical perspectives. Students are never considered as a self-interested group (in contrast to a congerie or statistical category) with its own structural location in society and his-

3. Cf. the two vólumes edited by Seymour Martin Lipset: *Student Politics.* New York: Basic Books, 1967; "Students and Politics," *Daedalus,* Winter, 1968.

4. Karl Mannheim, "The Problem of Generations," *Essays on the Sociology of Knowledge,* Oxford, 1952 (originally written in late 1920's); also Karl Mannheim, "The Problem of Youth in Modern Society," in *Diagnosis of Our Time.* New York: Oxford University Press, 1944. Kingsley Davis, "The Sociology of Parent-Youth Conflict," *American Sociological Review,* Vol. 5, August 1940, 523–535; also "Adolescence and the Social Structure," *Annals of the American Academy of Political and Social Sciences,* CCXXXV, November 1944, 8–16. Almost no contemporary writers distinguish between adolescence and youth—lumping them together or failing to treat youth over about eighteen. Such a distinction did exist in the late 1930's and is evident in Paul Landis, *Adolescence and Youth,* 2nd. ed. New York: McGraw-Hill, 1952 (originally published 1945).

tory and its own unique experience. Perusal of the technical literature reveals hundreds of studies of the young and of students using social class as an independent variable for predicting such items as academic success, occupational choice and mobility, adjustment, and so forth, but none has taken students as a class in and for itself or has examined student revolts as manifestations of a "class conflict" with the older generation.

The implicit nonperson status of youth and students is so pervasive in our culture that social scientists as well as society fail to consider the reciprocity of rights and obligations when studying generational interaction, as is shown by this quote from a recent important text on the American adolescent: "When the young meet the standards and demands of adults there is little conflict between the generations. When, however, youth do not fulfill the expectation of adults there is both intergenerational conflict and concern for the future of society."[5] Where is the perspective of the young? Or does the ruling generation really deny that others might have rights as well as obligations?

Seen in this light, the structural nature of the problem becomes clearer. The question of rights and their fulfillment — sometimes called "justice" — is eminently political. And if history teaches anything, it is that politically oppressed classes contain major potential for support of revolutionary movements. Students are becoming a politicized generation class. They constitute neither a society nor a party; and they are more than a sector of the economy, a segment of the population, and a status group. Students as a group have most of the characteristics of a revolutionary class, the essential difference being the substitution of a generational base for the poverty base. Students' "underdog" position is a consequence of being young in a generational conflict in which "adults" (full-fledged members of society) define what is real for others who, although not economically

5. D. Gottlieb and C. E. Ramsey, *The American Adolescent*. Homewood, Illinois: Dorsey Press, 1964, p. v.

deprived, are kept dependent.

The goal of synthesizing class and generation theories raises serious issues. It might be worth mentioning the difficulties in such an enterprise. A catalogue of objections to so conceptualizing the generational issue would include: (1) There is nothing new about the situation (and, by implication, nothing about which to be concerned). (2) Student unrest is nothing more than childhood rebellion against authority and hence transitory (and by implication not rooted in an inappropriate or imperfect sociopolitical structure). (3) Class theory is defunct (status groups, political parties, and the like, now propel history), even though society is organized along class lines. (4) Students and youth are no more than a status group. (5) But even if they met the requirements of definition as a class, it could not be a revolutionary class for the following reasons: (a) Students are no longer involved in the productive process. (b) They lack an institutional base. (c) Students are still a small numerical group. (d) Identification as a student is too brief (mobility). (e) The student movement has no utopian image or plan. (f) Internal splits exist. (g) Students are not exploited, oppressed, or impoverished. (h) There is more generational emulation than there is conflict; and in the event it were potentially revolutionary, it would be shortly defused of the adaptability of American society. These objections should be treated in detail.

1. A certain continuity underlies student unrest throughout the ages; but contrary to the conclusion that it can therefore be safely disregarded, such unrest is of deep social and historical significance precisely because of its continued manifestation. Furthermore, a unique quality is involved—a new kind of history in the experience of today's youth.

2. Feuer has asserted that generational conflict as a driving force in history is more ultimate than are class struggles. There is no need to deny psychoanalytic notions of authority conflict rooted in sex or other biopsychological mechanisms as having some validity in explaining student behavior. But total explanatory power must be denied this reductionist per-

spective. The facts of scarcity and economics, power and social structure, and ideology and history cannot be derived from familial relations or child-centered physiological drives. In short, sexual attitudes are significant in defining the new youth culture, but they do not determine its culture and character.

3. The existence and importance of social class need not be counterposed to the notion of generational conflict; the two often overlap and interact. As Sorokin indicated, the youth class is "one of the most powerful social groups in the Western world. With its growth it has established social class differentiation and the class-struggle as one of the most acute forms of intergroup conflict."[6] The implications of considering students as a social class are varied. It emphasizes their historical importance. This is crucial in a dynamic society that must rely for rejuvenation on the political mobilization and moral fervor of its youth. The structural location of a group makes possible the rational restructuring of society to reduce strains and to redirect wasted energy. It further points out the need for an institutional response on the part of adult society as well as an institutionalized mode of participation for the young. These are minimal, prima facie consequences of a model that brings conflict to awareness, thereby pinpointing the sources and mechanisms of change.

4. The fusion of these two concepts of generation and class brings into focus the importance of the problem of students in society. Status groups are in part definitional and in part analytical categories. The difference between analytical and empirical levels of discourse, which may be distinct in abstract analytical concepts, are linked in empirical reality. This is often the case in the connections among class, status, party, and power. Important classes tend to be empirically coincident with high status and coercive capacities. Students are in an anomalous position; they are highly educated and have relatively high standards of living, yet they are politically and economically exploited. It is the nature of social exis-

---

6. Pitirim Sorokin, "Social Differentiation," *International Encyclopedia of the Social Sciences*, 14. New York: Macmillan, 1968, p. 408.

tence as a whole that defines class and selects its members, not a few analytical fragments or indices.

5. If social class can be defined as some "multi-bonded group whose members are bound together into a solidary unity by similarity of occupational, economic and socio-political interests and activities"[7] then students certainly meet the criteria. They share an occupation — education — economic dependency, forms of housing, styles of speech, dress, music, and other symbolic identifications. They also have negative identification, such as personal alienation, lack of property, political-legal status, high frequency of interaction within the group, and large numbers in close physical proximity. For these reasons the language of social class best describes the general condition of young people and the specific condition of students — notwithstanding competing "class" factors that serve to distinguish working youth from college youth.

The Youth Generation

If historical process consists of an interplay between constant factors, such as innate biological impulses, and more dynamic ones such as technological developments, then a generation must be a part of this historical process, transcending its biological origin. A generation possesses characteristics peculiar to itself, derived from more than age alone. Were there no social interaction, there would be no social structure and no continuity of history in which to locate a class or generation. The sociological problem thus begins where the biological issue leaves off.

The unity of a generation is linked to a consciousness of belonging to one generic group. Generations are not concrete groups as are communities — where unity is dependent on physical proximity and on the members' concrete knowledge of one another — or associations deliberately founded for specific purposes. Generation is a social category that structurally resembles class. Both these phenomena are linked to

7. Sorokin, *op. cit.*

social location, which is defined by a common position individuals hold in the economic and political structure of society. The common position of a generation is based on a rhythm in social existence that endows those with roughly the same times of birth with a shared location in the social process. Generation and class unity derive essentially from this shared position in the social system. In turn, that system defines generational as well as class alliances.

Social psychologists distinguish five developmental stages of life history: infancy, childhood, adolescence, adulthood, and old age. Youth is a new such stage — distinct from simply being young, which is a purely chronological datum. Youth is postadolescent and preadult. Although certain age boundaries are useful in delimiting the youth population, it also includes certain psychological, social, and cultural boundaries imbedded in a historically unique economic-political context. Because youth, and particularly its principal subset of students, has a unique political-economic location, it is therefore more than just a generation with its own sociohistorical location.

The social nature of the youth phenomenon is emphasized for three reasons. First, its defining characteristics are more sociological than biopsychological. Second, it is becoming a massive social problem, without any institutionalized solutions. The young have always been associated with change if for no other reason than that they provide fresh perspectives to the old. Third, being young is no longer just a social problem: it is now becoming a social force. As a major social sector, the youth group is a recent phenomenon, arising only in advanced industrial civilization and acting for its own interests.[8]

Because the "abnormal" behavior of youth and students has been viewed primarily as a consequence of their crises of identity and adjustment, social aspects of the problem have

---

8. Many authors have made this point, e.g., Landis, *op. cit.* It is best documented in such books as P. Ariès, *Centuries of Childhood,* New York: Random House, 1962; D. Gottlieb, J. Reeves, W.D. TenHouten, *The Emergence of Youth Societies.* New York: Free Press, 1966.

been obscured.[9] In refuting the contention that "the adolescent-youth period is the most critical one in the life cycle for the individual in our culture," Landis has argued that "as an individual crisis it is probably not more important than such periods as widowhood, menopause, and retirement." But as a collective crisis the adolescence-youth period presents a much greater challenge to an industrial society than any other phase in the life cycle. It is hard to disagree with his conclusion that a "social problem emerges when conditions of society create maladjustments that make the group conscious that certain elements of the population do not fit the social structure." Certainly youths and students are no longer functional participants in the economic and political structure of industrial society; they have no formal role in the world of work and politics.

The critical formative years of the youth culture take place between the years eighteen through twenty-six, with the upper limit the more problematic. Basically youth is a period of extended dependency that as a meaningful experience can extend further upwards and frequently reaches down into adolescence further than eighteen. Yet the limits are not altogether arbitrary. Close to eighty per cent of American adolescents who complete high school graduate before becoming "adults" in the legal sense. An American male can also be drafted into the armed services after eighteen. The upper limit has meaning for three notable reasons. It represents the upper age limit on the draft; a fact of great significance to the young themselves. It reflects the approximate age at which a small but important segment of youth "comes of age" by officially embarking on a productive career in the economy. This includes those who are finishing graduate school as well as those who for one reason or another (army, Peace Corps, work, and the like) did not go straight through college but returned later to complete a degree. Finally, it is during this period that a person's world view becomes articulated and stabilized, following years of personal experi-

9. Cf. E. Erikson, *Identity: Youth and Crisis.* New York: W. W. Norton, 1968. Erikson is the best known and most influential "identity" theorist.

mentation with life and the consequent conscious questioning and reflection that begins in adolescence. However, many other variables intervene between the biological constant and experimental variation.

Adulthood, especially in complex societies, is related less to physical maturity than to economic and political determinants and moral and marital definition.[10] Ariès has documented the fact that in Western civilization even the idea of childhood as a distinct and dependent phase of life is less than 600 years old and is related to the reform movement in education that believed young people had to be protected from moral decadence and blunder by the school and its stern master.[11] Adolescence owes its conceptualization to industrial society. Not only did industrialization make possible mass education, but advanced technology and specialization required that society extend the length of time its young spent in formal schooling. One no longer graduated from childhood to adulthood at puberty; rather, one was "asked" to defer one's full participation in society and concomitantly relieved of certain responsibilities. This relief from social responsibility has come to be a defining characteristic of higher education, from freshman year to the postdoctoral stage.

The single most important sociological variable in determining membership in the youth group is an individual's status in relation to the labor force or the economy. This is as true for the college student as it is for the unemployed high-school dropout. To be in the job force means to contribute to society and to carry one's own weight; whereas to be a student or otherwise economically nonproductive is to be a nonperson in an important sense. Although prestige attaches to youthfulness and the youth culture, the relationship

10. Landis, in *Adolescence and Youth*, writes that "youth problems lie less in the glands than in the social structure in which their personalities are being formed." Nearly all writers, psychological as well as sociological, would agree with him. Cf. D. Rogers, *The Psychology of Adolescence.* New York: Appleton-Century-Crofts, 1962; Gottlieb *et al., op. cit.;* S. N. Eisenstadt, *From Generation to Generation.* Glencoe, Illinois: Free Press, 1956.
11. P. Ariès, *op. cit.*

people have to the productive process is still the prime determinant of their status and power in American society.

Although youths are excluded from status and power, they are physiologically, psychologically, and intellectually adults.[12] They are at the peak of physical strength and sexual activity; their vitality is becoming more disciplined and less frenetic. They are less narcissistic than they were as adolescents, having passed through most of the identity crisis and become more oriented to objective events and to wider circles of issues. They are more disciplined emotionally and intellectually and more settled in their basic values. They are better educated than previous generations. They are capable of deep, continuing meaningful relationships and of commitment in interpersonal relations. Their discovery of the larger world is accompanied by a turning from fun and games to exploration and serious action. They achieve a real capacity for sophisticated judgment while their learning and creative capacities and their openness to new experience and data are still relatively high.

Part of the precocity of the present generation of youth is probably a social-psychological consequence of earlier sexual maturation and increased physical size. Sexual maturation occurs on the average nearly one and one-half years earlier than it did 100 years ago, and the average American fourteen-year-old is five inches taller and twenty-four pounds heavier than his counterpart in 1880.[13]

The extension of a "probationary limbo" between biopsychological and "official" maturities has a profound and drastic effect on the psyche as well as on society. Generational conflict obtains whenever and wherever there exists a lack of correspondence between biological and sociological maturity.[14] While the "generation gap" may well be the product of the mass media and its penchant for catchy phrases, the

12. See Kenneth Keniston. *Young Radicals: Notes on Committed Youth.* New York: Harcourt, Brace and World, 1968.

13. A number of researchers have documented both earlier maturation and larger size. See H. Sebald, *Adolescence.* New York: Appleton-Century-Crofts, 1968, p. 122.

14. S. M. Eisenstadt, *From Generation to Generation.* New York: The Free Press, 1956.

concept has attained an existence of its own, and serves as a focus for creating and enhancing the phenomena it describes. Public acknowledgement of the generation gap is apparent in newspapers and magazines. Most parents who try to talk to their teenage children are acutely aware of it.[15]

Students frequently conceptualize class consciousness in terms of the generation gap. A student at Williams College asserted, "We're a new generation of people, developed in precarious times."[16] Another student at a recent conference on "Students and Society" held at the Center for the Study of Democratic Institutions made the following remarks: "A bona fide generation gap exists today—beyond mere difficulties in transition—and is qualitatively different from those that have occurred before. . . . The gap between youth and the society is not only imposed upon youth, but in many cases is sought by them as well. . . . The rascals to be thrown out are neither Democrats nor Republicans, but simply adults. The world is run by people over thirty, said an anonymous student in The New York Times, and we cannot trust them to rehabilitate themselves. . . . But an even more important trend has been the growth of solidarity among youth . . . students are already becoming recognized as something akin to a social class. . . . Previously, the gap was a matter of interest primarily to sociologists. . . . Now, however, it has become fundamentally a political matter, as youth has become powerful enough to act on its demands. . . . Both incidents reflect a society that oppresses its youth. . . . Youth will have to be mobilized as if they were an under-privileged class, which indeed politically they are."

Another student at the same conference pointed out that: "This conference is meeting at a time when communication between youth and adults in society is tenuous indeed. In fact, for millions of young people the dialogue has already broken down in what they regard as a society gone mad. . . . Almost every institution in society seems determined to thwart a youth's ambition to realize his potential-

15. See R. Lorber & E. Fladell, *The Gap*. New York: McGraw-Hill, 1968.
16. Quoted in C. G. Katope & P. G. Zolbrod (eds.), *Beyond Berkeley.* Cleveland: World Publishing Co., 1966, p. 221.

ity. . . . A full-scale rebellion is possible: youth pitted against their elders." Yet a third student, deploring the failure of dialogue even at this center of highly respected liberal scholars, half in fear, half in anticipation, said: "As for this session we're now in, an escalation of rudeness is the only thing I can call it. I really don't know what to make of this escalation of rudeness—I don't know what it is about people of widely different ages sitting together in a room that brings it out."[17]

Campus newspapers assert that American youth is "alienated." Alienation is now a political more than an economic term, but it still remains a class outrage. The fact that the "underdog" experiences of students, throughout the country, and throughout the world, are now reported on a steady basis has the effect of increasing awareness of a common plight and of strengthening international identifications along generational and student lines. What started as a critique of "hippies" has broadened into an assault on "youth". It is important to realize that the measure of class—in the sense of a "bourgeois" or "proletarian" class—has international dimensions. The "youth" class, like its counterparts in the past, confronts the parochialism of nationalism. This factor may contribute to the radicalization of this otherwise amorphous youth class.

Students: Key to the Youth Class

Never before have so many people been so distant from economic production during their years of greatest intellectual and physical strength. In addition to roughly seven million college students, there are more than one million young people in military service. Nor can the unemployed be ignored. This age group has the highest rate of unemployment. In 1965 only 55.7 per cent of those aged sixteen to nineteen who were counted as part of the labor force actually had gainful employment. And the unemployment rate in the twenty-to-twenty-four age group was roughly 14 per cent in

17. Center for the Study of Democratic Institutions, "Students and Society," *A Center Occasional Paper*, Vol. 1, No. 1, 1967.

contrast to the 96.5 per cent employed in the twenty-five-to-forty-four age group.[18]

However, since a social class, like a social movement, needs an institutional anchor, the student movement has become the most important expression and principal manifestation of generational conflict. The relation between youth as a generation and students as a class is also clear in the extension of formal education as an economic and social necessity rather than as a luxury of voluntary participation.[19]

In the past forty years college enrollment has increased nearly eight times as fast as the growth of the total population, while graduate enrollment in the past sixty years has undergone a more than forty-fold increase. College enrollment increased between 1950 and 1966 from 29.4 per cent to 54.3 per cent in the eighteen-to-nineteen age group, from 9.0 per cent to 19.9 per cent in the twenty-to-twenty-four age group, and from 3.0 per cent to 6.5 per cent in the twenty-five-to-twenty-nine age group.[20] Not only are such percentages continuing to increase as government and business require more employees holding college degrees, but the time spent by the young at college is being extended as the demand for technical sophistication and advanced degrees increases. There is the added incentive on society to increase school populations in order to minimize the pressure on the labor force. The changing character of participation in formal education makes it clear that the treatment of students as a special occupational category opens the possibility of applying the principles of class mobilization to students and their culture.[21]

18. U.S. Bureau of the Census, Statistical Abstract of the U.S.: 1968. (89th ed.), p. 216.

19. See Irving Louis Horowitz, "Young Radicals and Their Professional Critics," *Commonweal*, 89, No. 17 (January 31, 1969).

20. W.B. Brookover, *et al.*, *The College Student*. New York: The Center for Applied Research in Education, 1965, pp. 23–24. U.S. Bureau of the Census, *op. cit.*, p. 108.

21. For example, Jencks and Riesman make interesting analogies between workers and students today in reference to a "blue-collar mentality" that "focuses on improving the conditions associated with the group's present work" rather than moving on and up and out. Christopher Jencks and David Riesman, *The Academic Revolution*. Garden City, New York: Doubleday, 1968, p. 47.

The eight million young people in higher education are not just spread throughout the land; they are packed into several thousand acres of campuses, dormitories, and surrounding apartment houses. The mean number of students per campus is about 3,000. However, the majority of students are found on campuses having populations ranging from 15,000 to 30,000 (and several even larger). Like the nineteenth-century factories, colleges exhibit high physical density centered in a single type of locale having relatively few "branches." Only hours separate them in this modern world of high speed and inexpensive transportation. Perhaps even more important than the ease and frequency of physical mobility is psychological proximity, which has been increased by such communications media as television, underground press services, and common cultural interests. Instant communication makes possible a symbolic interaction and enhances class consciousness and social cohesion.

Most students share special housing conditions. One form is the dorm, wherein the university is expected to enforce rules and regulations that for the most part were unenforceable when the student was attending high school and living at home. Students are packed into tiny rooms, provided with institutional food, and offered scant facilities for releasing pent-up energy or for meeting other needs of the normal "whole" adult. Understandably, the demand for off-campus housing is greater than the supply; as a result, students are economically exploited by paying inflated rents for nonuniversity housing. Even such student residences tend to be old and in undesirable areas of the city. Students for the most part remain isolated from the larger social community, thereby increasing intraclass relations and decreasing intergroup contact.

In short, an institutional setting for a student class does exist. The relation of students to the university and, in turn, its relation to society are analogous to the relation of workers to the factory and its relation to society in the nineteenth century. Students put in long, hard, and tedious hours with little immediate remuneration, as did workers of an early time. They often have as little control over their conditions and treatment as the factory proletariat of the past. There is even a parallel between the unionization of labor and the current proliferation of student "unions" in colleges and departments.

To say that students as individuals, and the university as an institution, are not involved in the productive process is to take a parochial view of that process in modern society. Getting an education does contribute to the Gross National Product, if only in a delayed way, through eventual incremental wealth. Further, universities are much more important in the institutional framework than they were previously, and in some respects the university is more important than the factory.

The university has taken over much of the legitimizing function of religion. The university defines reality; it socializes the young and preaches democracy. The school teaches professional ethics and religion, and even trains clerics. If there remains at least a formal separation between church and state, there is certainly no such separation between university and state. The most important product of a university is knowledge, and the struggle is over the control of its primary source: the people who create and produce knowledge. There is a greater interdependence between the university, the economy, and the polity today than there was between the factory, economy, and polity of previous times. Students constitute not only the huge majority of the university population, but also its principal raison d'être. Therefore, they have increasingly engaged in acts of sabotage and violence on campus, to symbolize not only their special role as a youth class, but to dramatize the social role of the university.

To speak of the university as a knowledge factory is more than a neat analogue. For in this setting youthful sensibilities are also most flagrantly violated, if only because more is expected. Students arrive at college to be rudely awakened by the discrepancy between what they had been led to expect and what they find, between professorial preaching and administrative practices. College is portrayed in recruitment brochures as a place to develop critical thought, wisdom, and a personal philosophy as well as marketable skills. But reality is different. The university community is often rigidly departmentalized; the "life of ideas" is fragmented into prosaic practice—the rote stockpiling of "facts," figures, and pat answers, rather than experimental testing and true dialogue; fragmentation of the content of experience and an increasing separation of "learning" from "doing." Examinations are frequently meaningless; student papers receive little appraisal from overly committed professors. Innovations in education are invariably frowned upon by school administrators.

Students are pitted against one another in competition for scarce resources in the form of high grades. Since grades must be allocated on the basis of "objective" and therefore standardized criteria, representations of personal or idiosyncratic creativity receive little encouragement. The student learns that while short-term success—such as a good first job, quality graduate school, financial support—is highly dependent on good grades, they may not be indicators of long-term success. The good student, even more than others, resents a society that places a high value on a narrow criterion. He finds that his self-esteem suffers under such an idea; he therefore rebels, knowing that grades should not be the basis of personal worth. He frequently finds that inattention to disciplinary boundaries and insufficient "appreciation" for inherited theories or thinkers earn him a lower than warranted mark. He discovers that much of what he is expected to learn has little or no relation to present reality and future contingencies; his knowledge is not applicable to living or social problems; the fact of his diploma is more important than are "skills" and knowledge acquired in most courses. Since these problems are particularly evident in the humanities and the social sciences, the fact of their overrepresentation in student struggles may be partially explained.

The size and impersonality of most universities is also a factor. Many of them have grown to resemble mass-production factories. Undergraduate faculties are expected to produce dutiful, conforming, pragmatic believers in free enterprise, capitalism, and two-party politics, industrial marketeers, bureaucratic functionaries, and technological specialists. Freshmen and sophomores increasingly find themselves in classes with several hundred peers, able to catch little more than a glimpse of well-known but distant professors, who themselves are protected against overexposure to these "lower" classes by graduate teaching assistants. Advanced students frequently represent the only extended contact younger students have with "faculty." Graduate faculties produce good scholars and scientists, but they rarely reward good teachers. The socializing effect of the graduate student upon the undergraduate student is direct and often radicalizing, since the graduate student has precisely the highest degree of radicalism combined with the most ambiguous social status. Thus, the distance between professors and students serves to exacerbate the "class struggle" by heightening class awareness.

Many students feel that society is exploiting them for economic reasons. Another sense of exploitation emerges from a lack by administration and faculty of respect for the reciprocal nature of contracts. Student payment of tuition represents a contract that entails rights and obligations on the part of both parties. Many faculty members fail to consider that they have an obligation to spend a certain number of hours per week with students in order to earn their salaries. Administrators and trustees are much more concerned with their public image and with maintaining an outward semblance of order than with actually meeting the needs of students that have led to their dissatisfaction. Indeed, the fact that at most major universities tuition is not the most decisive source of income only weakens any faculty or administrative sense of obligation.

In the university questions of freedom, justice, equality, and democracy are raised to a high level of intellectual appreciation. Students come to expect a close fit between these ideals and practice. Instead they are treated as second-class citizens, experiencing a combination of semicorporate administrative-financial organizational structures and a feudal system of relationships within and between departments. The student confronts a stratified set of "classes" in the university, of which his own — the largest — has the fewest rights and the least power. Consequently the university becomes a symbol of particularist interests rather than leadership, while student power comes to signify a countervailing set of interests and the desire for a part in determining the purposes, policies, and organization of the institution.

The denial to students of full-fledged citizenship in the university community and in society at large is rationalized by two implicit assumptions: that students are innocent (at any age) and therefore not judicious; and that youths are not responsible because they do not have "ownership" in society in the adult sense of working and paying taxes. In essense the ruling generations decide for youths and students what is good for them and then define the channels for gaining status as mature adults.

When adult decisions are perceived as right and good by youth, the young people rarely oppose adult authority to implement their prerogatives. A considerable portion of the adult population has criticized the righteousness of the nature of American involvement in Vietnam, producing a challenge to its legitimacy from "above" as well as from the students "below." Professors and other critics may debate the issue without fear of personal reprisal, but for the nineteen-to-twenty-six-year olds, the war constitutes a real and immediate threat to life.

Students are largely ignored in legitimate political machinery; they are thus driven to engage in peace marches and demonstrations to assert their political claims. When they demonstrate, however, local draft boards may reclassify them. When they appeal as conscientious objectors, they are drafted. When they refuse induction and go to court, judges refuse to confront the question of the legality of wars and drafts. In short, young people are oppressed by the political machinery of the state and are treated unjustly in the courts when they register complaints about such treatment. Their rights to assemble and dissent may often be abrogated through threats and use of police force. Under such circumstances some have turned to revolutionary (and romantic) tactics, burning draft files and engaging in acts of property destruction.

If the university issue is primarily one of power, and the

war issue one of self-preservation, there remain concerns that are predominantly moral: racial discrimination and abject poverty. For many students reared to believe in Keynesian mechanisms for stimulating an economy, poverty simply should not exist in modern America. Since these are not personal problems for most students, the fact of their deep involvement reflects the strength of their idealistic commitment to the actualization of such ideals as equality, justice, freedom, and democracy and to social awareness and action and moral integrity. If students accept these cultural values they also reject those social practices and institutions that maintain the pervasive racism often linked to poverty. Not only do students urge the older generations to change their ways, but they also participate in the Peace Corps, Vista, and hundreds of smaller community-volunteer projects. But of the three centers of generational conflict, this one may be a result more of youthful impatience than of objective incompatibility.

The charge is made that the brevity of the student experience as well as the usual movement shortly thereafter into family and economic responsibilities and other involvements in the larger social system are fatal to the development of a potential revolutionary class. But such arguments only obscure the essence of social position in general and this one in particular. All classes experience considerable mobility. What is crucial are the objective conditions and the consequent experiences and social relationships rooted therein. Class is based on the realities of existence filtered through the social system, and not on particular individuals. Social reality is determined by position in power relationships. Since each type of position produces its own kind of experience and perspective, consciousness is a property of social position. Ideology, action, style, and organizational form are seated in the collectivity. This fact implies that the struggle is between social systems, between classes, rather than between individuals as human beings. It further implies that as long as certain structures and relationships obtain, there will be class conflict.

The Berkeley revolt of 1964 consisted mainly of undergraduates; so did the Columbia crisis of 1968. Similar school-wide disturbances are beginning to appear in high schools and even junior high schools, often under the tutelage of college students. As young people spend an increasing amount of time in school, the amount of time spent in the conditions conducive to class formation is extended. Even before the classroom experience, modern youths are oriented to one another. Organized peer activities exist for children from about age six in school (earlier for those in pre-school programs) and from about age eight outside school. Such activities include various forms of scouting, athletic competition (Little League baseball and football) and summer camps. The college activists of today have been in cohort formation, oriented to and interacting with one another, for up to fifteen years. Intergenerational interaction has been significantly reduced while intragenerational interaction has been greatly increased. In this circumstance lies part of the reason for the development of special forms of speech, music, dress, and outlook among the young. In past generations contact between parents and offspring was frequent. The son worked alongside his father in the field or learned a \trade from him or from a relative or in an apprenticeship position. Today, intergenerational contact within primary groups tends to be limited to special occasions and within secondary relationships to learning in a formal setting. As a result, cultural discontinuity, competing authorities, anomie, and lack of a dominant role or set of expectations are produced. Emulation becomes fragmented into many role models, rather than focusing on a single reference individual, resulting in an age without parental or familial heroes with whom to identify. This shift reflects a larger movement away from achievement orientation and a return to ascription in postindustrial societies.

The sense of time is related to the nature of subjective experience in an age of increasingly rapid change and the acceleration of history. A student today has experienced more kinds of events and encountered more varieties of people than his ancestors could have met during a lifetime. He has been more places, seen more things, and made more kinds of

decisions than his grandparents did in a lifetime. The ex-
ponential growth curves of science, technology, economy,
travel, the printed word, and television — not to mention the
capacity for destruction as well as development — indicate as
much. After collecting and reading more than a thousand
autobiographies of college students, and watching the course
of life on a college campus, Landis became convinced "that
the youth of today has faced more moral alternatives by the
time he is twenty years of age than his grandparents faced in
a lifetime"(p. 141). Groups develop their own traditions, and
it is just as easy for the underclasses to accumulate grievances as it is for the upper classes to accumulate self-
congratulations. Finally, revolutions by their very nature
always occur over a comparatively short time span and are
carried through by relatively young people. Revolution requires not only the fervor of young adults, but also their
stamina. The quasimilitary nature of revolutionary change in
the political system is thus directly linked to the world of the
young.

If at certain points along a continuum qualitative changes
take place, then 1945 truly marks a watershed in history.
Since Hiroshima the hydrogen bomb, chemical warfare, nuclear submarines, and intercontinental ballistic missiles have
been perfected, resulting in the specter of total annihilation.
In addition to many "minor" hot wars, the constant tension of
a seemingly interminable cold war has been felt. Research
has shown that low-intensity stress of long duration is more
damaging than are short bursts of high-intensity stress. This
is an age of drugs (legal and extralegal), and of heart trans-
plants; computers and sensitivity groups; jets, aircraft, and
moon rockets; bureaucracy and urbanization. Only 7 per cent
of the population is engaged in agriculture, while 50 per cent
of the eligible attend college. We have had scientific and
technological revolutions in energy transformation (atom), in
information manipulation (computers), in health (bioengi-
neering), in transportation (commercial and space), and in
communication (especially the mass media). The first commercial use of space technology was for communication satel-
lites. Today's students are accustomed to spectacular material

production and control of the elements and physical disease, side by side with a massive failure to solve social, economic, and political problems.

They indict the governing classes for this failure to distribute wealth equitably, to dispense the same justice to all men, to conquer prejudice and discrimination, to cure urban blight, and so on. For the new generation history is a series of mistakes perpetrated by their elders. Since these elders have failed to demonstrate mastery over themselves, over society, over wars, and over science, the avant-garde of the youth class rejects traditional authority. Even fathers must be worthy of respect, or they lose the right to deferential treatment. Youth turns to itself for authority, rejecting readymade hand-me-down explanations and formulas in favor or personal experience. In short, the young share a unique historical configuration, which represents an increasing awareness of a view of their historical role as initiating agents of change. The comparative strength of their international identification and the interconnectedness and epidemic proportions of revolts are indications of their awareness of a unique world historical role. Political messianism is thus a major aspect of the new youth class.

The mass media constitute not only a part of the new history, but probably the most important mechanism in the formation of class and enhancement of consciousness. Since the explosive growth of magazines and journals and especially television, the media have become massive, furnishing an instantaneous feedback loop in the social system—a loop that seems to magnify, sensationalize, reify and publicize—thereby lending a quasiofficial ring to "the news" in a mass society defined by the middle class. The communications revolution transforms society into a system of parts in reciprocal interdependence and visible to all.

High rates of interaction and common activities produce not only a similarity of experience, but also a shared awareness. The mutuality of this awareness needs to be emphasized. It is not just the awareness of each person of his own experience plus the fact that experiences derive from objectively similar conditions that is important. Group consciousness exists only when the experiences are communicated, a group interpretation is developed, and a social meaning is attached. The process of communicating—of externalizing—objectifies this social structure.

As the underclasses become aware of incompatible differences, they react. This reaction produces a counterreaction in other classes, setting off a reciprocating dynamic, resulting in a state in which the distance between classes widens at an ever increasing rate until a rupture occurs in the social fabric. Such a polarization has the effect of uniting individuals within a class. As class members combine into an association for the organized pursuit of their common aims and interests, intraclass competition decreases while interclass competition increases, thereby amplifying class antagonisms and class consciousness.

As classes become organized and internally differentiated, they develop their own literature and public communication networks for vilifying the enemy and glorifying themselves. The mass media of the larger system serve as the main channel of communication between antagonistic groups—a process that further objectifies the conflict. In this way the struggle for control of the means of communication in the twentieth century becomes as important as the struggle for the means of production in the nineteenth century.

What is most important in this process is the reification of concepts. They become real because they are "out there" in print and on television. People react to what has become publicly constructed as reality. The labeling process helps to create and amplifies the phenomenon so stereotyped. The very existence of the concept of a generation gap and the fact of its public discussion serve to increase the distance between generations by raising the gap to the level of full consciousness and focal concern. Public acknowledgment of a concept, especially through the printed word, is a major part in the identity formation of social classes. Once something appears in print, it acquires a social sanctity, a sacred immortality as an objective, quasiofficial monument. In this way most symbols that first appear as manifestations of class consciousness feed back into the system and become sec-

ond-order causes of class polarization and consciousness. Included in this collection of symbols are nearly all cultural
items, such as arm bands, lapel buttons, flags; special speech,
greetings, handshakes; dress and hair styles; taste in music,
literature, and art.[22] Other aspects — such as public worship of
the idea of being young, college-oriented commodities, industrial recruiting on campuses, and other items that single
out youth as a group — probably operate in this process as
symbolic influences.

The modern youth situation is unique in that it includes a
sense of accelerated history, instant mass communication,
rapid technological innovation, administrative and professorial involvements in industry and government-funded projects, and large numbers massed together — the university
turned conglomerate. There is an increasing indication of
political generation and class consciousness, including similar tastes and conventions, relative homogeneity of beliefs
and values, identification with common symbols, similarity of
political style and goals, expressed hostility toward other
classes, and stereotypical responses by classes toward each
other.

The crucial question of a youth culture concerns the importance of its differences from other cultural styles and their
long-term effects and implications. Confusion is associated
with the idea and nature of generational emulation. A distinction must be drawn between individual-to-individual
identification or rejection (as in any specific parent-child relationship) and interclass imitation or conflict.[23] The nature of
the question is not whether a particular student loves, ad-
mires, and identifies with his own parents and their world
view or whether most particular students (taken as an arith-
metic sum of individuals) identify with their respective parents. Rather, it has to do with the existence of a group identity that includes the identification of an antithetical class,
characterized by a strong negative image. It is quite possible

22. Mark Rudd, "Symbols of the Revolution," J. L. Avorn *et al., Up
Against the Ivy Wall.* New York: Atheneum, 1968.
23. An excellent discussion of youth subcultures is in D. Gottlieb and J.
Reeves, *Adolescent Behavior in Urban Areas.* Michigan State University,
College of Education, 1962, pp. 111.1–111.18.

for an individual to "transcend" class interests without the class itself ceasing to exist in its positive mission of liberation (youth) or oppression (age).

Nearly all students accept the values of democracy, justice, and the like, but there the continuity of generations ends. The conservative cluster emphasizes continuity of inherited ways, while the radical cluster emphasizes discontinuity.[24] Recent student revolts have had the active and passive support of a group of radical-left sympathizers that far exceeds the number of those "registered" with the new left or small groups involved in planning and organizing disruptions. A *Fortune* poll conducted in late 1968 identified a "forerunner" group of students that differed with the adult generation on many basic issues in important degrees. The size of this group is 42 per cent, indicating the high degree of latent dissatisfaction with the status quo. Thus the radical impulses of the present youth class show marked discontinuities with the expressed attitudes of the previous generation of the 1950's.

A major illustration of political differences between the ruling and student generations was exhibited in the 1968 presidential campaigns. In April, *Time* conducted a nation-wide student poll of presidential candidates. The results of "Choice 68" were: Eugene McCarthy, 28 per cent of the vote; Robert Kennedy, 21 per cent; Richard Nixon, 19 per cent; others in order of preference, Nelson Rockefeller, Lyndon Johnson, George Wallace, Ronald Reagan, John Lindsay, Hubert Humphrey, Charles Percy, and Mark Hatfield. Combining the McCarthy-Kennedy vote (representing essentially the same student interest) yields 40 per cent, compared to 19 per cent for the next nearest candidate. If votes for the "liberal" candidates in both parties are totaled, it rises to about 70 per cent. Projecting this figure to a national contest between Nixon and McCarthy would probably yield a major polariza-

---

24. The conservative view is expressed in M. S. Evans, *Revolt on Campus.* Chicago: Henry Regnery, 1961. It is interesting that rightwing sensitivity to political arousal on campus seems to have preceded that of the left wing by several years. New-left views are expressed in a number of publications, *e.g.*: J. Newfield, *A Prophetic Minority.* Signet Books, 1967; P. Jacobs and S. Landau, *The New Radicals.* Vintage Books, 1966.

tion between adults (who elected Nixon over Humphrey) and students of the magnitude of at least 65+ per cent of students for McCarthy and 60+ per cent of adults for Nixon (against McCarthy). This preference represents both intergenerational polarization and intragenerational homogeneity. A similar example of student unity in political affairs is the claim that in 1967-1968 about one-half of all student body presidents in state universities and colleges identified with the New Left.[25]

Other polls show evidence of further polarization. In a Gallup Poll conducted in March 1969 more than 80 per cent of the sample took a "hard" negative line on student disruptions. The difference between age groups over and under thirty was marked. Further, 70 per cent believed that students should not have a greater voice in campus policy.[26] The Mervin Field Poll in California reports large increases in "backlash" attitudes toward students over the past two years; 72 per cent of Californians strongly favor expulsion for all students who challenge and defy authorities, compared with 66 per cent in 1967. And 38 per cent strongly oppose giving students a greater voice in deciding campus rules, an increase of 20 per cent from 1967.[27] A recent survey conducted by the Educational Testing Service among more than 5,000 trustees representing more than 500 colleges and universities showed that "the typical university trustee is older, wealthier, and more conservative than even the students and faculty believed."[28]

A further source of polarization is the youthful style of political action and the older group's reaction to it. Traditionally, engagement in electoral politics and activity within established political parties is considered an acceptable way of attempting to achieve social change. Any deviation from this pattern of action, on the other hand, is perceived by the prevalent classes as illegitimate and threatening to the established order. Students are willing to engage in national politics through acceptable channels, as is proven by the tre-

25. Center for the Study of Democratic Institutions, *op. cit.*
26. Reported in the St. Louis *Post-Dispatch*, March 19, p. 18.
27. Reported in *Time*, March 14, 1969, p. 60.
28. Reported in *Parade* Magazine, April 6, 1969, p. 15.

mendous response by young people to the campaign of Eugene McCarthy. But when traditional political channels appear blocked—either through party machinations or because of such anomalies as assassinations—students resort to confrontational politics. These include tactics generally considered socially deviant: individual refusals to participate in war or induction into the army; collective disruption of public gatherings or official places—party conventions, the Pentagon and the Justice Department, and the like; demonstrations and sit-ins; and such overt acts of civil disobedience as destroying draft cards and draft-board files.

Students resort to such action all the more readily as they feel themselves too much ignored and considered trivial by the society at large. Lacking voting privileges and other forms of political clout, students may engage in more spectacular forms of action to draw attention to their special condition. Such behavior is not without precedent; at one time workers' strikes were considered deviant, though they are now accepted as institutionalized means of promoting change. But when students now go on strike in the university, even this action is perceived as illegitimate by the larger public—including, incidentally labor leaders.[29]

Much of the student movement is rebelling against bureaucratic forms of organization, perfected and extended by the older generation, preferring spontaneous "community" and "happenings," wholeness, and a moral laissez-faire called: "doing your own thing." This attitude has led to the charge that the new left lacks both a utopian image and a revolutionary plan. Older classes devise elaborate plans before embarking on a journey, in order to know every step of the way as well as the ultimate goal and to be able to "measure" deviations therefrom. In contrast, the "movement" emphasizes a lack of plan, preferring to discover en route. There is a utopian element in this nonplan; it has the psychological attraction of excitement and exploration of the

29. For a discussion of the breakdown of the traditional distinction between political marginality and social deviance, see I. L. Horowitz and Martin Liebowitz, "Social Deviance and Political Marginality," *Social Problems*, 15, 3, (Winter, 1968), 280–296.

unknown. Another reason for the rebellion against plans is that the history of revolutions is the history of perverted plans and ideals. One way to avoid such an outcome, then, is to avoid specific articulation of what ought to be; if history-as-it-unfolds is an emergent phenomenon, it is not possible to know what will take place. Yet the "movement" is not entirely without an image of what it wants, and it certainly knows what it does not desire — impersonality, war, injustice, inequality, hypocrisy. Further, it perceives "liberation" as freedom from political chicanery; and "slavery" as a response to external masters of any sort. This rebellion against totalitarianism as such spares the youth class the political fanaticism of its elders but does not spare it what is often equally difficult to digest — moral fanaticism.

All social classes aim at the seizure of power, at revolution. The youth class is no different. In the past, youths were a class *in* themselves; now they are becoming a class *for* themselves. The past reveals extensive generational conflicts as well as the tremendous impact of youth on change, whether through military conquest or political upheaval. Yet these facts have been obscured by the absence of an over-all "class" consciousness, beyond opposition to military conscription. Scholars in the past paid little attention to the major role students played in reform and radical movements: "In part because student movements are quite transitory in character and have left fewer records than adult organizations. Moreover, to stress the role of youth and students, rather than that of the social classes or religion, seemed in a sense to underemphasize their seriousness and significance of the happenings and to turn them into children's crusades. Then, too, from the Marxist perspective, intellectuals and students are not significant independent social forces."[30]

In another context Lipset points out that students have remained a source of new radical leadership and mass support, while other elements of society have not. He lists more than a dozen cases in which students played significant roles

30. Seymour Martin Lipset (ed.), *Student Politics*. New York: Basic Books, 1967, esp. vii-ix.

in major social reform and revolution throughout the world. He mentions that university students in nineteenth-century Russia "were almost the only group to engage in demonstrations demanding freedom and economic reform, from the middle of the century onward" and that "the Russian workers learned the value of street demonstrations from students." He suggests that efforts by the rulers of Communist countries to repress student political activities may be explained in part by their awareness of the importance of student movements in undermining the pre-Communist regimes of these countries. Finally, Lipset points out the emphasis Mao Tse-tung is placing on youth as the source of continuing revolutionary ideology.[31] In short, the youth class is one that grows in solidarity and consciousness under both capitalist and socialist conditions.

Student disruptions have occurred throughout history. But now, when society has become highly differentiated and functionally interdependent, student revolts reverberate more strongly. Their efforts extend further into a more equitable system of institutional and informational relationships. Modern communication enhances both public visibility of disturbances and the connections among the various events. To the degree that students do act as a class, for themselves as well as in themselves, student movements are no longer sporadic or mutually independent. Rather, the movement has reached epidemic proportions, becoming mutually reinforcing and interconnected, often sharing some of the same leaders, both within a country and across national borders.

The problem of size, as regards the making of a revolution, is crucial but unresolved. It is not known precisely what proportion of the population ever constitutes a critical "mass" in revolutions. It is certain, however, that a relatively small minority can create the conditions for, if not bring about, a revolution. The American Revolution, for example, was successful with the active support of not more than one-third of the colonial population. A leadership group can

31. Seymour Martin Lipset and Sheldon Wolin, *The Berkeley Student Rebellion*. New York: Doubleday, 1965, pp. 2, 12.

be strong at 5 per cent and seldom exceeds 10 per cent of the population. The proportion of the total population involved does not therefore uniquely determine the success of a revolution. What is crucial to revolution is that the strength of those who actively oppose it is less than that of those who actively support it. Thus, where the army, militia, or police force throws its support may determine the fate of large numbers. This is why actual revolutionary struggles often take the form of "people" vs. "police," when in fact the police represent large classes of people.

The French riots of 1968 well illustrate what a few hundred militants can accomplish when the "objective conditions" are ripe. Eventually tens of thousands of students took to the streets, and one-half the total labor force went on strike.[32] France's economy virtually came to a halt. Only the feebleness of the old left prevented a full-blown revolution. To place matters in an American context, it should be noted that the United States' population is a little over four times that of France. The proportion of students in this country to the population is more than three times that of France, while Paris is to France what New York, Boston, Philadelphia, Washington, D.C., and Detroit rolled into one would be to the United States. Therefore, 30,000 students in the streets of Paris would be roughly equivalent to nearly 500,000 American students.

The radical student population in America is smaller, proportionately, than that of many European countries; it is, perhaps, the smallest outside of Communist states. The reported strength of the new left is 2 per cent, or approximately 125,000. But 100,000 well-organized revolutionaries represent an extraordinary vanguard force in this country. This number does not reflect those who would probably lend active and passive support. If recent campus riots are any indication, these two groups might amount to another half-million and one million respectively. The *Fortune* survey further indicates that nearly three million students are

32. Daniel Cohn-Bendit *et al.*, *The French Student Revolt*, New York: Hill and Wang, 1968.

significantly more left-wing in orientation than is the older generation, indicating a potential revolutionary "mass base" of 40 percent of the student youth; a sizable cluster by any standards.

It is not our purpose to prophesy an imminent student-led revolution in America. Rather, we have tried to formulate the youth issue in terms that emphasize its long-range serious- ness and to permit policies that would constructively address themselves to the social contribution of youth, especially students. For if any "lesson" of this generation is clear, it is that beyond social revolution is moral redemption — that, at any rate, is the utopia. The reality remains to be determined.

CHAPTER SIX

Professors and Protesters

In considering faculty response to the student rebellion, a distinction should be made between the unorganized and unstructured responses of the professoriate to student rebels and more organized reactions from teacher associations. Unorganized responses occur largely in formless but intensive and continuous faculty interactions. Since the professoriate, like other occupational groups, devotes considerable time to shoptalk, it is understandable that considerable faculty energy is devoted to discussion of events at Berkeley, Columbia and San Francisco State—as well as local campus demonstrations. These discussions constitute the base upon which the more organized action of the professoriate develops. As such, it is significant but difficult (if not impossible) to examine systematically. Our report is based primarily on personal impressions. Somewhat more systematically, we will examine the more organized forms of professional action. Of these we turn first to a consideration of the faculty in action and then to the manner in which members of the professoriate have responded to the student rebels in more detached ways, particularly in their writings.

149

Professorial Responses to Student Power

In hundreds of thousands of interactions and in a myriad of scenes, the thousands of university teachers constituting the professoriate of American universities meet daily to worry over the state of their world. Only a few see any hope in any aspect of the current student rebellion, and fewer still are enthusiastic about it. While most faculty members have been trained to function deliberatively so that issues will not be immediately translated into behavior, the worry expressed in academic hallways, men's rooms, and the faculty club helps to create the environment within which most faculty action occurs.

Despite the massive expenditure of energy by the professoriate in discussing the current state of the university, it is necessary to emphasize how little the faculty actually knows about students, about student life and conditions, let alone the substance of actual demonstrations. Most faculty members base their knowledge about students upon the belief that, having lived through the experience themselves, they know a great deal about the student subculture. The deficiencies of this approach, particularly for older faculty members, should be clear; many faculty members passed through the universities before the massive influx of students following World War II began. Not only was the university more of an elitist institution in those prewar days, but the character of student culture has also radically changed since then. Even for younger faculty members, themselves the product of the large-scale universities of the post-World War II era, dependence upon personal experience overlooks the sharp changes that have developed in student culture during the 1960's.

Professors depend for their information about students on their daily formal, structured contacts with students. Most of this interaction is structured by the professors' role requirements — that is, the conveying of knowledge in structured classroom circumstances. Moreover, such contacts as exist outside of the classroom are also highly structured. Thus, when faculty members become friendly with students or attempt to deal with them as individuals, this interchange is accomplished in circumstances in which the faculty member represents the source of knowledge, information, and *power*, while the student is the recipient of these benefits. Grading, as well as the other resources that the professor commands, serves to enforce the subordinate position of the student. In such circumstances communication between student and professor is highly structured and reinforces the faculty member's conception of himself as well as the student's subordination. When demonstrations begin, faculty members cannot then understand how students, who behave so respectfully toward them in other circumstances, can confront them with the horrendous slogan, "Up against the wall, motherfucker."

Participation in demonstrations constitutes an area which most faculty members have had little or no contact. When demonstrations occur, the overwhelming majority of faculty members will never be found near them at any time. A small number of faculty members may pass near the demonstration, and even smaller numbers may come and watch for a few minutes. Our estimate of the percentage of faculty that has spent more than a half-hour involved personally in any way in demonstrations at the universities with which we have had connection during the past few years is on the order of 1 or 2 per cent of the total faculty. When a demonstration occurs on any campus, the faculty, *like any other segment of society*, obtains its information primarily through standard communications media, rather than getting it directly. An important supplement to these media consists of secondhand accounts retailed by students (acting in subordinate roles vis-à-vis the faculty members) and by those few faculty members who have spent some time at the demonstration and whose stories are passed around at second, third, fourth, and fifth hand in the cloistered and restricted confines of the faculty club.

Despite the bulk of the faculty's limited primary knowledge about student demonstrations, daily interaction by the overwhelming majority of this faculty is devoted to discussions of the demonstrations while they are in progress. Even more curious about the willingness of many professors to hold forth extensively on the nature of demonstrations is their self-acknowledged lack of competence to deal with subject matters outside their professional spheres of interest. If a student asks a professor a question marginal to his area of competence (and particularly if there is another member of the faculty who commands competence in this area), the tendency is to refer the student to an expert. Most faculty members feel ill at ease when working in areas marginal to their professional competence and refuse to purvey such outside knowledge. For a faculty member to teach a class in a subject outside his realm of competence normally involves a substantial commitment in time to accumulate the necessary knowledge. It is most peculiar, therefore, that faculty members express strongly held attitudes and opinions about the student demonstrations and the role of students in the university.

Students have become the subject of intensive study only recently, and most studies are single ones rather than continuing ones. While many studies have been conducted of students at specific institutions, few universities conduct systematic analyses of their student bodies in terms of the social origins of students or of their attitudes toward curriculum, the educational process, the university, or the broader society. Searching through the documentary material to examine changes in student culture over time, a significant volume of literature was found, but it contained no longitudinal or panel studies. The only studies conducted over time are by education experts, from schools of education, concerned less with students than with curricular questions and with the effectiveness of the educational process.

Such weaknesses partially account for the professoriate's meeting continually to express unhappiness both with the student demonstrators and their own incapacity to grasp the nettle. Most faculty members fail to appreciate the profound dissatisfaction of students or the fact that the small activist minority involved in demonstrations represents a significant number of student sympathizers or disaffected elements. Many faculty members, bemoaning the demonstrations, ask, "Where is the liberal middle?" Others manifest an inability to grasp that the "bad manners" of the student demonstrators are deliberate. That their students will use four-letter curse words to describe the faculty or the administration can only mean, for most academics, that such students are thugs. Despite considerable empirical evidence that activists are among the best students, many faculty members continue to insist that demonstrators are bad students. As the focus of action has shifted to the black students, this insistence has often taken on a subtle racist quality, with the faculty members stating that "they," coming from a different background than "we," cannot possibly have the same conception of the university. While data are not available on the academic performance of black activists, the data on white activists are clear but ignored.

Another response of the professoriate is to turn against the administration, which it sees as being heavy-handed in its handling of demonstrations. If the administration calls in the police, it is condemned for escalating violence on the campus. If the administration temporizes or "buys time," it is accused of vacillation. The administration has in the past been the "natural" enemy of the professoriate, constituting the main impediment to faculty action. While the initial response of the faculty toward demonstrations is to join forces with the administration, this feeling turns to pique and frustration as the faculty realizes that the administration is unable to contain the students and restore a status quo ante in which the faculty remains free of collegiate responsibility.

Parenthetically, if the faculty has only limited and structured contacts with students, the administrative officers of the university have even fewer, and such contacts are even more structured. It is a source of continual irritation to faculty members to hear their presidents or other administrative officers pontificating to the national media and at conferences—and occasionally to the president of the United States—on the student rebels.

Only a few faculty members have had other than classroom contacts with students, and many of these are sympathetic to the rebels. Thus, a situation arises in which the faculty is unable to anticipate, much less cope with, student discontent. It also leads to a student cynicism, which seeks to manipulate faculty alienation rather than mobilize faculty support. This, in turn, only serves to intensify faculty legalism and conservation on matters related to the campus, thus completing the cycle of frustration and alienation.

Professors in Action

Before beginning an examination of the professoriate in action, it will be useful to consider the professoriate as a social stratum, particularly the manner of their socialization and recruitment. These background factors explain a great deal about the incapacity of the faculty to exercise initiatives as a corporate group during student confrontations. An understanding of background factors also helps to explain the limited role professors can play either as individuals or in the form of ad hoc groups.

As a general rule it can be said that the higher the quality of the university, the more likely its faculty is to have a cosmpolitan orientation toward recruiting, promoting, and retaining scholars who are primarily interested in production for their professional fields rather than in the provision of other services. The professors recognize that to succeed in the top-ranking universities they must publish in journals that reach members of their profession outside their own university. Indeed, the surest way to obtain mobility within one's own university is to receive job offers from top-quality universities. (For someone teaching at Harvard, a job offer from the University of South Carolina carries little weight; a faculty member at the University of South Carolina can often translate a job offer from Harvard, into a promotion in salary or rank at his university.) Conversely, the lower the quality of the university, the more likely is the predominance of a local orientation. In universities where demands for publication are low and the volume of teaching requirements is high (quality of teaching is not considered as significant as the number of courses taught), involvement in the profession is attenuated and professors are more concerned with local issues.

This situation is the product of the deliberate recruitment and promotion patterns of the better universities. Lower-quality schools, which make greater demands for teaching volume and often have lower salary structures, must hire the faculty members that are not preempted by the better schools. These universities cannot, except in unusual circumstances, provide special rewards for faculty members with strong professional orientations. But even lower-quality schools contain some professors with cosmopolitan orientations, as a function, to a considerable degree, of the emphasis upon professional achievement in their graduate-school training. Although the professoriate of the lower-status institutions is important, we will focus our attention on the higher-quality institutions. Most of the campus demonstrations, at least in the initial years of the student rebellion, have been centered around the mainstream universities.

Professors at both major and minor universities and colleges share certain features that make action difficult to undertake. First, the tenure system operates to reduce radical activity on the part of younger faculty members still striving for economic security. Second, a university post, especially at a major university, represents a permanent investment, whereas for the student the same university is only a four-year hitch. Third, the faculty cannot count on the sort of peer-group support for radical actions as can the student activists. Political behavior is in itself open to criticism, while radical activity is sometimes open to censorship. Fourth, many of the issues now occupying student activists are uniquely geared to student problems, and these concern faculty members only peripherally. Finally, although students expect faculty support in times of crisis, faculty rarely if ever receive any assurance from student radicals that they will have mass student support should a job be placed in jeopardy. These are but some of the complications limiting faculty action on behalf of student causes. But in the main the problem is simply that faculty see themselves as a separate domain, no more responsive to or responsible for student demands than the reverse. Thus interest group pressures serve to limit, rather than enhance, faculty-student interactions.

Professorial Socialization

In an age of staggering proliferation of knowledge the professional scholar can survive only through a narrowing of his focus on a field of specialization. Not only has the Renaissance man disappeared from the university, but those attempting to undertake such a role today are often regarded as dilettantes or buffoons by their professionally oriented colleagues. It has become increasingly impossible to encompass the totality of a given discipline; though sociologists, for example, are supposed to command a general body of knowledge commonly accepted as "sociology" by professionals, practitioners have neither information nor interest in many parts of the field. The phenomenon of specialization becomes exacerbated as the sciences become "harder," with more division and specialization in the biological sciences and even greater differentiation in the physical sciences. This high level of specialization is a function of the limited capacity of human beings to absorb knowledge at the rate at which it is being created; the consequence is an adult socialization process in which the graduate student is geared by his instructors to an increasingly encompassed focus on the latter's own work.

The sanctions brought against those who seek to broaden their scope are considerable. The doctorate is a reward ostensibly given only to those able to make a significant new contribution to knowledge. The only way new knowledge can be produced is by having an intense grasp of what has previously been established. In training new generations of professionals, then, the professoriate insists upon a tight compartmentalization of work. The socialization process in higher education guarantees rewards to those who focus upon limited areas. Graduate students' papers rarely deal with broad philosophical issues, focusing usually upon restricted frames of reference. In addition, graduate students who devote themselves in any significant degree to what are defined by their seniors as outside activities find themselves sanctioned negatively.

The training process of the professoriate emphasizes the development of narrow, highly specialized frames of reference as well as the development of loyalties to a body of knowledge rather than to a specific institution. In high-quality graduate-school programs professional socialization is stronger than in lower-ranking universities, but to some degree all share this orientation to the professional body of knowledge.

How the Professoriate Works

The socialization process becomes amplified when the newly trained professional becomes a faculty member; and this progress continues throughout his academic career. The work of the professor can be divided into four areas of service: research and publication, teaching, public service (to the larger society), and "citizenship" (public service to the university where he works). For the professionally oriented professoriate in the higher-quality universities only the first of the four functions carries significant rewards; the other three are mostly peripheral.

Rewards at a university take symbolic and material forms. Symbolic rewards consist of the allocation of tenure and advancement in rank. The material rewards, usually correlated highly with the symbolic, consist largely of salary advances. When these rewards are to be allocated, whether by review committees of seniors or by the administration, considerable difficulties arise in assessing a professor's performance. Assessors, for example, rarely have much knowledge (let alone systematic information) about the quality of a professor's teaching—professors do not sit in on one another's classes. It is also a violation of the normative code of the professoriate to ask open and direct questions of students about a colleague's performance. Students often volunteer such information informally, but more often for those courses with which they are pleased. Obtaining systematic data about a professor's teaching has only become somewhat widespread since the events of Berkeley in 1964, when a growing sensitivity to the need for improvement in teaching arose. But even the use of more systematic instruments, such as surveys, raises difficulties. Not only are there methodological deficiencies in such data-gathering devices, but even where they have been introduced, restrictions often preclude the use of survey results in the assessment procedures by which members of the professoriate are judged.

At some universities, under the impact of criticism by students on the quality of teaching, awards for good teaching have been established. The winning of such an award is noted in the dossier of the professor and becomes an important datum for evaluation committees. But the number of such teaching awards is insignificant compared to the rewards to be obtained through publication. Most universities gear the award system to research rather than to teaching. As a result most faculty members are excluded from any formal recognition of teaching ability; this condition is passed along to the graduate students — who in turn communicate this situation to lower levels.

Public service and "citizenship" activities are prized by assessors but are also difficult to judge. When a member of the professoriate is named to the national presidential cabinet, it is obvious that he holds an important appointment. It is more difficult to judge the value of an appointment as a technical consultant to a governor's committee on crime or to a board concerned with reapportionment of the wards in the local town. Similarly, membership on a committee on student conduct is a significant service to the university but one that must be weighed against other contributions.

Only in the area of publication does a tangible product capable of systematic professional assessment become realizable. A professor's work must not only be "weighed" but also assessed as to its quality by professionals with established reputations. The research and publication record emerges as a crucial means by which members of the professoriate assess their colleagues. Thus, despite increasing emphasis on teaching, the reward system of the university continues to be structured toward research and publication rather than other areas.

One consequence of the high level of professionalization has been to delegate faculty administrative responsibilities to a separate, distinct bureaucracy — the administration. Although top echelons of most university bureaucracies have

academic credentials (at high-quality institutions the doctorate is a sine qua non for appointment to the top level of the
university bureaucracy), the administration is a separate body
distinct from the faculty. Unlike the university systems of
most European countries, where faculty members carry many
administrative responsibilities, much of the detailed work of
maintaining records and processing information on students
has become the obligation of a specialized bureaucracy. This
differentiation process places considerable powers in the
hands of bureaucrats. To a considerable degree it is a result
of the orientation of faculty members, who do not wish to
implement administrative regulations but prefer to focus on
those activities that provide the greatest rewards – research
and, to a lesser degree, teaching. Professionally oriented fac
ulty members not only admit to disinterest in bureaucratic
procedures but actively seek to avoid it. Some members of
the professoriate nevertheless find themselves sitting on
committees when they would rather be doing other kinds of
work. On the whole, the tendency within the high-quality
institutions is for much of the committee work to fall upon a
small segment of the total professorial group who, having
obtained tenure, become "good citizens" and participate in
internal administrative functions. This division of labor produces limited administrative experience that, coupled with
the narrow professional outlook, assures that practically no
faculty personnel are able to function in times of crisis or
under the pressure of immediate decision making.

The Faculty Corporation

The discussion of the professoriate as a social stratum – that
is, a group of individuals having a similar position in society
and therefore exhibiting similar characteristics – leads to consideration of the university faculties in their corporate capacities within the university. As such the faculty constitutes
one of the major legislative bodies of the university; in most
cases, drawing their power from higher bodies (boards of
trustees, regents, and the like), the faculty as a corporate
group acts as a legislature to determine the basic policies of
the educational process. The faculty as a corporate group is

rarely involved in certain areas that are left to other bodies within the university; financial questions, for example are almost never the concern of the faculty (except, of course, as professors struggle for more money). Normally, overall financial issues are handled by the administration and the trustees.

The faculty as a corporate group in most universities operates legislatively in three major areas: educational policy, personnel matters involving the faculty, and student conduct. Educational policy refers to the establishment of curricula and the supervision of various aspects of the educational process—how grades shall be allocated, for example, or the determination of whether students have fulfilled requirements, whether academic standards have been maintained or are being violated, and the like. Personnel questions refer to the processes by which academic personnel are recruited, advanced, and excluded from the university; they never deal with personnel questions involving the administrative bureaucracy. Questions of student conduct involve issues of nonacademic student behavior—that is, students in their dealings with each other or as they impinge upon other elements of the university community.

Even on these three issues problems of size limit the faculty as a corporate group in its ability to act. In mainstream universities, where faculties exceed 500, their capacity to function legislatively is limited. In addition, faculties do not feel comfortable operating in situations of controversy and prefer to achieve decisions on the basis of consensus. This does not mean that voting does not take place; rather, when a faculty is badly split on an issue, it prefers to move slowly and to build a larger majority through lengthy discussion. Other factors impede the capacity of the faculty to act as a corporate group. As already indicated, the professional orientation of faculty members means that they will not often willingly devote time to the legislative process. In order to function as a legislative group, the faculty should meet regularly and frequently; but most university faculties meet only once a month and then usually so late in the afternoon that the meeting has to be kept to an hour or two.

Relatively little legislative experience is acquired, for most faculty members stay away from such meetings except when crucial issues arise. (One crude index is faculties' almost total ignorance of parliamentary procedures—although most faculties as corporate groups insist on adherence to these formalized procedures.) Finally, the faculty as a corporate group is often limited in legislating by the formal and informal powers of the administrative bureaucracy. In many cases, administrative control is formally embodied in legal codes of the university that limit the jurisdiction of the faculty as a corporate group.

But even when powers are not limited, the faculty as a corporate group can only perform very limited legislative roles, establishing only the most general of policies, and then allocating authority downward to lower-echelon faculty bodies. Thus at any given university the university faculty establishes very general rules that then serve as guidelines for individual college faculties within that university. College faculties are also often too large and meet infrequently and therefore delegate the implementation of these regulations to the main administrative unit of the faculty—the department, where policies become implemented on a day-to-day basis. In some areas university or college faculties may establish specific bodies exercising jurisdiction over students; student conduct is, for example, often regulated by a universitywide structure supervised by a permanent faculty committee organized for this purpose. Similarly, academic misconduct (cheating or plagiarism) is frequently supervised by a universitywide faculty committee. The main work of the faculty as a corporate group, therefore, is the establishment of basic policies of regulative organizations and their supervision, usually through receiving reports from committees.

In higher-quality institutions the faculty as a corporate group is more likely to have a great deal of authority, particularly vis-à-vis the administration. At lower quality institutions the administration retains most powers, and any jurisdiction of the faculty as a corporate group is subject to administrative veto. But as universities become composed of very high percentages of cosmopolitan professionals, the trend is reversed and the administration gains authority, if only by default. A good example is the University of California at Berkeley, where most decision making rests with bodies other than the faculty as a corporate group.

The faculty as a corporate group is therefore able to respond to initiatives, but it rarely puts forward its own initiatives. This limited capability of initiating action is also characteristic of such legislative organizations as the United States Congress. Composed of conflicting interest groups, the Congress's authority is limited to those areas where its prerogatives as a corporate group are threatened; otherwise it must depend upon the initiatives put forth by the executive branch of government. Legislative groups are notoriously unable to function in crisis situations and can only at best react to them. In the campus crises, for example, some state legislatures responded by adopting legislation to cut off financial support to students involved in demonstrations. This action hardly constitutes a positive attempt to control or change the conditions giving rise to campus crises.

The structure of faculty meetings illustrates the group's inability to initiate action. At faculty meetings formal leadership often rests with its chief administrator (usually the president), who chairs the meeting. This structure controls the main inputs of information upon which the faculty as legislature must act and gives the administration the power to orchestrate decisions and hence to control the collective will of any faculty body. It also permits administration domination, since the chairman can respond quickly and briefly to comments to the point that the faculty as legislature is converted into an administratively directed organization. Some sensitivity is demanded of the administrators, since the faculty can react if issues are forced upon it, particularly issues involving faculty prerogatives. Nothing can arouse a faculty as much, for example, as an administrative attempt to impose parking limitations upon the faculty.

Another factor limiting the capacity of the faculty as a corporate group to act or react is its unsulation from other corporate groups on campus. For example, students are rarely, if ever, present at university faculty meetings. Though they may have representation in lower-level faculty bodies, their role even there is normatively limited. It would be a courageous student indeed who would open discussion on most issues. When student representatives do speak, they not only limit their remarks but also continue to provide the symbols of deference that characterize student exchanges with faculty members because faculty members will subsequently give them rewards or punishments (grades). This fact severely limits the capacity of students to deal even with issues in which they have a direct stake; they operate in the faculty-as-legislature not as peers but as vulnerable clients. Not surprisingly, even where student representation does exist, it fails to convey sentiments of the students as a group.

The most significant aspect of the faculty as a corporate group is its defense of its own vested interests, whether they concern academic freedom, curricula, and personnel matters or nonacademic questions, such as parking and salaries. When vested interests are threatened, the faculty as a corporate group becomes aroused; it is at such times that massive participation in faculty meetings occurs. The faculty as a corporate group is also concerned with the defense of university traditions, including the openness of the university as the marketplace of ideas, the value-free character of the university, and the nonviolent exchange of views. Concern for tradition leads to concerns for the maintenance of the status quo. Having established mechanisms for the resolution of problems, the faculty as a corporate group insists upon adherence to established procedures, invariably arguing that the procedures contain possibilities for change and revision and therefore are legitimate.

The concern with retaining procedural integrity often becomes focused on the maintenance of good manners. The faculty as a corporate group is able to achieve decisions on matters of educational policy, personnel, and student conduct, but it finds itself unable to act legislatively on goals defined as outside the purview of the academy. Thus, when students demand that the faculty implicitly or explicitly criticize United States government policy or that it advocate disaffiliation of the university from financial involvments in

South Africa, the group is unable to act. Faculty members as individuals develop their own positions but reject the notion that the faculty as a corporate group should have a position. When students see faculty members as individuals who agree upon goals but are unwilling or unable to establish such goals formally and to implement them within the university, they turn to their own modes of implementation, particularly confrontation. The faculty as a corporate group reacts to confrontational actions by insisting upon "good manners" or a return to the established patterns of authority of the university.

Occasionally, but not with any significant frequency, individual faculty members sharing similar points of view organize ad hoc groups to function within the legislative meeting of the faculty. Such organized activity, whether informal or formal, is normally abhorred by most faculties, which prefer to avoid a polarization of internal faculty politics. This preference is reinforced by the fact that professional interests often prevail over political interests, thus mitigating further the potential for rift within any faculty deliberative body.

Professors as Individuals

Despite the substantial energies unleashed by the student rebellion, the ability of members of the professoriate to act individually has proven to be limited. The numbers of professors involved in any confrontation constitute an insignificant minority of the total faculty. Even in a crisis situation, such as that at Columbia, where an ad hoc faculty group was organized, it involved the energies of only several hundred faculty members—at best 5 per cent of the total university faculty. When members of the professoriate become activized at times of crisis, they become so more as members of the faculty as a corporate group than in any other way; that is, they will turn out for faculty meetings, but they do not participate in confrontations, even in a spectator's capacity, or in any other kind of action that has a potential for illegal acts or violent responses.

In examining the behavior of the few members of the

professoriate that become activized, it is necessary to emphasize how the socialization process draws faculty away from critical actions within the university. Accustomed to assembling information under conditions of withdrawal, most faculty members find the heat of a confrontation too difficult to sustain even as spectators. Indeed, as indicated earlier, only a few come as spectators, and fewer still become involved in direct action sponsored by students.

When members of the professoriate become mobilized, they do so to support student demonstrators rather than oppose them. When confrontations occur, the number of professors who make themselves known as hostile at such confrontations is far smaller than the number that provides active support or passive acknowledgment that the goals of the students are accurate, even though their tactics are illicit. A few hostile faculty members with the individual capacity to sustain great pressures may argue with student demonstrators, but most simply stay away. Only in rare circumstances will a hostile professor become involved in the organization of counter demonstrations, as one faculty member did at Columbia.

Even among sympathetic faculty activists it is rare to find any example to substitute faculty energy for that of the students. In confrontation one or two faculty members may *fully associate* themselves with the students. These faculty members rarely play significant leadership roles in the event, although they may hold some prominence in the internal activities of the student demonstrators. More significantly, faculty activists who become involved in the support of the demonstrators seek to define their own role as autonomous and separate from that of the students. Either they will not sit physically with the students or they will define the marginality of their presence in other ways. In many cases this separation takes symbolic form, with faculty members standing on the periphery of the sit-in group rather than sitting on the floor with the demonstrators.

The overwhelming bulk of the faculty rarely has any notion about how to mobilize. Those who do become involved are in most cases drawn into the vortex of the demonstration as it unfolds rather than participating in it in its formative stages. Most faculty members cannot grasp the fact that the organizing sessions at which confrontations are planned are open. It is, in fact, simple to learn where an SDS meeting is occurring and to attend such a meeting. (This is not the case with black student meetings.) As far as most nonblack confrontations are concerned, meetings are accessible to anyone seeking to attend. But the socialization of faculty members precludes their involvement, since their associations have been structured and particularized within professional areas. For the overwhelming bulk of faculty members the concept of attending an SDS meeting is as alien as attempting to convince a professional audience with a gun. Thus most professors' knowledge about student confrontations is obtained at second hand. It is probable that three-fourths of any university faculty has never actually witnessed much less participated in a confrontation except for short intervals.

In considering what faculty activists actually do during student demonstrations, one can see that the initiating capacity of the faculty member is limited. In many respects this circumstance reflects the different status bestowed on the teacher vis-à-vis the student generation. But in addition the ability to allocate large quantities of time to activism is severely limited. Further the training of faculty members makes them conservative about the violations of laws and university regulations, and hence it is difficult to mobilize them.

The activism of faculty supporters of the students tends to be limited to four types of activities.

1. Loosely structured *ad hoc* support groups are formed. In many cases student confrontations involve the organization of support activities, especially financial and psychological. Adult support groups have been mobilized to provide general support to the student movement over long periods of time rather than in the heat of confrontations. This in itself makes for a marginal rather than central relationship.

2. Individual faculty members have been involved in the antiwar movement, usually in such nonconfrontational activities as vigils, demonstrations, and parades. Although the students will confront the university directly on the issue of the

war—especially to prevent companies or organizations involved with the war from recruiting on campus—faculty members tend to recoil from direct personal involvement. Most faculty antiwar activists engage in actions fully within the realm of legality or in which the consequences for legal violation are not onerous, such as refusal to pay federal tax on telephone bills. When faculty activists decide to break a law significantly, they tend to do so with a maximum of advance warning and publicity.

3. The physical presence of faculty members at confrontations often provides considerable legitimation to student demands. While many of the serious militants feel they need such support, the ranks of the student confronters are rarely composed of such people. Many are unsure about their own commitment to confrontation as a tactic and have become involved because they feel intensely about an issue to which society or the university seem oblivious. The presence of the faculty member, though he may discuss the issues dispassionately and may only generally support the student goals, provides support for many students. During actual confrontations faculty supporters of the students have made their presence felt in a variety of ways. In such circumstances faculty members assume a "witness" role in which they "make themselves available" to provide evidence at future judicial procedures. Their intent is to make sure that student demonstrators' rights are protected by the judicial mechanisms of the university. They provide support in judicial proceedings when they attempt to interpret the events in the most favorable light before disciplinary committees.

4. As we mentioned earlier, in the heat of confrontation, faculty "witnesses" are drawn into the vortex of conflict. When the administration initiates an escalation in punitive approaches, when violence is introduced by the police or by counterdemonstrators, or when some norm clearly established in the minds of faculty members is violated by parties to a confrontation, faculty sympathizers tend to become directly involved—though they will retain their usual autonomous role; rarely will a faculty member join the students fully to become a participant in their actions.

Professorial Polemics

There is little direct faculty opposition to the student movement; however, this position does not rule out a considerable
amount of indirect and internecine opposition. Professional
academic men are at their best when writing and, contrary to
their explicit ban on ideological importations, when polemi-
cizing. Thus a considerable body of literature has been built
up in the recent period reflecting, if not the dominant sentiments of faculty men, then at least the sentiments of a good
number of them, particularly those reared in intellectual and
political traditions inherited from an earlier time. What follows is a collective portrait of intellectual opposition to student protest, not necessarily a consensus of faculty opinion
on the worth of such opposition.

While there has been a great deal of analysis of student
unrest by the professoriate, there have been surprisingly few
written defenses of the students from the adult portion of the
university community. Most serious adult defenses of student
unrest have stemmed from nonacademic or, at best, marginal
academic sources—from such writers as Hal Draper, a librar-
ian at Berkeley; Norman Mailer, the novelist; and Paul Good-
man, one of the few practicing unattached intellectuals in the
United States. Others who have been relatively sympathetic
to the student cause, such as Herbert Marcuse and Noam
Chomsky, while philosophically instrumental in motivating
the rebellion (despite sharp ideological differences between
them), have found themselves in practice at sharp variance
with student aims and ambitions, at least as exemplified by
the student militants at Columbia University and at San
Francisco State College. Others, such as Amitai Etzioni (his
clear sympathies with the students notwithstanding), have
been involved more in adjudicating student conflict with the
administration than with active participation in the rebellion
or the theoretical justification for such uprisings.

The bulk of professorial writing on the rebellion has,
therefore, been oriented more toward criticism than toward
support. It is impossible to encompass the totality of this

commentary, since much is aimed at local audiences, particularly alumni and students, and is therefore not readily accessible. We turn our attention, therefore, to a consideration of one major tendency and two minor developments that can be dealt with briefly.

LIBERAL CRITICISM

The first minor manifestation is the relatively rare occurrence of a professor writing from the viewpoint of the *traditional right* in American politics.[1] This approach is more significant by its absence; what is remarkable is that so few of the professorial critics express themselves from the traditional rightwing point of view. Indeed, the main salient of the critical professoriate has an old-left background.

A second and more significant manifestation among the professoriate has been addressed to the academic community through the weekly journal of the American Association for the Advancement of Science, where an article by a group of Fellows at the Center for Advanced Study in the Behavioral Sciences at Stanford issued a call for

> a national study, supported by some appropriate federal agency or private foundation ... to examine the individual and group patterns of response to these protests by students, faculty, and administration. A distinguished panel of behavioral scientists and educators should be appointed to serve as an advisory body. The scope and methods of the study should be developed by this advisory body, and should be designed to provide a national perspective on this phenomenon.[2]

The proposal, made by nineteen eminent academicians, argued that there was relatively little knowledge about various assertions made concerning the student rebels.

The proposal originated in a study group organized at the Center in October 1957 on "The College Environment as a

---

1. See, for example *Barron's*, May 20, 1968.
2. "Student Protests: A Phenomenon for Behavioral Sciences Research," *Science*, July 5, 1968, p. 20.

Place to Learn." With the acceleration of events in the fall of 1967, the seminar became increasingly aware of the impact of student unrest on the college campus as demonstrations occurred on the campuses of the participants in the seminar. The issue came closest to immediate concern when the laboratory of one of the participants (from Antioch College) was picketed and forcibly closed for a few hours by a group of students because of its research contracts with the Department of Defense.

The Fellows of the Center decided to look more intensively at this entire phenomenon of student unrest. The mode of analysis used is interesting, since its elitist assumptions limited any rounded study of student unrest. "We invited a number of college presidents to meet individually with us in the seminar." Drawing upon five nearby college presidents, a series of discussions led to the formulation of the proposal in *Science*.[3]

The proposal of the Center Fellows initiated a sequence of correspondence in *Science* that was largely negative.[4] The initial response (August 23, 1968) came from a *counter-demonstrator* involved in the Antioch events, Joseph R. Whaley, and was strongly negative. Crediting the Antioch administration with dealing directly with the issues, Mr. Whaley pointed out that, had Antioch's president followed in the spirit of the Fellows' proposal,

> he would have convened a panel of noted behavioral scientists to examine the psychodynamics of the social phenomenon of campus protest at Antioch. That panel, its very existence a slur on the sanity and intelligence of the protestors, would have been a perfect proof of the underlying contention that the college was not interested in serious discussion of the issues. I suggest that the Stanford fellows call instead for a study of the blindness, stubbornness, and hypocrisy of university administrations across the country, in order to determine why they seem unable to grasp the urgency of the need for reforms in their institutions. The students, after all, have been stating all along what changes they want. (Instead of a national study, the Stanford fellows need no

3. As proof that the proceedings were genuinely scholarly, we are promised further publications in a footnote to the article.
4. *Science*, August 23, 1968; September 20, 1968; December 6, 1968; February 28, 1969, March 7, 1969.

more than subscriptions to the *New York Times*. Instead of *study-ing* they students, why not start *listening* to us?

Another letter (December 6, 1968) questioned whether the Center Fellows were proposing a study of an activity about which they already had strong views. Robert Liberman attacked the methodological bias of the Fellows' approach in studying student rebellions.

The pro-establishment bias of the 19 behavioral scientists is clear from their report: they interviewed only college presidents, not student activists; and they label student confrontations as violent despite the fact that violence came to these protest demonstrations only when the university administration called out the police. It requires middle age and comfortable professional success (often nurtured by close cooperation with university and governmental hierarchies) to win a sabbatical at the Center for Advanced Study in the Behavioral Sciences. I am afraid that the 19 fellows of the Center are victims of their own histories and constrained by creaking and rusting liberalism.

Despite the preeminence of the signatories to the proposal, it appears to have died aborning. A number of investigations are currently under way into the student rebellion, however, by congressional committees and similar organs of state legislatures. There has not been any proposal within government for such a scholarly analysis.

A somewhat different viewpoint was put forward by Robert Morrison of Cornell University (March 7, 1969). Admitting differences between the way in which students and senior faculty defined the university, Morrison argues that "there is really not much of a generation gap about such fundamentals as freedom, love, war and race prejudice." The gap exists between those who wish to attack all the problems at once and "those who disclaim any concern for the ends to which their discoveries are put and who view any prior commitment as a dangerous impediment to detached investigation." Attacking the self-righteousness of both extreme positions, Morrison notes defects on both sides.

If the radicals are too self-satisfied about their moral commitments, conventional scholars may be dangerously smug about the magnificence of their detachment from human concerns. As scientists we might in fact be more effective teachers if we began by admitting that we too are against war, poverty, and hate and that we really went into science, at least in part, because it offered the best available means of overcoming these evils. Our seeming failure to grapple with the big problems all at once is not a sign of indifference or lack of commitment. Rather it stems from the perhaps deplorable but still undeniable fact that the scientific method has achieved almost all its successes by breaking big unmanageable problems down into little, controllable ones.

These views are sure to be unwelcome to those who feel that reforms which fall short of immediate total revolution are nothing more than "little finky changes" unworthy of men of virtue and vision. It may be, however, that the survival of universities that include the right of student dissent depends on the transmission of our belief that the only revolutions worth having come as the slowly accumulating sum of those same "little finky changes."

Morrison's view directs professors to a more explicit statement favoring change but arguing for gradualism. The response by the student rebels to this argument has been clear: if such concern exists, why does the university not engage in breaking down unmanageable problems but continue to follow the courses of the past? Morrison has fallen into the error of attributing to all the demonstrators a position held by only a few; while some demonstrators want massive change in all respects and simultaneously, most would accept the breaking down of problems and gradual change if such change were to get under way. The student critics point out with some justification that the rate of change within the university is relatively small despite the massive protests already registered.

LEFT CRITICISM

Consideration now turns to the largest and most coherent group of academic critics. These include such figures as Lewis Feuer, Seymour Martin Lipset, Irving Howe, and Diana Trilling. The arguments of this coherent and articulate segment of the professoriate deserve examination in their own right, but it is worth making a brief sociological excursus, appraising the origins of these critics, since this technique is one they often use with respect to the students.

These critics share a number of characteristics. (1) All are over forty. (2) All are professional liberals—that is, with long standing reputations and public commitments. (3) Their writings frequently appear in traditional rightwing socialist media, although they also publish in such national liberal media as *The New York Times Sunday Magazine, Harpers,* and the *Atlantic* (4) Their critiques invariably contain strong allusions to the 1930's and the struggles between the Communists and the anti-Communist left, and they reflect in many respects their personal leftism of that period. (5) Each has a vested interest in academic liberalism as the quintessence of campus politics. (6) Finally, most of them are Jewish.[5]

Turning to more significant issues—the content of their criticism—three major aspects can be delineated.

First, the old critics of the new left have developed strong commitments through struggles within the old left or traumatic confrontations that led to the abandonment of former allegiances. The nature of these allegiances varies from critic to critic: some were involved with the old Communist Party, whereas others went through a Trotskyist or Socialist Party experience. Very often there were direct organizational attachments, but other critics operated on the peripheries of the political movements.

This experience has shaped the second major characteristic of the critics. Each tends to deal with the new left very much as if it were a continuation of the old left. The critics insist on projecting the new left as a continuation of the old, while the students present the new wave of radicalism as discrete and separable from previous eras of student

---

5. It is necessary to call attention to the ethnic origins of critics more because of their own preoccupation with their discovery, still empirically unproven, that the student rebels are preponderantly of Jewish origin than because we ourselves find any special significance in the Jewishness of critics. We suspect that more significance attaches to the fact that rebels, critics, and critics of the critics are noted more for ethnic *origin* than for attachments, dedication, and affiliation to Judaism, either in its religious or cultural sense. Although what seems to be occurring here is an internal Jewish polemic, this polemic is taking place not *within* the Jewish community but in the academic community—which is far from being Jewish. Whether student rebels have significant Jewish origins remains to be proven. We note finally that this distinction does not apply to black student rebels.

struggles and political leftism and in sharp disharmony with what came before.

Third, the critics confront the imperfections and vagaries of student action with the perfections of history and doctrine. Nearly every critique has noted, as a central point, the absence of a program and has accused the student left of a lack of concrete goals. This criticism is largely justified, although the reasons for the absence of these specific goals are rarely discussed by the critics. The deliberate avoidance of highly specified goals represents the conscious break by the new student left with the old programmatic orientations, the students having learned (like the critics) of the betrayal of socialism and of failures to develop economic alternatives more viable or morally more worthwhile than capitalism or the ostensible socialism of the Soviet Union. The new left has recognized the difficulty of implementing the highly complex goals that characterized the old left. And in this respect the students are very much like their critics — who equally eschew specifying goals of change after having experienced the disappointments of the "workers' Fatherland" in the 1930's. Instead of working out parameters of a future society, the old professorial left remains content to criticize the students, while the new student left remains content with unstipulated over-all goals, seeking a series of ad hoc changes centered on vague references to "socialism."

Professorial critics, such as Diana Trilling, frequently criticize the new left for acting as a moralizing force rather than a political one. They note that student rebels rarely link their struggle to the quality of their instruction but concern themselves with the control of institutional mechanisms. Why this thrust should be considered nonpolitical is difficult to appreciate; after all, the question of control is eminently political. Because the old left always considered the university as a liberalizing or radicalizing agency rather than a conservative force, old leftists find it difficult to conceive of a university as a place requiring a redistribution of power and control.

Other detractors, such as Lipset, have been more concerned with the size than with the character of unrest. Lipset insists that, although students played a significant role in the civil rights struggle of an earlier period and in focusing attention on the bureaucracy of higher education, the student movement in recent years has not succeeded in mobilizing a major segment of the total student population. While there are obvious problems in defining just what constitutes a "significant segment" of any population, it is clear that Lipset has become so committed to electoral processes as to forget revolutionary history. During rapid social change population clusters of 3 to 10 per cent—the estimated size of the core and periphery of student rebels—have been able to achieve the shutting down or transformation of university life. At peak points it is not organizational membership but the participation of masses of students that has determined the success of a student uprising. If politics is defined in narrow electoral or student-government terms, the demonstrators of the post-Berkeley period can be regarded as insignificant. Such a judgment, however, neglects the experience of historical processes, in which only small percentages of populations have ever been involved in revolutionary action leading to change.

Perhaps the most significant and thorough criticism of the student left has been leveled by Lewis S. Feuer. His lengthy and scholarly book[6] constitutes the obverse of his own criticism of the students. Whereas Feuer regards the students as juvenocrats inspired by filiarchy, this volume is perilously close to sustaining gerontocracy and patriarchy. The bulk of Feuer's study is devoted to historical matters related to the current student uprising only by virtue of his basic thesis on the conflict of generations. The current relevance of the book is found in three chapters that state the basic thesis and discuss the emergence of the new left and the Berkeley events. Feuer's basic thesis is that student movements manifest two conflicting attributes. For the past 150 years, they "have been the bearers of a higher ethic for social reconstruction, of altruism, and of generous emotion. On the other hand, with all the uniformity of a sociological law, they have imposed on the political process a choice of means destructive both of self and of the goals which presumably were

6. Lewis S. Feuer, *The Conflict of Generations: The Character and Significance of Student Movements.* New York: Basic Books, 1969.

sought" (p. 5). Feuer accuses student movements of suicidalism, terrorism, nihilism, self-annihilation, elitist amoralism, assassination, messianism, immorality, irrationality, psychological father destruction, emotional rebellion, sickness,
juvenocracy and filiarchy, middle-classness, innocence and
purity, morbid self-destructive masochism, cultural isolation
from the population, and other crimes and pathologies.

Having engaged in filicide in his first chapter, Feuer proceeds to symbolically disfigure the destroyed corpse. Feuer
can discover little to commend the new student revival of the
1960's and proceeds to a melange of criticism. He begins by
noting the rejection of a host of traditional groups: the labor
movement, the old Marxists, and the old left, as well as the
old liberals. This rejection by students is akin to that of C.
Wright Mills who, "disillusioned with labor, and at odds with
the middle class and what he called the 'power elite,' had
only the intellectuals to turn to as agents of social change."
Feuer notes that Mills was himself criticized by new leftists
for elitism. Thus the burden of Feuer's argument rests on the
similarity of rejection of traditional liberal forces by the new
left *and* the new sociology (pp. 386–390).

The impetus of the revitalized student movement begins
with the Negro student movement of the early 1960's. But
"the Negro student movement . . . was relatively free of the
beatnik, nihilist elements which characterized the white student movement." The impact of the blacks on the white
students produced a back-to-the-people movement in the
form of the civil rights participation in Mississippi and the
South indicative of a "will to martyrdom" and representing a
combination of "elitism, populism, and the tragic ingredient
of suicidalism." Feuer faults the new left for its opposition to
a constructive back-to-the-people movement initiated by
President Kennedy and the Peace Corps. Counterposing the
new left with the Peace Corps ("Thus, the student movement
generally stood opposed to the 10,200 volunteers who in
1966 were at work in forty-six countries"), Feuer ignores the
fact that some of the earlier Peace Corps returnees had joined
the student revolt and at some universities, were in fact
providing leadership experience developed within the Peace
Corps. He next turns to a consideration of the back to the

people movement developed by the new leftists that consisted of moving into the slums from which, within a short period, the poor rejected them. "Two years later ... this back-to-the-people spirit was being replaced by a more unadorned elitism of the intellectual class" (pp. 403–404). Following this rejection, according to Feuer, the new left shifted more significantly to an elitist orientation. Although there is a relationship between the new left and the beats and hippies, Feuer nevertheless makes distinctions:

> The New Left endorses the moral critique of the Beat Generation, but adds to it the all-powerful strain of activism. The beatnik immersed himself in Zen, the ideology of secession and masochism; the New Leftist goes on to aggression, participatory democracy, and the young Marx. ... When he is rejected by his hoped-for lowly class allies, the New Leftist turns either to individual violence or individual withdrawal; the terrorist and the hippie are the commingling alternatives within the next stage of the New Left (p. 407).

Feuer next attacks new left commitments to participatory democracy, which rejects the old forms of parliamentarianism and representation. Participation becomes "Lenin up-dated" in that there is a kinship between participatory democracy and Soviet democracy. Feuer proceeds to mount an attack on the teach-in movement of the spring of 1965 as a form of "elitism" and "authoritarianism." For him, the teach-in constituted a demand for special status and privilege.

After an attack on the "anti-Americanism" of the students, Feuer proceeds to a discussion of student-movement ethics, noting a shift from "absolutism to amoralism." And this, in turn, is said to have produced aberrant forms of sexual behavior. The evidence that Feuer adduces for interracial sexuality is drawn from manifestations in Berkeley CORE during 1962–1964. Orgiastic behavior is adduced by citations from courses taught in the Berkeley Free University that, among others, included a course taught by the president of the Sexual Freedom League, "The History of Western Anti-Sensualism." Feuer concludes his lenthy attack on the new student left by examining the preponderance of Jewish students as "the bearers of generational conflict in the United States."

The possibility of dealing with Feuer's many arguments is limited not only by the paucity of empirical data relevant to his contentions, but also by the extreme levels of generalization. Methodologically it is worth noting that Feuer has based most of his criticism on limited developments occurring on only a single campus, Berkeley, with which he is most familiar. Indeed, most of the evidence cited for Berkeley and attributed to the new left is of marginal legitimacy. Feuer should have drawn his data from broader sources; he could have obtained a more representative picture of the new left had he delineated its parameters more carefully within the context of Berkeley, which represents the far extreme case of student activism and which is, therefore, hardly typical of national trends. Empirical studies indicate that the demonstrators are not as monstrous as Feuer would have them. Thus Glen Lyonns reports: "Generally the demonstrators seemed to be more liberal politically and to live in less restrictive housing than the total university population." Similarly, Robert H. Somers notes that "even if one disposes of the whole Free Speech Movement as representing only a minority of the campus, the group thus sloughed off is a minority vital to the excellence of this university."[7]

Additional evidence can be produced from empirical studies that the grades of the protesters at Chicago are somewhat higher than those of nonprotestors. Furthermore, at Berkeley "The Free Speech Movement drew extraordinarily large proportions of students with strong intellectual orientations at all levels (freshmen through graduate)."[8]

Crediting the student left with a death wish, a will to martyrdom, or a drive to suicide represents the crude Freud-

7. cf. Glen Lyonns, "The Police Car Demonstration: A Survey of Participants" in *The Berkeley Student Revolt*, edited by Seymour M. Lipset and Sheldon Wolin. Garden City, New York: Anchor-Doubleday, 1965, pp. 519–530. Robert H. Somers, "The Mainsprings of The Rebellion," in *The Berkeley Student Revolt*, pp. 530–557.

8. Richard Flacks, "The Liberated Generation: An Exploration of the Roots of Student Protest," *Journal of Social Issues*, 23,3 (July 1967), 56; see also Somers, p. 544. Paul Heist, "Intellect and Commitment: The Faces of Discontent," Berkeley, Center for the Study of Higher Education, 1965, unpublished paper cited by Christian Bay, "Political and Apolitical Students: Facts in Search of a Theory," *Journal of Social Issues*, 23,3 (July 1967), 76–91.

ian generalization referred to as the "psycho-historical" method. But Freud's Oedipal complex and death wish have proven to be unamenable to empirical analysis; similarly, Feuer's analysis is also beyond demonstration.

What accounts for the critical professorial writing? Why should there be a lack of professorial confidence in radical student behavior? It must immediately be appreciated that generational factors are relatively constant. When students were politically quiescent, the professoriate condemned them for being a "silent generation"; now that students have become politically demanding, the critical professoriate condemns them either on tactical grounds or for lacking the requisite calm and judiciousness needed in public affairs.

Several additional answers come readily to mind, although it is difficult to name the most important single factor.

For much of the old professoriate, attending a university was a chance for achievement, for moving beyond the occupational and prestige levels of the parent generation. But now going to college has largely become a *familial obligation*, rather than an *individual choice*. The growth of the university since the end of World War II from a community of one million to more than seven million indicates the radical shift from the formerly specially favored position of higher education to its general acceptance as a requisite for "life."

Confusion therefore arises on the part of the professoriate. There is incredulous disbelief that, given such a vast opportunity, students will rebel. In fact, the rebellion is not so much against the opportunities gained by going to college but by the fact that attendance at college has become as socially obligatory as attendance at elementary and high schools is legally compulsory. The credentialist society sharply curtails possibilities of achievement without a college degree. There is a concerted effort among families, friends, and draft boards to insure university attendance by all males. Nearly the same amount of pressure is applied to girls by their families to insure a proper locale for meeting the right prospective husband. The weight of middle-class familial expectations looms far larger as a factor in student rebellion than it could when going to college itself represented a rebellion against lower-class family wishes. In this respect the ambivalence of many black students becomes clearer. Although they share with the professoriate an appreciation of upward mobility and increasing life chances, they also share with the student radicals a concern for the bureaucratic, antidemocratic spirit of university hierarchies.

The old professorial critics were touched by the fear of failure, but the new student radical is branded with the guilt of success. The natural history of moving from college radicalism to occupational conservatism is a rite of passage undergone by nearly every member of the professorial estate. Many look back to radical pasts; few can claim radical commitments in the present, and fewer have prospects for a radical future. A precise assault on the natural history of political socialization—from radicalism to conservatism in four easy years—has been made by the new left in common with such radical regimes as Maoist China. It is not the nature of their respective political systems that links the Red Guards and the student radicals in America but their shared apprehension of being overtaken by middle-generational conservatism. In this sense every professorial attack on the student radicals serves as a negative reinforcement; this gap between generational ideologies remains.

Another new element that presently separates the old professorial critics from the new student movement is the infusion on campus of such new ethnic groups as Negroes, Puerto Ricans, and Mexican-Americans. These groups have a different attitude toward higher education than do older ethnic groups. They share a functional, rather than a reverential, view of the educational process. For them the idea of a liberal arts education has become subverted in some measure by the idea of application. The ethnic demand for relevance (in contrast to the white students' demand for relevance) has at its core an insistence upon occupational training, to assure a meaningful role in society—in one's *own* society.

Too often the position of minorities has been interpreted

in simplistic terms. It is assumed that they either want to be fully integrated into the American system of higher education or are in rebellion against that system on ideological grounds. Rather, it is probable that their vision of college education is functional rather than ideological, occupational rather than professional. These differences create unspoken and unmentioned tensions that appear as a struggle between campus blacks and campus whites, though in fact, the struggle could better be conceptualized as concerning the nature of the liberal arts university per se.

The attitude of the old professoriate that has commented on the subject of the black students is instructive. It is perhaps best summed up by Irving Howe, who expresses the belief in the desirability and attainability of egalitarian goals for the Negro students. But he perceives these goals only in the traditional terms of integration and participation. As long as demands were made for equity and for greater attention to the economic and intellectual needs of minority groups in American society, black minority demands elicited the wholehearted support of the professoriate. When demands began to be made for separatism, for separate black housing (to offset the effects of fraternity segregationist policies) or for separate black-studies institutions (to offset ongoing establishment institutions dedicated to the study of East African Affairs, Russian Affairs, and so on), attitudes towards "extremist" demands of the black students became hostile and negative.

Black student demands for separateness pose serious challenges to the traditional norms of academic freedom and raise the specter of "Balkanization" in higher education. By this thinking, tomorrow there can be the same type of demand for Polish or Irish studies. The role of ideology and racial parity can in this way blunt the edge of universal criteria for the training of people—criteria that are historically linked to the autonomous functioning of the university.

This danger duly noted, the fact is that the Negro is only repeating practices well established in higher education. For years academia countenanced separation foisted by the fraternity and sorority system. Only at this time, belatedly, under intense pressure and without much feeling, has this WASPish system of old student power opened itself to the demands of minority groups. The fragmentation of the American university has been going on for some time, beginning with the development of professional schools (in contradistinction to the historical liberal arts core); it has continued with the growth of institutes, centers, and other specialized groupings. Everything from the Institute for Defense Analysis to "police science" training centers has become standard university fare. The foreign-area studies and military-training programs have institutionalized separatism at every level of university life—the movement towards cross-fertilization of ideas and interdisciplinary research notwithstanding.

While abstract criticisms directed at the Negro demands are well taken and presented with telling logic, the same logic was rarely applied by professorial critics in an earlier age when the institutionalization of separatism and particularism, exacerbated by World War II and the cold war, arose. Thus the professional ideology of the established professoriate, now firmly linked to a medieval myth of university autonomy, finds itself unwanted by the new left and unappreciated by the black militants. Its self-righteous reconstruction of the past is out of tune with the history that was or the utopia that is ostensibly coming into existence.

This circumstance has agonizing consequences, since the traditional definition of the university and such concepts as academic freedom are contradicted by demands for black control of parts of the educational curriculum. The struggle becomes one of autonomy at the level of student control versus integrity at the level of intellectual performance. As in all struggles, the problem is to choose between alternative goods, entailing a radical departure from traditional, professional concepts of the university. Little wonder that the older professors invariably attack the new student left for being oblivious to the nature of their university! The students respond that the classic system of higher learning in America has become more mythic than real. The roles of military contracts, of large-scale enterprise in defining curricula, and of government in determining the limits of university experimentation have made obsolete inherited standards of academic freedom. The struggle of student rebels has thus shifted from academic freedom to organizational control. This in itself is a sobering indication that we have reached a new stage in the maturation of higher education in America.

Finally, professorial opposition to student radicalism stems in part from the retreat of liberalism from the prosaic political arena to the academic realm. The university has become the natural expression of classical liberalism, the utilitarian limbo, the resting home of past and future advisers. Perceived in this context, the anti-intellectualism and fanaticism of students seem to present the same threat to current liberal values as did the threat represented by the political right ten to thirty years ago. The rhetoric of fanaticism of the new student left becomes confused with that of the old antistudent right and is seen as a common assault on the life of reason and of shared judgment and experiences—reason being equated with professionalism.

The transition of the university from a conservative to a liberal force emerged only gradually. It took place as a result of the exhaustion of the conservative upper classes of the Eastern seaboard and of the Latinist curriculum that prevailed in earlier colleges. The older conservatism was unable to service a modern technological society, even though it may have remained operational in the realm of political struggles. As liberalism spread and became a modus operandi in the university, it never announced its ideology but became important as a by-product for the needed expertise of the institution. The liberal persuasion assumed control on the campus, not as a fighting creed, but as a genteel secondary result of technological proficiency.

The irony is that the classical liberal as professorial educationist has become obligated to defend all kinds of programs for social welfare and international domination, again as a by-product of the continuing need for expertise. In this way professional liberalism stands in marked contrast to student ideology on American campuses and has become the enemy to the new student radicals. It is these liberals who now see the university as something more than a technical tool and as an institution that needs to be defended—from students rather than from administrators.

CHAPTER SEVEN

Black Experience and Campus Shock

The black student movement represents a new departure
within the Negro tradition at least as much as it does a
response to the structure of university power and its discriminatory tendencies. It is a rebellion against the crap-
shooting, cotillion-going, drug-taking petit bourgeoisie described in E. Franklin Frazier's classic text, *Black Bourgeoisie.* Black power on the campus is a response to these
social shadows without economic substance. If the white
radical student movement perceives this black movement as
at one and the same time exaggerated in its posture and
conservative in its political implications, the blacks themselves consider their newfound consciousness to transcend
the assault upon the bastions of white racism.

The black students perceive their own movement as a
necessary antiseptic to past Negro betrayals of black interests. And if their amorphous black-studies programs, African "natural" hair styles, and demands for a return to the
ghetto seem to strike a bizarre note, it can only be pointed
out that an overresponse on the side of self-identity is invariably linked to an exaggerated sense of mission, just as in
the past a high degree of self-hatred accompanied an emphasis on cultural mimesis. Although this new stage may appear

185

as implausible and unappealing at the historic stage, it must frankly be pointed out that creativity and consciousness are far easier to stimulate where strong group identification can be found than where such identification is absent. Furthermore — and this is all-important — the politics of assertion find a readier response in the white world than do the politics of accommodation; a fact even more true in the timorous world of university affairs than in the social world in general. It is in an awareness of such a double context of internal consciousness and external clout that the following is offered.

The analysis of ongoing rapid social change is difficult, since events always move more rapidly than data can be developed. The difficulties in examining the black student movement are compounded by factors beyond those that apply to the more general student movement, for the black students have been as closed to the nonblack world as the white students have been open to it. While it has been possible for anyone — professors, police, even total strangers — to attend white student meetings, the black movement has closeted itself. Not only have black students excluded nonblacks from participation in their organizations, but on most campuses they have maintained a secretive style of tactical planning. This separation has been accomplished in two ways: through the maintenance of a normative discipline toward the white world among most of their members, which precludes their revealing anything to whites, even to nonblack friends; and through attempting to control news sources and other forms of public disclosure to permit release of only small amounts of information. As shall be seen, there are tactical reasons for this style of information management, but from the point of view of the writers, there are also liabilities. Because it is difficult to obtain direct information about internal developments in black circles, we have had to operate primarily from inferences made about their behavior.

The black student movement is interesting not only because of its differences from the white student movement, but also for the rapidity with which it has burgeoned. Prior to the assassination of Martin Luther King in April 1968, there were many black student organizations on U.S. campuses, but these were still in early organizational phases, and few attempts had been made to project them onto the broader campus scene. Scattered individual blacks had been active in the early antiwar confrontations, but the Vietnam movement generally did not bring blacks into prominence among student activists. Nor were the civil rights experiences significant to black students on white campuses, since these events transpired during a period when their numbers were small and a critical mass of blacks had not yet developed on campus.

The increase in the numbers of black students on white campuses came after the early 1960's—after the civil rights movement had gone through its heroic phase in Montgomery, Selma, and Mississippi. During that phase whites were drawn into support of black activities in southern states; they later transferred their experiences to their home bases. Significantly for the overwhelmingly white campuses, the southern actions raised questions as to why so many institutions were lily-white. At many northern universities the southern experience was translated into programs to recruit black high-school graduates. These "outreach" programs were intended to overcome two basic problems in recruiting black students. First, most black high-school graduates with adequate academic records did not apply to the elite universities. In some cases this inaction was a result of sheer inertia (blacks went to such schools as Tuskegee and Howard and made it; why go elsewhere?); in others it was a result of discrimination and well-founded fears. Before the 1960's only the most courageous Negro, with an impeccable academic record, would undertake the difficulties of any Ivy League school, let alone the problems of living in what was often a distinctly dangerous environment. This is not to say that there were no such foolhardy Negroes or that they were refused admittance. Some such students were admitted, and some even graduated. But they never constituted any large number, let alone a large percentage of the total population of the mainstream universities and colleges.

The second problem that outreach programs intended to resolve was the inadequate academic preparation of the blacks (as compared to whites), which very often meant that they were excluded on academic grounds alone. All other things being unequal, whites had better academic records and therefore filled whatever vacancies were available. This circumstance reflected the de facto segregated educational systems in the north and the perpetuation of a double-standard system of education. This inequality was a factor leading to the proposals in the early 1960's to mix grade school students (generally by busing arrangements), so that white parents would have a stake in upgrading all schools — black and white — within a given system.

Outreach programs attempted to increase participation by black students in mainstream white universities by encouraging them to apply for admission, by setting up variable admission standards (this proved to be a delicate issue), and by organizing tutoring and other special educational programs to compensate black students with deficient academic backgrounds. In the first half of the 1960's outreach programs did succeed in increasing black admissions at the undergraduate level.

During the early years of these programs the black students' capacities for organization were severely limited. Not only did they suffer from organizational inexperience, but the sheer problems of survival in the higher quality universities made enormous demands on their personal resources. Perhaps even more significantly, the necessary ideological orientation was only then being formulated: these students were still *Negroes* rather than *blacks*. Not until black ideology began to be formulated and black pride began to become widespread did black organizations on campus get under way. Although there had been primitive formulations of black ideologies before, it was not until after the summer of 1964 — when SNCC began to realize that its movement would have to become black and shed its white supporters — until after the assassination of Malcolm X in February 1965, and until in 1966 Stokely Carmichael proposed the slogan of "Black Power" that a meaningful black ideology began to develop. The slogan of Black Power created a distinction between blacks on the one hand and all other categories — ranging from "Negroes" to "Colored" to "Uncle Toms" — on the other.

For most blacks at mainstream universities during these early years (1963–1965), Berkeley, Vietnam, and the horrors of in loco parentis were insignificant matters. Even the civil rights issues valiantly being carried forward by Martin Luther King and others were more important to white students (and faculty) than to blacks. Most black students came from northern environments and had little involvement in the southern struggles. Even the major northern events, the large-scale urban riots that began in 1966, took place in the summers, when students were not functioning as students. It was also difficult for black students to relate to these events for other reasons, having to do with their social origins and the consequent social differences between themselves and many of the rioters.

The assassination of Martin Luther King served to trigger a new level of demands. Literally in that instant of murder the entire relationship between the black students and the university changed dramatically. Perhaps this was because the assassination had such an impact upon the predominantly white university communities in which an open outpouring of sorrow (mixed with guilt) took place. At campuses throughout the nation hundreds of whites joined memorial marches organized at university centers. At Columbia, a memorial service was disrupted by Mark Rudd and by a walkout of SDS students in protest at the presumed moral hypocrisy such a memorial service represented. At hundreds of other universities and colleges there was a collective outpouring of grief, surpassing in intensity perhaps even the feelings on the campus at the time John F. Kennedy was assassinated. Kennedy's death was felt with intensity by the entire nation, and this universality tended to vitiate the particular feelings of the campus. The King assassination may have been felt even more keenly than the murder of Robert Kennedy, although the latter had been developing a substantial campus following. Like his brother, Robert Kennedy was a national figure. Though Martin Luther King was not a campus figure, his approach to civil rights — militant confrontation and multiracial nonviolent action — had a special appeal for campus liberals. His persistence, even while surrounded by more militant figures espousing separation and orientations toward violence, made him even more attractive. King had worked to prevent his less militant stance from impeding his attempts to broaden his social-action base. Recognizing the necessity to expand the civil rights struggle, he made the attempt (largely unsuccessful) in Chicago to begin work in a new urban milieu. For the campus liberals Martin Luther King was an ideal leader, militant but liberal and legitimated by a Nobel Peace Prize. His death could only mean militant polarization of black and white, and campus liberals mourned his passing. The black student movement became crystallized as, on campus after campus, the blacks utilized the memorial services not to commemorate Martin Luther King, but to attack the white world, which was held responsible for his death, and to put forward demands to university authorities.

This black student movement took form as the inexorable schedule of the academic year was running out. Had King been assassinated in February, a momentum might have grown, producing unparalleled difficulties for the university leadership. With only a brief period left in the semester, the capacity of the blacks to organize, make demands, negotiate, consolidate, and make new demands was severely limited. Thus it was that the main black action awaited the academic year 1968–1969.

Before examining the black student movement and its relationship to the wider student movement, it will be useful to consider the social origins of black students and the consequences of these origins for black organization.

Black Students in an Environmental Context

The character of the black student movement rests upon the peculiar characteristics of black students themselves: distinctly underprivileged, especially when compared to their white peers, the black students nevertheless constitute a highly privileged segment of the larger black population. Beyond their present social position as students, their future mobility is virtually guaranteed if they graduate from the university. This privileged condition is a continuation of an already favored social position, for black collegians come from relatively privileged backgrounds. Because substantial numbers of black children fail to complete high school, those holding high-school diplomas—even if these are "deficient" by the standards of mainstream universities—are placed in a position markedly superior to their black peers.

While we have seen no statistical data on this subject, personal contacts with black students have indicated to us that their parents are members of the "black bourgeoisie." Black college students do not usually come from broken homes where the mother is the economic mainstay of the family. Many have fathers with low-ranking civil-service positions or other stable and permanent employment—positions that are not impressive by white monetary standards but that provide stability of economic and social existence.

Outreach programs remain beyond the grasp of the bulk of black schoolchildren, since they lack that basic sine qua non for university entry—the high-school diploma. The fact that black collegians have "made it" into the university places them in a superior position to their black peers. "Making it" into Yale, Cornell, or Michigan constitutes more definitive recognition than does acceptance into the old elite Negro colleges such as Tuskegee or Howard. Black college students know that they are better off than the urban, dropout, ghetto dwellers. Indeed, their fellow blacks may become ideological abstractions rather than living persons, since those who have "made it" have largely been socially insulated from the black urban masses.

Despite these differences, black collegians respond to the ideology of blackness more consciously and intellectually than do their less fortunate "brothers." For the dropouts the ideology of blackness is still abstraction and has little meaning. While a few ideologists have begun to get through with some simple ideas ("black is beautiful"), the younger black dropouts remain as unimpressed with ideology as college blacks are impressed.

The relative privilege of the black students raises questions about how they relate themselves to the black communities outside the university and how these communities, in turn, relate to the black students. For the moment, the way in which the student legions relate to the black community is rhetorically, but not behaviorally, clear. Black students now have a strong sense of adherence to the black communities outside the university as a result of the new "black is beautiful" rhetoric as well as of what they envision as their future in the black communities. Black undergraduates, for example, talk about working in the black community-action projects to improve the community's condition. On the other hand, they do not seem to be actually carrying on that much activity in the communities. While a few participate in community activities, three conditions tend to limit their involvement.

First, since many universities are not located near black communities, trips from the center of learning to the center of action are made only with difficulty. Schools near the black community, such as Columbia and CCNY, are relatively few. Even at Berkeley geography poses difficulties, for black ghettos are some distance from the university. The travel time involved erodes intense long-range involvement by students in community affairs. Second, the structure of the academic calendar poses problems for students, for it chops the year into time periods, leaving only the summer for extensive commitments to community affairs. Third, engagement in extensive activities for which there is no curricular reward is perilous, especially when one is academically marginal to begin with. In mainstream universities even good students have to devote considerable time to their studies; many black students, coming from a deprived background, have to work even harder. While there is rhetorical intent to become involved in black community affairs, for the bulk of the black students actual action is all too frequently precluded.

Other factors impede the involvement of black collegians in black community affairs. Because of differences between the students and community people, many black students are ill at ease with the less privileged and less educated people presently emerging as community leaders. Despite the common bond of blackness, there can be considerable tensions between black collegians and this new uneducated leadership. In many respects the new ghetto leaders regard black collegians in the same way as they do sympathetic whites: as outsiders who should do as they are told and should not seek to dominate ghetto organizations. Relegation to a secondary and advisory role hardly gibes with the black students' own self-conceptions.

This point underscores the relationship of the black communities to the black college students. In a sense it is erroneous to use the term "community" today. In a sociological sense the term community is applied prematurely, since little sense of common harmony, authority structure, or, indeed, common identity has yet emerged in the black world, although the outlines of these elements may now be seen. The black "community," therefore, is still an abstraction consisting of a variety of heterogeneous organizations and many amorphous tendencies. The great amount of social energy now released in the black communities is improving the prospects for more homogeneous organization. Meanwhile, however, black students must relate to the black community through specific organizations that are often only peripherally involved in the black power revolution. How black students get into these organizations depends on the nature of the organizations. When they originate with lower-class Negroes now seeking their own modus operandi, the relatively privileged black collegian is rarely welcomed and may be resented.

Presently the actual linkages between black communities and the black students—particularly cases in which communities support students in their demands—have been negligible. Of the confrontations during the academic year 1968–1969, in only one case has there been a significant rapprochement between black students and the community: at San Francisco State College. Even there the linkage was tenuous. For several days at the peak of the 1968 crisis community leaders supported the strike of the Third World Liberation Front and helped confront the San Francisco State administration. Within a few days community participation decreased, and strain between community leaders and the student strikers became somewhat public. During the Columbia events in April-May 1968, initially concerning the construction of a gymnasium in Morningside Park, the Harlem community remained largely aloof from the campus protest.

Despite the black collegian's tenuous relationship to the black community, it is generally believed that such linkages will eventually be established. Whites, led by their own discomfort and guilt in the presence of all black people, believe that articulation between the two black communities is inevitable. White expectations generate pressure upon the blacks, who are also bound by the ideological celebration of blackness. But when black collegians and black community leaders attempt to operate together, tensions inevitably develop. The only certainty is that black students have greater potential for linkage with the black community than do white students with any grouping, organization, or social category in the white community. Much will depend on the degree to which black students relate to the organizations forming in the black ghettos. To the extent that black students effect a liaison with popular and militant community groups, they may call upon these organizations at times of campus crisis. For unlike white radicals, campus blacks have a natural constituency among the black communities who have a shared belief in the values of education, and the skills it provides, in gaining full citizenship.

The Character of Black Student Actions

The beginning of the academic year 1968–1969 brought to the American campus a shift from the antiwar confrontations of the previous three years to a series of black confrontations. (Although there was one major antiwar action at the University of Connecticut during the fall semester, not until after 1969 began did additional antiwar actions get under way.) Though black student action is lineally part of the more general student uprising, it is qualitatively different, since it also represents the translation of the more general black revolution to the campus. Although they act independently of the white militants, black students generally receive the support of the former in their demands for change. The whites have called into question the previous consensus and the legitimacy of the authority system of the university; the major thrust has now shifted to blacks; and the black student actions are spelling out in detail many generalized demands put forward by the whites over the past few years.

The black students have focused on those aspects of the university that affect them as specific interest group. Putting forward demands that vary from university to university, these boil down to the establishment of procedures that would severely limit existing powers of administration and faculty, the expansion of the powers of black students, and the increase of their actual numbers.

Most of the demands deal with some variant of the following:

1. Increased recruitment of blacks in all categories of the university—as students, faculty, and staff.

2. Turning over of recruitment (both of students and faculty) to the blacks themselves.

3. Establishment of ethnic-studies programs (variously referred to as "Afro-American" or "black") providing more relevant instruction for blacks and dealing with the black experience.

4. The autonomy of such study programs, guaranteeing their independence of normal decision-making centers, such as the faculty or the administration.

Control over all internal processes would rest initially with black students (including hiring and firing of faculty, determination of curricula, setting of standards, recruitment and exclusion of students—mainly white). At some vague stage in the future some powers would be shared with black faculty, but whites would not exercise controls over such programs in any way. Whites would only pay their costs.

To put forward these demands, blacks have used a wide range of styles, from insurrectionary forms at San Francisco State and Berkeley in which they openly battle with police to gentle sit-ins where there is no intent to impede the normal processes of the university. In many cases confrontations over the demands have involved sit-ins in which blacks take over a university building and hold it during negotiations.

Another key tactic of the blacks is levying demands defined as nonnegotiable. Publicly they state that the sole acceptable response from the university is complete acceptance of the demands *before* the blacks end their sit-in. In fact, a great deal of negotiation occurs in which exchanges of views between students and administration permits both to re-formulate their positions.

This tactic of nonnegotiability has been taken from the more general student movement, but blacks have developed it with a greater eye to publicity. There are similarities between the use of this style by black students and the more general student movement. For the antiwar militants, however, nonnegotiability was not a virtue in itself but was a part of their conscious rejection of procedures that encouraged the crystallization of leadership roles. Because they recognized that negotiations with hundreds of demonstrators would be difficult, the earlier antiwar militants either stated that their demands were not negotiable or proposed that administrators negotiate with the entire demonstrating group. For these early militants this position was also valued because it undermined the cooptative mechanisms present in any negotiations procedure, that divide the negotiators from those they represent. The blacks do not hold to this antileadership position ideologically; indeed, while black attitudes toward leadership have not been clearly expressed, we are left with the distinct belief that organizational roles are strongly demarcated and leadership is hierarchical. Furthermore, we believe the levels of trust between leaders and members of the black student organizations are relatively low and that leaders have relatively little confidence in their ability to direct members. If we are correct, this circumstance may in part be a reflection of the incipient phase of organization of the black student movement; tried and trusted leaders—charismatic figures with personal authority—have not yet emerged. Under these circumstances the formal leaders of the black students insulate themselves from negotiations with administrations through the use of intermediaries. They have used the technique of insulation and personnel succession by rotating intermediaries to exchange views on the other side. In this way the black leadership maintains maximum flexibility with respect to followers. By circulating their emissaries and continually replacing them, the black leaders have overcome the subversive aspects of cooptation.

Black and White Student Relationships

The intentionally self-isolating style of the black student confrontations has antagonized a great many nonblack students on many college campuses. While many of these students feel guilty about their relationships to blacks or, in some cases, support black demands, many whites have regarded black conduct as offensive. Whites who have come to regard the campus as a free marketplace of ideas, for example, resent black students' issuance of nonnegotiable demands without consulting other elements of the campus community.

Nor have the blacks made any significant appeal to those campus elements that might be most supportive—the militant, antiwar students in organizations such as SDS. The black lack of concern with white support is part of the process by which blacks seek to develop their own capacities for handling their own problems. Because they know that all too frequently in the past their responsibilities have been preempted by sympathetic whites, the entire black movement since 1964 has been seeking to determine its own fate without white assistance. The most militant black ideologists have totally rejected white participation. Though they often feel the need for external support, it is rarely manifested publicly, and blacks have "gone it alone."

White militants such as the SDS members were initially disappointed when blacks did not turn to them for support. To many SDS militants the "natural" alliance of black and white students seemed to call for closer collaboration and organization. Though they supported many black demands, organizations such as SDS found themselves excluded from black actions. Over a period of time, and after a series of abortive efforts at political cooperation, SDS militants came to regard black actions with sympathy but to accept the notion of black autonomy and their own exclusion as a necessary step for the black students. If the blacks have to "do their thing" alone, that is sufficient as long as it puts the university and the centers of power in the United States "uptight."

This autonomous black style arises from a number of factors. First, as has been pointed out, although black students are relatively privileged when compared to rest of black America, they are substantially underprivileged when compared to white students. Many SDS militants, for example, come from well-established, middle- and upper-middle-class families and know that their positions in society are secure. In contrast, blacks are still worried about "making it" and seek to protect themselves by maintaining a rigid group discipline within which all can hide. A second reason for autonomy is the relative lack of organizational skill of the black students. For many the university experience not only is new but, as they work out internal power relationships, further contains prospects for making very substantial errors. Under these circumstances the less revealed to "the enemy," the greater is their ability to adapt to changing exigencies. Autonomy tends to be compensatory for inexperience. A third factor results from the relative sparsity of black ideology and the blacks' need to work out orientations to the world through concrete self-experience in confrontation. The white militants have an advantage of several years of experience with ideological formulation and in formulating their ideas with respect to the war, the United States, and the university. The blacks come to the process of ideology formation relatively late. Their system of ideas is less worked out and more eclectic. They are more nationalist than revolutionary in that they are concerned with the developing black expression, not with changing the entire social system. Until they work out a more coherent ideological basis for action, autonomy and internal discipline provide the individual with his psychological support.

A critical difference between white and black students lies in their respective attitudes toward vocational training. Black students are profoundly oriented to upward mobility and view college life as advanced training for well-paying positions. White students clearly have far less vocational drive, given their own relatively affluent backgrounds. The vocationalism of black students cuts through the autonomous nature of the black style and underwrites each of its elements. This vocational orientation is also serviceable in distinguishing what will be "taken" from the white professoriate. The blacks are prepared to "buy" their expertise but not their ideology. In this way, two main ambitions of the black students are served: upward mobility in the economic world and ideological purity in the political world. How this will work out when a full generation of black collegians graduate is another matter, but for the present the vocational approach is both serviceable and feasible.

Despite their lack of opposition to the system as such, black students have a much greater capacity for militancy than do the whites. In this respect the comparison of American and European trade unionism provides a compelling parallel. European unionism was far more revolutionary in its rhetoric, yet American trade unionism has demonstrated far higher levels of militancy than has the European model. The capacity to engage in more demanding actions while being unconcerned with changing the social structure characterizes both the American trade unions of the past and the contemporary black militant. In contrast, white activists are more revolutionary but less militant. They have more respect for and attachment to property, particularly property associated with centers of learning. Despite the small minority of white revolutionaries prepared to tear the university apart, most white activists are unwilling to engage in the systematic destruction of property to which a university is so vulnerable.

Whites who support the greater militancy of blacks do so basically because they suffer from the generalized guilt and fear now prevalent among white liberals in the university. Although campus liberals abhor violence, their confused feelings toward the black man permit him to engage unobstructedly in levels of militancy that would draw substantial sanctions if exhibited by whites. The black militancy is restrained by blacks' social aspirations; most want to make it within the existing system, perhaps slightly "blackwashed" but fundamentally untouched. In an atmosphere of white repression this overwhelming bulk is sometimes dominated by the anomic terrorists now beginning to appear in small numbers in the black nationalist movement. Whether these terrorists will be able to direct the energies of the black students toward increasing militancy depends considerably on the capacity of institutions to adapt to significant and rapid social change. In the meantime, black nationalism is itself increasingly defined in economic terms.

While functioning independently of the white activists, the black students have begun to serve as shock troops for the whites. This is because their actions, if successful in any degree, set precedents for the whites and their demands. Indeed, accession to any black demands destroys long-established barriers against which the white militants have thus far been largely ineffective. Only after black students achieve their initial intent of public negotiations with the administration and their basic demands have been granted do they move negotiations out of sight to give themselves greater maneuverability. When the administration subsequently tries to refuse to negotiate with the white sit-in demonstrators, the precedent of the administration's negotiating with the blacks is invoked.

To the extent that demands for autonomy of black-studies programs are accepted, precedents are being made for the involvement of students in decision making at the university. At many universities there has been a de facto understanding that no one will be hired for the black studies program who is regarded as persona non grata by the black students' organization. While few university authorities will admit this fact publicly, it has been established as a precedent in all current black appointments. For the moment, the arrangement is an informal one; if the blacks continue to exercise control over other aspects of their program, the precedent for the more general involvement of students in similar decision making spheres of the university will have been established.

Despite the comparable forms of many demands of black and white activists, generalized united fronts are unlikely to occur in the near future. Given the increasing militancy, ideology, and rhetoric of the black-power movement, blacks are not likely to surrender in any way their right to formulate decisions with respect to their demands (and the solution of those demands). What is more probable is that, if black students come into greater conflict with the university administrations (and there is no guarantee that they will), they will seek ad hoc arrangements with the white militants, seeking to manipulate and utilize white students to man the frontline of their own confrontations. The degree to which such ad hoc united actions will develop depends upon a number of factors.

For one, there is the question of the degree of sophistication of university administrators. To the extent that it is possible to make concessions to one group (such as the blacks) without conceding anything to another group, it will be feasible to maintain wedges between the two wings of the student movement. A second feature conditioning ad hoc united actions depends on the degree to which black students initiate contact with individual white sympathizers. The prospect of organizational contacts between black student groups and the white militants is small. This may change in the future if black students feel themselves under very severe pressures. For the moment, however, contact between groups will occur at the individual level, and united actions will occur when understandings are achieved rather than through formal agreements.

In the long run, if there is to be a long run, a university administration will remain better able to control the black students than the whites. As long as the black students can be bought off with programs to fit many of their needs, most will be satisfied. This situation may change when the outreach programs to recruit blacks increases the numbers of black students on the college campus and changes the social composition of the black constituency, drawing more and more upon ghetto elements from lower and lower social classes. These groups will not only be more accustomed to accept higher levels of militancy, but will be less concerned about the applications of violence to the university, having had even less contact with universities than has the current generation of blacks.

CHAPTER EIGHT

Student Power: Prospects

Relatively few student activists or sympathetic students participate in confrontation activities; the politically inert population is much larger. These "inerts" make it difficult to assess the future of the student power movement. Should significant numbers of inerts commit themselves in one way or another, the direction of the movement could be significantly altered. If the inerts become sympathetic to the activists and join their efforts to obtain greater student participation, activists' power would be greatly increased. On the other hand, should the inerts become hostile because they come to believe that confrontational activities jeopardize their futures, the student power movement would be in serious danger. Confrontations on campus would probably diminish after a period of intrastudent violence.

The more militant activists, who advocate the university's destruction, will fail to win support among the inerts. These students argue that the university is the handmaiden of an exploitative social system intent on wreaking its imperialism on the entire world. Sometimes they push this position to its logical extreme: if the university is handmaiden to this system and the system must be destroyed, then the university must be destroyed. Although this position has gained publicity in various demonstrations, most student activists accept the university as one of the saner places in an irrational and corrupt world; the university, though culpable, is an institution within which they can operate. Accordingly, those extremists who demand the destruction of the university are not supported by most militants; the overwhelming bulk of sympathizers and all the inerts will also reject this point of view. If, however, the extreme militant position were to gain support among the leadership of the student power movement, we would expect strong student reaction against activists in general.

Student Organizational Anomie

The amorphousness of the student power movement is exposed by the dilemma of dealing with large-scale off-campus issues from the campus outposts. Student *power* is almost exclusively manifested on campus; whereas student *interests* are more universal. The success of efforts to confront administrators and to close the university shows that within a familiar milieu demonstrators can mobilize significant support. Students have shown some ambivalence between working with off-campus issues or dealing solely with on-campus issues. Issues related to the war or general social problems have failed to mobilize large numbers of students for continuous periods of time. What "grabs" the majority of students are on-campus issues affecting them individually, as students, and having a significant moral basis. But activist student leadership cannot decide where to place the focus. Many advocate dealing with societal questions rather than concentrating on more limited campus issues. Such a decision would represent a return to the strategies of the left of the 1930's: using the campus to mobilize support for off-campus issues could recreate the political isolation of the past should the efforts fail.

For significant student power to develop, the overwhelming bulk of students must discover issues that are meaningful to them. Such issues would deal with curriculum, grades, and experiments and innovation in teaching; with restructuring the university to place greater emphasis on teaching and relationships with students rather than on research; and with involving students in the decision making process of the university. Most of these issues, while complex, are also dull. Whether students, transient within the university, will be willing to expend the time and the energy necessary to participate in making decisions is still the question. If they are, the student power movement may significantly reconstruct the university. If not, the movement will have been an unfulfilled phase in American history, an important but transient byproduct of the Vietnam war.

Still another imponderable in the future of the movement is the relationship of black and white demonstrators. To the present, black-white alliances have occurred when white militants express generalized support of black demands or when black groups, such as the Panthers, invite whites to join them in black-determined and black-directed "antiestablishment" activities. When white militants have levied demands, the blacks have stayed aloof from them except when they concern some black issue (such as South African investments). As long as this separation continues, there can be little significant expansion in the student power movement. If, however, the blacks and whites develop less particularist demands or broaden their approach to encompass issues that affect students personally *and* morally, student power may expand considerably.

Other imponderables are related to the organizational weakness of the student power movement. At present there is little to tie activity on one campus to activities elsewhere. The most significant linkages have developed around organization for particular events, such as the Vietnam Mobilizations of the fall of 1969. Ultimately, if student power is to have national impact, it will have to develop more significant organizational linkages. That prospect seems dim at the moment. Activists themselves reject closely knit organization, which contradicts their anarchistic proclivities. If the movement grows and burgeons, however, they may have to concern themselves with the problem of organization on a national basis.

Responses to Student Power Drives

In spite of the amorphous aspects of the students' drive for power, in their relationships to other campus elements (as well as in the general society) students generate pressures for social change to which these other elements must respond and adapt. How different groups in society respond to this thrust will determine what counterbalances to student power will develop. Though agencies such as Congress have adopted legislation prohibiting allocation of federal funds to students implicated in demonstrations, such interventions are likely to be on too large a scale and too generalized to have significant consequences. Moreover, most university administrators have not welcomed this potential threat to their autonomy. Nonetheless, the demand for curbing campus radicals does reflect the views of many social sectors outside the university.

Somewhat similarly, the police represent a force that can enter the campus and exercise an autonomous will. They may wait until they are summoned by university administrators, but once such an intervention occurs, control shifts to a social stratum unsympathetic to students. The police riot in Chicago in August 1968, at the Democratic National Convention, indicates what can happen when leading echelons of police relinquish control over their ranks. Similarly, the violent intervention of New York City's police at Columbia was not desired by the administrators, who had asked the force only to expel the students from Columbia's buildings. To the extent that administrators have to depend upon the police, the latter will act autonomously in struggles between students and administration.

Other peripheral groups may play intervening roles as well. The alumni of Columbia University, through their official organization, have already undertaken such a role; the alumni of other universities, acting through their organized associations, may also seek to become involved. Such interventions, if they take place, will probably be in support of the status quo, rather than favoring the demonstrators.

Alumni organizations are almost invariably led by wealthier, conservative elements, who maintain psychological identification with their alma mater. This identification is rarely manifested by alumni with ideologies markedly left of center.

Still other agencies within and without the academic community such as nonprofessional employees of the university, may find themselves involved in future battles. Student demands must invariably be translated into financial expenditures; in making claims upon the scarce resources of the university, students will enter into a competitive battle with other university strata. In many universities the nonprofessional staff, who have neglected to develop the potential organizational power that nonuniversity employees possess, may believe its own economic stakes are threatened by the demands of student rebels and may organize against them rather than against its nominal employer, the administration.

The main adaptive thrust must come from within the upper echelons of the university: the administration and faculty. Within both groups a variety of tendencies can be discerned, each of which is present to different degrees in administration and faculty at various universities. The three prevalent tendencies will be referred to as: the nonadaptive approach; the crisis-management approach; and the adaptive approach.

NONADAPTIVENESS

Corporate institutions such as universities must recognize that groups exercising power in the name of the entire institution develop entrenched interests. The university is committed to the use of rationality in the analysis of problems; it is also committed to using extreme care in the application of knowledge. Those who dominate the university today are opposed to change not necessarily for the sake of opposition but because they hesitate to innovate, fearing that the consequences of change may endanger their own stakes in the university. In addition, as with any established social group, entrenched groups are reluctant to share what powers they have; they reject notions of sharing decision making with what they consider a transient and immature group. Thus faculty and administration ideologies sustain the status quo and reject student claims for involvement in decision making.

The transience argument declares that other elements in the university community have a greater stake in its operation because they must spend their entire adult lives there. Students participate in university life only briefly, but faculty and administration expect to continue living within the framework of the university. Similarly, if students do make changes, the benefits and the responsibilities that may result will belong to other, successive groups of students. It is only reasonable, the argument therefore goes, that groups other than students should make the major and minor decisions for the university. Proponents of this viewpoint admit that students should be "listened to" by the proper decision makers but that they should be denied the right to any significant sharing of power.

A similar argument concerns the immaturity of students. The university is an institution developed over time and contains in its corporate outline the congealed wisdom of the ages. This wisdom is present predominantly in the faculty who, through a lengthy socialization process—including the professors' own tenure as students—have developed the psychological attributes for mature and stable decision making. To introduce into this process young people, many of whom have never before experienced serious responsibilities, is considered the height of irresponsibility. Some proponents of this view admit that students can legitimately regulate their own existences within frameworks delineated by those maturer and wiser than themselves and that students should be "listened to." Beyond this, however, students cannot be trusted in decision making processes because they do not have the time (in terms of their primary commitment to study at the university), the maturity, or the stake that other elements of the university community have.

Many other arguments are made on the grounds of tradition, efficiency, and cost. On the whole, the "unadaptive" approach is characteristic of large, nonelite state universities more often than of small, elite, private liberal arts colleges and the elite public institutions. Similarly, this attitude is found within faculties of business and engineering schools more often than in liberal arts faculties. Variations exist; indeed, the case study of Stanford indicates that professional schools, usually markedly conservative, may occasionally be more adaptive to events than are schools and colleges traditionally regarded as liberal.

CRISIS MANAGEMENT

Some university leaders, recognizing the full seriousness of student rebellion, have manipulated it to keep it in hand. This crisis-management approach attempts to control the movement while retaining as intact as possible the existing structure of the university. An abstract ideal type sometimes blends into nonadaptive and partially adaptive approaches; but on the whole crisis managers will move as much as necessary to keep the movement under control. Crisis managers are particularly concerned with creating conditions to keep the majority of students inert and to eliminate conditions that prepare sympathetic students to join the activists.

A main characteristic of crisis managers is their assiduous search for areas in the university where hostility to the administration and faculty may crystallize. Crisis managers develop organizational antennae that ceaselessly search to discover students' concerns. As part of this process, they have created forums, symposia, and other meeting grounds to deal with all groups of students, not just the activists. Recognizing the mobilization potential of the sympathetic ones and some of the inert ones, they attempt to foresee issues and to focus upon them before activists begin to generate dissatisfaction that might end in some form of demonstration.

A second major tactic of the crisis managers is their attempts to coopt student leaders who may potentially crystallize demonstrations. The managers do not seek to incorporate the more active student demonstrators; instead, they attempt to include those who are active but not "unreasonable." By drawing such students into the committee network, managers denude activists of part of their own ranks.

The cooptative process may deal with real questions and may involve students to some degree in university decision making. Two points must be made about the process. First, those students coopted do not necessarily represent the activists, the sympathetics, or the inerts. They are selected by university authorities, not by their own following. As a result, their participation does not necessarily bring them back into contact with ostensible constituents. The second point is that coopted students hold authority only at the discretion of someone else. This position undermines their autonomy and subtly changes the manner in which they perform when involved in cooptative tactics.

A third quality of crisis management can be found in the formulation of a new ideology and rhetoric. In recent years the notion of the university as a community, endogamous and autonomous, has burgeoned. The fact that it is a "community"—a term used preeminently by university administrators—tends to emphasize that normative agreement is necessary to keep it together. The university does manifest some sociological characteristics of "communities," but more interesting is the present-day ideological formulations the concept has excited in administrations and faculties. Like a community, the university is autonomous in its function of creating knowledge; unlike a community, it is not autonomous in other ways. This fact has given rise to the rhetoric of "public service." In fact, the notion of the university as an institution creating knowledge to be put to the service of society is an old one. It first took legal form in the United States with the Morrill Act of 1865, which created the land-grant institutions of higher learning. In the past public service has meant the involvement of the university in affairs of state. Not only did faculty members join presidential administrations (as they continue to do), but the universities also became over time the corporate recipients of vast sums of money for research on questions of pressing concern to agriculture and industry and later to military and foreign-policy governmental authorities. As student rebels—and, indeed, many inerts—clamor for increased relevance in instruction, "public service" is coming to mean a commitment of elements of the university to work with groups in society that are only now beginning to develop political power.

The differences between the more sophisticated approach of the crisis managers and that of the nonadaptives becomes apparent in considering past student demonstrations. The crisis managers have been more often prepared to negotiate with the student rebels and to manipulate the administrative-legal organization for their own purposes. The nonadaptives have preferred to lecture the students rather than to talk to them, although invariably they also fall back on legalisms. One salient feature of the nonadaptives is their detestation of the rebels' modus operandi; they are as affronted by their bad manners as by the substantive issues the rebels raise.

Nonadaptives tend to rely upon the police to restore "law and order," particularly when demonstrators seize university property, even though the presence of police on campus galvanizes student protest. This has certainly been true at the University of Wisconsin, San Francisco State College, Columbia University and Kent State University. Many inert students are drawn into mass forays only after the police have been called. Like the students of Latin America they assume that campuses are "sacred" territories, not subject to "secular" harassment. What has become clear is that when authorities resort to "extra-legal" methods of quelling student rebellion, the legalistic (and democratic) instincts of students leads to very high campus political participation.

ADAPTIVENESS

What we term the adaptive approach contains serious implications for change in the university. It also has its dangers, but these must be weighed against those implicit in the maintenance of the status quo in the university, whether by nonadaptive adherence to the past or through crisis management. Through an adaptive approach no segment of the university will occupy a nonstatus position. While the "student-as-nigger" argument has been overstated, careful examination of the role of students within the university lends credence to this viewpoint on cultural, if not economic, grounds. Accordingly, students must be openly and uncompromisingly involved in decision making in the university along with present decision makers. Lower-echelon personnel—semiprofessional, service, secretarial, and maintenance workers—must participate as well.

This is not a demand for the volitional abandonment of the rights of faculty to teach or of bureaucrats to administer, but a recognition that students, in the process of learning, also have vested interests and rights. From a strategic position nothing could more effectively clarify the goals of student revolt than extensive involvement of students at all levels of the decision making process. When students fully participate in deliberative, legally constituted bodies for a great length of time, they will be far less concerned with the shadow of power and more intimately linked to the substance of power.

This recommendation is, however, too generalized; a more detailed set of suggestions about student power is necessary. How shall students be concretely involved in university decision making? Our answer is: at all levels that determine policies affecting students—and this means involvement in most of the organized bodies of the university. Let us consider two concrete issues of university existence to see how they are currently handled and how they *might* be dealt with. We have deliberately chosen one noncurricular and one curricular issue.

Student Housing. Students complain endlessly about university housing: lack of amenities or of planning, noisiness, overcrowding, and the like. If the energies generations of students have devoted to complaints about housing could have been transformed into "useful" devices, the university might not now be in its present difficulties. Is housing really so bad or are we witnessing just the usual griping that results when large numbers of people are handled in structured and regimented fashion? There may be some truth to this supposition, but surely more meaningful answers can be found.

It is clear that some types of housing circumstances generate more complaints than do other types. Housing units that provide some mechanism for self-selection, for example (and this includes fraternities, sororities and co-ops), can generally deal with dissatisfactions with greater facility than can university dormitories. Similarly, housing units broken up internally into smaller, self-managed units (for example, where four to six students bunk in small rooms but share a common living area) also have reduced strain. Probably many other devices could also ease the problems of student living in the university.

These two techniques are not here offered as "solutions" to housing dilemmas—rather, they are mentioned to point out in the planning of student housing students should be integrally involved and, indeed, should have powers equal to those of the administration (which has to manage the finances and the physical facility) and the architects. Here is an area within which the faculty has had—and should continue to have—little say, but where student contributions could be invaluable.

The prospect that student involvement will raise costs is one that should be confronted. After all, while students define much present-day housing as "bad," it could in fact be much worse. Many student rooms currently housing two students could add a third—but only at the cost of creating what would be for most students "unbearable" conditions. That such impositions do not occur is a function of the recognition by administrators that economies alone cannot be permitted to establish criteria for housing. Similarly, the involvement of students in planning housing may prove to be more effective in facilitating the development of an environment for learning. Indeed, students might begin to reconceptualize housing arrangements and seek to make their housing circumstances more than a "flop" or place to "park the body." And in this regard faculty members might be drawn into an arena they presently assiduously avoid.

The planning of housing is but one aspect of the housing problem; another is the management of existing housing units. In most universities management of housing is vested in a service bureaucracy that has little understanding of—and frequently little sympathy for—the educational process. Since this bureaucracy reports to an assistant to the presi-

dent, it has few dealings with students. Student involvement
in the management of housing would mean that service personnel would to some degree be answerable to students; in
addition, students could present the viewpoint of the con-
sumer to those who presently manage housing facilities.
However, with students *involved* in management, all ranks
would have to be more seriously concerned with the welfare
of their clients.

Faculty promotion. As was pointed out earlier, faculty
members receive rewards through two internal university
procedures: advancement in rank and allocation of tenure.
These two conjoined but independent procedures are managed by different universities in differing ways. At mainstream universities tenure rank decisions are handled primarily by the faculty itself, through systems of ad hoc committees that review a professor's performance and make recommendations to larger collegial bodies or to administrative
officers. Review procedures maintained at higher administrative levels tend to confirm faculty decisions; only in marginal cases will administrators overturn faculty decisions.
Lower-ranking institutions place more authority in the hands
of the administration; and in some, faculty are consulted only
in the most peripheral manner. The model here will be
decision making at the better schools.

Considerable problems face a faculty committee in assessing a person's work and the weight placed on publication as a
crucial criterion for advancement. The inclusion of students
on tenure committees would have a significant structural
effect by providing an additional input from the client-con-
sumer of a professor's performance. That is, to supplement
the standard ways now used to judge teaching (secondhand
reports plus, in some cases, survey data obtained from students about the professor's teaching), students who have had
classes under the instructor or who have lived, eaten, and
participated extensively with other students in the student
subculture would sit formally on tenure and review committees. The fact that anonymous students might turn up
some day on his review committee is a diffuse threat to a

professor's academic freedom. At the same time, such a procedure would provide more accurate information about professors' classroom performances than at present.

Any procedure involving the cooptation of students into the delicate assessment procedures of faculty review has its dangers. Student participants on review committees might be constrained to report less on the basis of what their peers say than on their own need to be properly assessed by faculty members sitting on the committee with them. Equally, the question of student responsibility poses difficulties for the in camera procedures used by review committees. By the same token, the problems cited hold for faculty members: when examining others, their judgments may be made in terms of maintaining their own peer group advantages; secretive procedures limited to faculty maintain full secrecy with difficulty. At moments of tension or when highly controversial professors are being judged, norms of secrecy frequently get breached. Thus, drawing students into review procedures has dangers only somewhat different from those of present procedures.

Inclusion of students in these procedures obviously calls for careful selection and socialization into the norms and responsibilities involved. First, inclusion in review committees is not a right of all students, any more than it is presumably a right of faculty members. Selection of student participants should be made on the same basis as that of faculty: on their measured judgment, on responsibility, and grasp of the nature of the institution and its procedures. Second, somewhat greater care in socializing students to review committee roles may be necessary, at least until procedures become institutionalized. None of these problems is impossible; indeed, basic structures could be retained intact with relatively small degrees of adaptation.

These changes illustrate what we consider adaptive procedures to draw students into university decision making. Their consequences for the university would not only lessen the present pressures of confrontation but, far more significantly, open the way to structural change making the university far more efficient as an instrumentality for conveying knowledge. Most important, university procedures would become devices for teaching and learning. In a period in which involvement in large-scale complex organizations becomes ubiquitous for persons dealing with technology (physicists, engineers), social organization (economists, sociologists), or problems of humanity (philosophers, writers, historians), the sooner students are prepared for real problems by concrete meaningful experiences, the better.

Adaptiveness to student power demands will mean *sharing* power with students in proportion to the relative stakes students, faculty, and others have in the educational process. We do not conceive of this sharing as a "one man-one vote" procedure, since under such a system the faculty could easily be outvoted by the students. (It is worth noting that even a "one man-one vote" procedure might not produce that fearful state of domination. Faculty members are generally more sophisticated than are students and could probably succeed in convincing student majorities on most issues.) Nor are we as yet prepared to specify the relative proportions that might be used (e.g., 60-40 per cent, 70-30 per cent, or the like). Proportions might vary in different areas of decision making. Thus, it might be best not to have review committees balanced equally between faculty and students, but to permit student representatives to attend the actual committee and to vote in higher-level faculty bodies to which the review committees report. Our intent here is not to specify concrete procedures or percentages; these issues should be worked out in different ways on the various campuses to fit specific needs. Our proposal is that broad-based student involvement be insured at all levels of university decision making and operations.

University Decision Making

We turn now to a consideration of problems involved in our earlier indication that all levels of the university should be involved in decision making; specifically to problems of including lower-echelon personnel.

Within the university structure are a number of bureaucracies auxiliary to direct instructional activities. We have already alluded to service personnel who are responsible for all aspects of student housing. This group of employees is only part of a vast array of employees found in the university. Other service personnel tend academic buildings as janitors. Most universities also maintain dining facilities, which employ all types of personnel, from purchasing agents through cooks and mess attendants to truck drivers. Other employees deliver internal and external messages. Nor can the hundreds of secretarial and clerical staff be omitted. Besides these nonprofessionals the larger universities employ hundreds of semiprofessionals—librarians, research assistants, laboratory technicians, and others. Few of them have been involved in any way in university decision making except to the extent that they form unions to improve working standards. In many cases either the legal protections for union recognition accorded to most workers have not been made available to university employees or they have failed to organize and develop some degree of control over their economic existence.

Union organization—one method by which these nonacademic employees can obtain participation in university life—functions mainly on the level of economic relationships with the university as employer and does not deal with the university as community. If the university is to be a "community" in more than a rhetorical sense, it is necessary that nonacademic employees be drawn into the vortex of decision making. Again it is necessary to emphasize our lack of specific recommendations. The basic principle underlying our approach is that different strata should be involved in different aspects of decision making and management in proportion to their contributions to different aspects of the university's operation. Thus, we do not propose that food-service workers should be involved in the determination of curricula; that responsibility should remain with the faculty in conjunction with students and with the consultation and advice of the academic bureaucracy. Librarians, however, and possibly some categories of research assistants—those whose work brings them into regular involvement with aspects of teaching—should be involved with curricular matters.

How the different strata and groups in the complex structure of the university should communicate with one another remains the basic problem. We recognize the difficulties implicit in our proposals as well as their revolutionary implications. Indeed, we push well beyond student power and argue for *a sharing of powers among all the strata and groups that constitute the university.* Our proposal is for the creation of *community* or, of what used to be called, half a century ago, *industrial democracy* and what is sometimes called nowadays *participative management* (although in this latter case it has proven to be a manipulative control system rather than a sharing of powers). It calls for the formation of a university senate providing for occupational representation with *unequal* representation from the many categories that make up the university.

How shall such a senate be constituted? As faculty members, we admit our vested interests but argue that primary representation must come from the faculty, which has the responsibility for both teaching and the generation of new knowledge, two crucial functions of the university. To our clients, the students, who are the most immediate beneficiaries (and victims) of our ministrations, we would accord a secondary position, since they partake of the university mainly in terms of teaching and only slightly in its capacity to generate knowledge. The administration, whose main responsibility is to integrate the various academic and service functions of the university, deserves a tertiary position— integrative functions are extremely important but should not be permitted to dominate university decision making. Finally, representation—but in diminished capacity—should be provided to nonacademic employees, whose main relationship to the university is almost entirely economic rather than academic.

We turn finally to the question of how to balance such representation concretely. One possible way, of course, is the traditional one: the university's trustees (or faculty) could set up investigatory commissions to make recommendations, which are then implemented. We hardly need propose such a procedure when obvious deficiencies obtrude; any such procedure will retain basic structures, with only nominal change, as long as the discussion of new patterns is held under the aegis of groups that already hold power.

To obtain significant and thoroughgoing change, power must be redistributed in a freer framework. To this end we propose the establishment of a constituent assembly at each university—a body that prepares the rules for a new university based upon the normative consent of all constituent elements; a body that, among other matters, must decide the basis upon which the various strata will be represented within itself. The constituent assembly should initially decide this issue and then proceed to the formulation of general rules by which the various strata are represented at different levels and in different kinds of university structures. The constituent assembly must also deal with the determination of the fundamental goals of the university (teaching and research) as well as auxiliary goals, such as public service. The constituent assembly must further assess such traditional academic mores as academic freedom and tenure. If such values hold today, their reaffirmation will have far greater meaning than do the typical devout faculty resolutions. Everyone knows the faculty believes in academic freedom and tenure; the issue now is to convince others, especially the students, that these values are worth being sustained and protected in the new university.

We believe that the implementation of these proposals will create the normative base necessary to sustain the university. Never in its history has this base of the university been as challenged as it is today. What is required therefore is less the reaffirmation of the old than the beginnings of reconstruction.

The student rebellion in America has not been without its traumas. When students engage in non-rational collective behavior, it behooves their wiser elders, the faculty in particular, to act with rationality rather than with punitive response. Faculty insistence on good manners, on adherence to procedures, and on the status quo fails to answer the rational criticism of the student rebels. The point has now been reached where faculty rationality demands attention to substantive criticism and the institution of significant change.

Much is owed the student rebels, despite their occasional vehemence and even less frequent violence. (It is worth remembering that the constant difficulties of the post-Berkeley period have been marked by a far lesser loss of life than might have been anticipated—and then a loss engendered by police and militia rather than inflicted by students.) The students have focused on the moral issues of society and have confronted one of society's institutions—the key one, as far as they are concerned—with its culpability for the present social and political malaise.

When all is said and done, the problems of, with, and about the knowledge factory do not concern the facts but the values of generations and classes in conflict. The young are not better informed about the corruption of social and political organization in America than are their elders—indeed, they may even have less information at their disposal. The difference is at the level of actions and values. How does one respond to "corruption"? And here the gaps are large-scale and manifest. The older generations are willing to accept, or at least to work within, the established frameworks of society. The younger generations (or at least a sizable portion) are determined to bring down that which is defined as corrupt. If a moral fanaticism ensues that sustains rather than removes the ambiguities in American society, it has the merit of confronting the facts with the future. And even in this complicated world of the knowledge factory, one clumsy and uncoordinated step forward is far better than marching in step two steps backward.

Five Years of Confrontation at Cornell

Pre-Berkeley Cornell

The Cornell campus is typical of a great many campuses in the United States. Although it is an Ivy League school, Cornell's status is somewhere at the bottom of the Ivy League hierarchy. Its land-grant origins, while suitably converted into a private endowment, nevertheless give it a distinctly plebian character enhanced by Cornell's unusual situation as a partially privately endowed university that at the same time contains New York State units. But perhaps even more significantly, Cornell's clientele gives it a plebian character that distinguishes it from higher-status counterparts in the Ivy League. Like the University of Michigan, it enrolls large numbers of metropolitan New York Jews distinctly lacking in the WASPish qualities necessary for high status, who impart a high intellectual demand and critical, indeed radical, orientations toward the world. At the same time the acknowledged excellence of Cornell's College of Agriculture attracts many rural persons, most of them moving away from the farm, lacking the intellectual sophistication of their metropolitan brethren, bringing similar low social status to the institution.

When Cornell began to attract this metropolitan student

body is not exactly clear, but the trend was already well-established by the end of World War II, the period with which this narrative of Cornell student activities begins. Into the 1950's Cornell was like many other American universities — a place where one could be dedicated to having fun while going to school, where athletics occupied a considerable amount of students' time. Changes since the 1950's have been reflected in the position of sports news, which has moved from a prominent position on the first page of the *Cornell Daily Sun* to the back pages. Accompanying athletic activities of the 1950's were the usual "rah rah" rallies and bonfires, particularly during the football season.

As late as the fall 1949 semester, sophomores were still raising the traditional hell about rules concerning freshmen wearing beanies. In the following year, however, as a consequence of a fight over the shaving of a freshman's head the year before, sophomores were prohibited from using punishment to enforce beanie wearing. Until 1953 laments could occasionally be heard about the failure of the frosh to wear beanies, but even they declined. Though beanies were still worn occasionally into the early 1960's, they tended to have only esoteric significance for the few, and there was no longer any extensive reaction from upperclassmen when more and more freshmen declined to wear beanies.

Politically the campus was largely apathetic. The few political manifestations on campus of broadly based American politics were limited to the editorial page of the *Sun*, which pontificated on arcane subjects such as the Marshall Plan and Communist China to students. The political indifference of students was symbolized in the comic strips the *Sun* printed. "Li'l Abner" and "Terry and the Pirates," though they engaged in anti-Communist polemics, were read primarily for their entertainment value.

The formation of a Labor Youth League unit at Cornell in the fall 1949 semester created quite a stir, for the cold war was already well underway. Only eight Cornellians signed up for membership, but some thirty-five to forty attended a public meeting; the *Sun* advised Cornellians to ignore the organization. A few other leftist organizations operated with minuscule followings until around 1952, when overt political leftism ceased to exist on the campus.

As the cold war intensified, the campus reflected the xenophobic qualities of American life, shaded by a peculiar component of academic liberalism. No one, for example, would defend in the pages of the *Sun* a communist or communism, but some occasionally worried about whether or not communism was an equal or greater threat than was the loss of civil liberties.[1] After Senator Joseph McCarthy took on the United States Army and was censured for his activities, fears for the loss of academic freedom began to take hold, and concerns about communism declined to some degree. During the 1950's some Cornell faculty members who were called before the House Un-American Activities Committee refused to discuss their alleged previous associations with leftist groups. The general posture of the campus toward their refusal was careful defense of their academic freedom. Given the character of the first McCarthy period, the defense was very courageous indeed. Nevertheless, many students who were quite willing to compliment one man's courage argued that he should be jailed.

The Korean war did not produce an upsurge of antiwar protest by Cornell students. Toward the end of the war the *Sun* editorialized that "by any kind of moral judgment, we are right." Student correspondents to the paper generally favored a thaw in the cold war, but others looked upon the active hostility between the United States and the Soviet Union with equanimity. Any commentator who criticized the United States—even when he dealt with issues such as civil rights, not directly related to the cold war—usually drew a flurry of letters advising him to go to live in Russia. During the mid-1950s a conservative group, the Society of In-

1. Short shrift is given here to the intellectual devastation of the cold-war period and to its effects on the "silent generation." For a reconstruction of that period at Cornell, see Susan Brownmiller, "Up from Silence: Cornell Then and Now—Panty Raids to Guerrilla Theatre," *Esquire*, no. 424 (March 1969). This article also provides personal descriptions of participants in the post-Berkeley period as well as presenting a trenchant comparison of the two periods. Cornell's reputation of political apathy is attested to by Nathan Tarcov, "The Last Four Years at Cornell," *The Public Interest*, no. 13 (Fall 1968): 122–123.

dividualists, inspired discussion, although it was out of all proportion to the number of members who made themselves visible in print or at meetings.

To the extent that distinct new trends became delineated on campus, these began *after* the Supreme Court decision of 1954 calling for school desegregation. Cornell's chapter of the National Association for the Advancement of Colored People (NAACP) was relatively insignificant before then; in 1949, when it sponsored a petition to be sent to Washington favoring equality, only a single two-inch notice appeared in the *Sun*. In the following year the Cornell NAACP entered the mainstream of American society by opposing leftist groups. In the early 1950's there were a few complaints that requirements to include photographs with student applications for admission to Cornell contained a potential for discrimination, but when the registrar assured the campus community that these were intended to be used only for identification, no additional complaints were registered. When over 1,500 students presented Cornell President Malott with a petition concerning off-campus housing discrimination, the action drew minimal coverage in the *Sun*.

The Supreme Court decision of 1954 changed all this for the rest of the decade. Almost every week articles, letters, or columns in the *Sun* discussed discrimination in fraternities or in local housing or the existence of prejudice in some other spheres of Cornell or Ithaca life. By November 1954 a discrimination commission had been organized by student government, and the pressures upon the university to enforce regulations prohibiting discrimination in the fraternities and sororities of Cornell began to increase. These onslaughts ultimately challenged the validity of the entire fraternity system. The initial response of fraternity members tended to be procedural rather than substantive; falling back on the regulation "imposed" by their nationals, they argued that those rules could not be easily changed. As time passed and the pressures increased, the fraternity leadership became more defensive and argued for time to persuade the national organizations to change discriminatory clauses. By the early 1960's local chapters that wanted to accommodate to the new nor-

mative climate were seeking ways to disaffiliate themselves
from their national organizations in order to retain legitimacy
on the campus. The validity of the fraternity system was
challenged in a different way in 1967, when black students
manifested considerable ambiguity about whether or not
they would pledge fraternities.

Into the early 1950's student government focused upon
social activities. One major function was sponsoring the complex series of elections by which offices were annually
passed from one cohort of students to another. The sheer
quantity of these offices was staggering. Not only were there
government units for the whole university, but each of the six
undergraduate divisions of Cornell had its own student organization. In addition, there were governments for the
freshman through the senior classes, as well as for men's and
women's organizations and for each separate university dormitory. The volume of student offices permitted many students to accumulate titles as a means of impressing potential
employers. But it did little to regulate student life effectively,
since control remained firmly in the hands of the administration.

This does not mean that the elections were not taken
seriously. The *Sun*, its breathless manner reflecting the ethos
of the time, urged maximum involvement, implying that failure to participate would lead to the collapse of the entire
democratic process. Besides urging everyone to vote, the *Sun*
endorsed candidates for the scores of contested offices.

An index of the changes in student processes since the
1950's is provided by rush, the procedure by which students
examine various fraternities to decide in which they are interested and by which fraternities decide to whom they wish
to offer pledging opportunities. During the 1950's rushing
was standard procedure for all men; by the early 1960's the
percentage of freshmen men refusing to rush had climbed to
the 20 per cent level and was continuing to increase.

"In loco parentis" appears to have been an unquestioned
university function until 1953, when feeble challenges began
to be formulated. The initial issue arose at the end of 1952
and made the pages of the *Sun*, when a couple of students

complained about faculty prohibition of laced eggnog in holiday celebrations. Complaints spread as students chafed under the sexual restrictions the university was beginning to enforce. When university authorities outlawed apartment parties, an upsurge of student hostility was manifested, but almost entirely in print; certainly there was no physical opposition at this time. The apartment-party ban had become a major issue by the end of 1953; the situation continually concerned the faculty and administration, and in November 1953 it led to the organization of Cornell's first student judiciary board. (The board could, however, be overruled by a president's committee.) During the next few years students increasingly complained about various restrictions on their personal conduct. But not until May 1958 did this verbal output become behavioral. Early in May a number of "spring is in the air" editorials appeared in the *Sun*. One asked the Dean of Women if the ban on apartment parties was specifically intended to suppress "intercourse"; if so, would she please make this aim clear. In the first week in May Cornell had another of its traditional "panty raids." After a notably quiet spring weekend, the campus was engaged in a series of demonstrations later memorialized by Richard Farina, one of the leaders, in his book *Been Down So Long it Seems Like Up to Me*. According to another leader of the demonstrations, the university's failure "to establish any channels of efficient communication" left the students no recourse other than demonstration against the apartment-party ban. The rebels, backed by the Student Council, climaxed their protests by a march on the off-campus home of President Malott, which culminated in a nasty scene. Over 2,000 students were motivated to participate in these events originating in questions of sex. As a result five students were temporarily suspended. Eventually two of them received paroles (just under suspension); two were given unofficial reprimands; and in one case no action was taken.

The immediate result of the confrontation was that the President's Committee on Student Activities withdrew its ban on unchaperoned apartment parties. During the following year presidential committees relating to student activities and behavior were dissolved, and their responsibilities were turned over to the faculty. A Faculty Committee on Student Affairs was formed to oversee general policy toward student conduct. A second committee, the Faculty Committee on Student Conduct, was established as a disciplinary review group. Finally an Undergraduate Judicial Board, composed of students, was formed as the initial committee to deal with student violators. UJB decisions were subject to review and modification by the Faculty Committee on Student Conduct.

While curfews for senior women were not completely eliminated until 1962, the types of restrictions on personal conduct that had characterized the 1950's came under increasing attack. In loco parentis was the major issue on campus in the late 1950's and into the 1960's. A gradual erosion of restrictions initially reduced curfew restriction, permitted senior women to live off campus, and ended restriction on apartment parties. Ultimately, in 1968, all curfew restrictions on female students were removed. The "Farina rebellion," as it came to be called, was practically the sole expression of campus activism through the 1950's. Although a few students participated in an abortive strike of Cornell employees, on the whole the campus remained quiet.

In the early 1960's the pace increased slightly, focusing initially on questions of civil rights and international tensions. The fall 1961 semester opened with a ten-hour vigil protesting radioactive fallout from bomb tests. This was followed by a letter from the executive board of student government supporting Negro students in Mississippi. In April 1963 Cornell demonstrators picketed a Woolworth in downtown Ithaca to protest the segregation practiced in the company's southern stores.

The early 1960's saw the birth of the Cornell Liberal Union (CLU), the first large left-of-center group to appear on campus in a decade. Although it was largely oriented toward off-campus issues—particularly civil rights—the group ultimately had its greatest impact on student political style. Meetings were scheduled around specific issues; for instance, the Woolworth picket in April 1963 grew out of a meeting called by three members because "something had to be done" about segregation at Southern lunch counters.

Perhaps even more significant was the consensual operation of the group's meetings. At these meetings students and professors sat together on dormitory or apartment floors and quite deliberately called one another by their first names. Although parliamentary procedure was generally followed and votes were taken on most issues, a decision to act depended not so much on the support of a majority of those present as on a consensus that the action was a good one. On a few occasions, when consensus could not be obtained, a splinter group would act in an ad hoc capacity.

Because of the informal, consensual nature of the group and the frequency of "crisis" meetings, they often lasted until the early hours of morning. It is especially worth noting that membership in the CLU was not required for participation either in its meetings or its activities. Although membership cards were printed and dues were established, few of the former were distributed and less of the latter collected. Funds generally came from contributions and specific appeals. For example, among a group of undistributed membership cards discovered in an Ithaca apartment in 1967 was the following note: "Collected at meeting for printing costs $7.42." Because the CLU espoused no rigorous ideological position, its activities revealed a spectrum of political beliefs, from those held by mild integrationists to those of members of communist groups of the 1930's. Because of the CLU's consensual character, leaders usually fell somewhere in the middle.

By the end of 1963 Cornell students became involved in specific action programs in the South. As a result of a number of fortuitous connections, Fayette County in Tennessee was "adopted" by the Cornell students, and interest centered upon Negro attempts to obtain access to the political process of the county. By the spring of 1964 the Fayette project was raising funds to support student summer work with Fayette Negroes. During the spring 1964 semester a debate over whether student government should be officially involved in the Fayette County Project began when the student government was asked to provide $1,000 for the project. On March 5 the executive board voted to grant the money. The campus was thrown into a turmoil, the likes of which had not been seen for some time; 2,355 students petitioned for a referendum on the executive board's action.

Students of all persuasions descended on the dormitories to win support for their views. Hours of debate took place in dorm lounges, on the student union steps, in the cafeterias, and before and after classes. For the first time in Cornell's history leaflets were distributed daily for a week. The sheer number of different leaflets and groups printing them made it impossible for the Dean of Students' office to enforce leaflet-approval regulations. Although some groups continued to seek administration approval for each leaflet, the activities of the week ended forever the inevitability of leaflet censorship by the Cornell administration. During the week the *Sun* discussed nothing but the impending vote and its significance for the student body.

In a referendum on March 24, one of the largest in Cornell history, financial support of the Fayette Project was approved by a vote of 2,514 to 1,984. The significance of the referendum went beyond the funds involved, since the issue concerned the formal involvement of Cornell's student government in an off-campus action some distance from Cornell. The Fayette Project continued for another year, and students were again involved in the summer of 1965, after which other priorities developed on the Cornell campus itself.

This resumé of activities leading up to the "year of Berkeley" illustrates that, as student activism grew, initial concern about questions of personal conduct but increasingly gained a political component concerning discrimination and prejudice, and internationally, concerning the bomb tests of the late 1950's and early 1960's.

1964: Berkeley and Beyond

The years in the period beginning September 1964 may be distinguished as bearing distinct "personalities," identified by crystallization of different issues that occupied growing numbers of student militants and activists and mobilized substantial numbers of less-involved students. The post-Berkeley period began relatively quietly, but levels of activism increased, until a major confrontation occurred in the spring of 1966. In this interim period portions of the campus community experimented on the one hand with the limits on behavior while, on the other, managerial sections of the community sought to contain the protest. After 1966 levels of activism declined slightly as they took on more organized form. Two key organizations emerged in this period — first the Students for a Democratic Society (SDS) and later the Afro-American Society (AAS). Until the spring of 1968, SDS was the major organizational force, although its deliberately anarchistic structure took clear organizational form only over time. In the spring of 1968, after joint action between SDS and AAS on the issue of Cornell's South African investments, the initiative shifted to the AAS, which became increasingly separatist in its operations, eschewing contacts with whites.

As will also be shown, in the summers after 1965 a Hegelian dialectic developed in which the quantity of actions of the previous year were weighed, assessed, and evaluated, and qualitative leaps into increasingly complex organizational forms were made. Structural changes generally filled needs that had been expressed in the previous spring, and they had to be acceptable by the returning students.

The Cornell Daily Sun in the first part of the academic year 1964–1965 provided little indication that the coming academic year would be different from all those that had come before. Even the Berkeley events, which filled the national press day after day, were barely reflected in the campus newspaper, although students discussed them continually and organized a pressure group to support the Berkeley rebels. Nor did the Vietnam war significantly concern the campus newspaper, although the buildup of American manpower, begun in the Kennedy administration, increased greatly. Yet, after a quiet fall semester, both issues burst upon the campus scene with dramatic impact.

The *Sun* first mentioned Berkeley on December 8, in anticipation of a resolution introduced to the Cornell faculty meeting the following day. This resolution supported the Berkeley faculty who had just endorsed the basic demands of the free-speech demonstrators in California. The resolution had little impact, although on December 10 the development of political awareness on campus could be detected in the objection to the use of student funds to support the ROTC drill team. However, the objection to the appropriation was based primarily on the frivolity of supporting a drill team rather than on ROTC's relationship to America's activities in Vietnam.

When punitive bombings of North Vietnam intensified early in 1965, the campus wakened dramatically to the anti-war issue. Although anti-Vietnam activities had now been going on at Berkeley for well over a year, it took the bombing of the North to mobilize Cornell faculty and students. President Johnson announced the policy of punitive bombings in the North on February 7. Four days later an ad hoc faculty committee on Vietnam began to meet. Four days after this, fifty-nine Cornell demonstrators for the first time picketed the naval recruiter in downtown Ithaca. The bombing loosed protest in classes and in the newspaper. Senator Wayne Morse's appearance at Cornell on February 22, at which he publicly attacked America's Vietnam policy, greatly encouraged those critical of the latest escalation of the war. By the end of the month an ad hoc student's committee was in operation, and student discontent about local campus issues began to be demonstrated.

The formation of Students for Education (SFE) early in March came somewhat as a shock to Cornell's administration and faculty. Although the Berkeley activities had prepared campuses everywhere for student action, no overt action had even been hinted at during the fall semester, when the Berkeley events peaked. Precisely what gave rise to the formation of SFE is still unclear, since after a brief but eventful existence it was soon absorbed by the antiwar effort. SFE formative committees began operating spontaneously in the latter part of February. The first meeting of SFE on March 8 opened a cauldron of grievances on campus issues. Hundreds of students piled into Cornell's first mass exercise in participatory democracy, rejecting formal organization and insisting that everyone have an opportunity to participate, so that consensus might be achieved on a variety of issues. The heated tone of the first meeting, concerned mainly with articulating grievances rather than providing solutions, indicated that, while Cornell was a long way from Berkeley, the potential for serious action existed within SFE. At this meeting complaints on every conceivable issue were heard: a campus bookstore crammed with textbooks but little else to read; grades that were demoralizing and coercive; the quality of food; restrictions on the use of pot; a proctor and a dean of students who did not act in the interest of students— particularly on the question of pot.[2]

With the incredibly varied protests and the heated and intense feelings that were generated, the only consensus that could be achieved in this first meeting was that a number of work-study groups should examine specific problems at Cornell. One day after the initial meeting an alarmed Provost and Dean of Students met with SFE representatives to discuss the campus bookstore; the administration, concerned with defusing tension, immediately agreed to devote one floor of the bookstore to noncurricular books, to expand the quality of periodicals (which had previously been removed), and to set up a meeting with President James Perkins, then in his second year as Cornell's chief administrator.

SFE proceeded to a series of open meetings that attracted faculty members and students who shared a generally enhanced militancy. International, national, and local issues were integrated into a package of grievances capable of mobilizing large numbers of students. On March 10 the Selma, Alabama, march led by Martin Luther King brought civil rights demonstrators into conflict with the Alabama police. At the same time the escalation in Vietnam and the resignation of Clark Kerr as President of the University of California

2. Tarcov, class of 1968, attended Cornell during the four years discussed here. His perceptions of events are similar to ours, but his interpretation is different. In his assessment of SFE, he terms it "an artificial movement created with the sponsorship of the student establishment—student government and the *Cornell Daily Sun* included—rather than an expression of immediate and spontaneous outrage over local incidents." While some members of the Establishment were pulled into SFE, the *Sun* remarked that student government had become obsolescent. Most SFE leaders—if we may dare to use such a word to describe the amorphous roles that emerged within SFE—were not active in student government or on the *Sun*. Similar errors of interpretation abound in Tarcov's article.

on March 9 provided background against which the SFE militants began to unfold their plans. The issue of inflated laundry prices was added to an already large agenda of grievances, and one of the study commissions of SFE came out in favor of a new grading procedure on a satisfactory-unsatisfactory basis to eliminate the invidious grade-grubbing that the SFE militants (frequently supported by some of their teachers) wanted to end. Although SFE was now much larger than the defunct Cornell Liberal Union had ever been, its activities involving several hundred students at times, the meetings became less, not more, formal. Officers were elected but were given no power. All work was done in committee, where there were no formal offices. A person could concentrate his energy and time on one committee, or he could belong to as many as he wished. Informal lists were made to contact members, but no serious attempt to assess membership was made. SFE had no dues or formalities of membership; as funds were required, spontaneous collections were taken at whatever meetings were being held.

Meanwhile the Vietnam war continued to obtrude. On March 17 Jean Paul Sartre, who was to visit Cornell in the spring to give a series of lectures, canceled his visit to protest America's involvement in Vietnam. The cancellation intensified campus discussion, some persons attacking him for penalizing Cornell for an action that had nothing to do with Cornell and others either justifying Sartre's position or seeking ways to encourage him to come to the campus despite his position on Vietnam.

That Cornell was beginning to change, at least as manifested through its daily newspaper, was demonstrated on March 25 by a front-page article about student pickets at Fairleigh Dickinson University—a coverage that had not even been accorded the Berkeley rebels. Students for Education began to lose its impetus, for SFE militants became increasingly concerned with the war. By mid-April SFE had lost student interest, although the issue of a minimum wage for student workers kept it alive for several additional weeks.

At the first national mobilization against the war's escalation in Washington, D.C., on April 18, some 20,000 marchers protested the raids on the North. The participation of 120 Cornellians and students of Ithaca College brought a counterprotest from students who endorsed government policy. Counterprotesters sat down in front of the buses loaded with antiwar students to prevent their departure. Although the counterprotesters dispersed at the request of the Proctor, this demonstration represented the beginning of organized student support of U.S. policy in Vietnam. A week later 350 students protested the bombing in the first vigil held on campus, while 30 counterprotesters made their own presence felt.

A group called the *Ad Hoc* Committee to End the War in Vietnam, which had a large hand in planning antiwar actions at Cornell for the rest of the spring semester and throughout the following year, developed out of local planning sessions for the National Mobilization in Washington. The *Ad Hoc* Committee planned Cornell's first confrontation: a walkout during the Charter Day Convocation on April 27. Manifesting the concerns with maintaining respectability typical of this experimental phase, the antiwar protesters agreed to walk out on Governor Nelson Rockefeller's convocation address — but to do this decorously. In addition, the protesters were to come in "straight" dress — suits, ties, white shirts, and haircuts. At a given signal the protesters arose, flashed their antiwar banners, marched in front of the podium, and departed while chanting antiwar slogans. The Governor responded to the demonstration by commending President Johnson's Vietnam policy: "It is a wonderful thing that we have a President willing to fight for the freedom of the world." This was the first and last "respectable" demonstration; future protests were obstructive as student activists dropped their concerns about appearing respectable.

The following day the activists were confronted by another antagonizing aspect of American foreign policy when, at the direction of the President, U.S. marines invaded the Dominican Republic to intervene in its civil war. By this time the campus was a seething mass of arguments, in and out of class, in the newspaper, even in casual conversation. In early May a soapbox was placed on the lawn in front of the student union to permit a somewhat more structured debate. At the same time Students for Education decided to suspend its organization, since other events were pre-empting the attention of SFE activists.

In mid-April the teach-in movement had spread across the country after its inception at the University of Michigan. The idea was quickly adopted by Cornell, where its main impetus was provided by an ad hoc faculty committee interested in broad discussion about Vietnam. As April drew to an end, preparations for a Cornell teach-in got under way. The weakness of the adult supporters of official American policy was revealed, for it was possible to find only one faculty member willing to give even qualified support to administration policy in Vietnam. Many faculty members supported government policy, but only one would speak publicly at the teach-in. The teach-in organizers sought progovernment speakers outside the campus as well, even addressing requests for participation to the State Department. None, however, were forthcoming.

At 8:00 P.M. on Friday, May 7, Cornell's first teach-in began and continued until dawn the following day. The teach-in started with a capacity audience of over 2,000, though many more were precluded from entering because the hall was filled. During the night between 2,500 and 3,000 students and faculty were involved. The almost universal criticism of US policy was typical of teach-ins on hundreds of campuses as American foreign policy came under attack, with few spokesmen available to defend it. For many previously uninformed students the teach-in was a turning point, after which they rejected, with increasing visibility and vigor, the Vietnam war.

Ambassador Averill Harriman's visit to Cornell on May 11 set off the first disruptive confrontation on the campus. The Charter Day Convocation walkout had been respectful and controlled; at the Harriman session students unable to control their reactions to many of his provocative statements let loose a torrent of boos and hisses. In ill-considered reaction to the rising tide of open hostility, Harriman asked "all the Communists in the audience to raise their hands"; hundreds, if not an actual majority of the audience, did so. The meeting degenerated into a shouting match with one of the more vociferous students and ended with a spontaneous protest sit-in that continued into the next morning. The treatment of Harriman raised a variety of problems for the campus. Whether or not he had been provided a full opportunity to present his point of view was, of course, a significant issue, although many faculty members were also concerned about the question of manners. A resolution immediately after the event expressed the general faculty sentiment that the campus could not tolerate such treatment of speakers, even if they presented minority points of view.

But the tempo of events was escalating, as was the war in Vietnam. The weekend after the Harriman affair, on May 15 and 16, a national teach-in was held in Washington, D.C., and the nation was treated to a wide-ranging debate over television in which administration policy was submitted to critic after critic, although in this case a number of articulate and coherent supporters of the U.S. policy in Vietnam had been assembled. At Cornell, however, the temper of the students was reaching a breaking point. The militants searched for an issue that would provide a focus for their determination to obstruct the normal processes of the university and to register their profound discontent with the war. This issue became the annual presidential review of the ROTC, an event held at the end of the academic year that usually drew no more than a handful of student observers.

The tactics meeting of the *Ad Hoc* Committee, at which the ROTC review disruption was planned, was so typical of the open procedure that had developed that the presence of plainclothesmen from Cornell's Safety Division, the Proctor, and the Associate Dean of Students drew little reaction from the student planners. The Proctor, in a written statement, warned the students against disruption of the ROTC review. But the students were by this time determined, and they expressed willingness to take whatever penalties resulted from their rejection of the Vietnam war. On May 17 in Cornell's cavernous Barton Hall, built armory-style to handle ROTC drill, seventy-six students sat down in the middle of the drill hall to obstruct the review. The ire of some 2,500 violently angry counterdemonstrators in the balcony rose by the minute, until President Perkins appeared ahead of schedule to begin the review in spite of the protesters. The potential for violence was such that probably only the President's early appearance kept the situation from getting out of hand. However, the demonstrators as well as the counterprotesters stood for the "Star-Spangled Banner." Although the militants resumed their places on the floor as soon as it ended, this concession to tradition had a slightly calming effect upon the counterdemonstrators.

The obstruction of the ROTC review immediately set in process the university's judicial machinery on student conduct. Three days after the demonstration, on May 20, the student Undergraduate Judiciary Board (UJB) heard the cases and reprimanded the demonstrators. On May 25 the Faculty Committee on Student Conduct (FCSC), which had the authority to review and to change all UJB decisions, reheard the Barton Hall cases in an all-night meeting. Its decision, while a mild response compared to previous actions, was to increase the UJB penalties; sixty-nine students were placed on disciplinary probation for the remainder of the semester. While in this case only a few days remained in the semester, the significance of the retrial became manifest during the next two years. Several Barton Hall protesters, when tried for additional protests, were given more severe penalties as second offenders.

Because the hearings involved such a large number of students, they enlivened interest in the issue of ROTC's presence on campus and, more importantly, in the war in Vietnam. As in all future actions, the students did not deny that they had interfered with a university event or that they had refused a Proctor's order; rather, they based their defense on the unsatisfactory rationale for ROTC and the resulting "unreasonableness" of the Proctor's directive.

Rather than accepting the legal framework of either the UJB or the FCSC, the students invariable discussed broader issues, such as the university's complicity in the Vietnam war. At the same time they began to challenge the legitimacy of the faculty-dominated judicial system itself. The rewards of their approach were indicated not only by the number of new supporters they won in each trial, but also in the decreasing severity of their punishments and the growing disaffection of student members of the UJB with the FCSC review procedures. On December 9, 1967, so many UJB members resigned in protest of the FCSC's reversal of the UJB's decision on a sit-in case that the UJB quorum was destroyed, rendering the body ineffective.

The academic year 1964–1965 was not devoted simply to antiwar activities, although the escalation of the war unquestionably played the crucial role in politicizing the students and bringing them into militant confrontation with the university. Concurrent campus developments reinforced other interests that have already been discussed. Early in the academic year Vice President for Student Affairs John Summerskill announced that the new freshman class contained the highest number of Negroes in Cornell's history and that Cornell would continue to seek Negro students. Meanwhile, in November, the campus memorialized a recent alumnus, Michael Schwerner, one of three civil-rights workers murdered in Mississippi that summer. The reports of the Fayette County group's summer work were widely circulated on the campus.

In January 1965, after a year of considerable student agitation, the Faculty Committee on Student Affairs (FCSA) abolished the curfew for junior women, extending the 1962 action that had eliminated the senior women's curfew. The removal of constraints on women students was amplified a month later, when an FCSA decision permitted senior women to live off campus for the first time in Cornell's history. The action was endorsed two days later by the university faculty with little debate.

A public lecture by Richard Alpert, then one of the high priests of the developing LSD cult, almost precipitated another crisis. The administration demanded that at the conclusion of Alpert's talk a physician from the Cornell Medical Clinic be permitted to read a statement warning of the dangers of drugs. That the situation did not explode was due, at least in part, to the restrained nature of the statement. Although it outraged many students, protest was limited to a few letters in the *Sun.* A few days later, however, the County District Attorney publicly reported on the use of marijuana at Cornell in preparation for subpoenaing seven students to appear before the grand jury on drug issues. The marijuana problem at Cornell had become public only during that academic year, but it reached a critical stage a week later. Two Cornell students' arraignments on marijuana charges triggered extensive correspondence in the *Sun* as well as in protest meetings. By early 1965 pot became an issue to which even nonactivists could relate. The constant threat of "the bust" affected not only hippy types in Collegetown, but often whole fraternities as well. At least two Cornell fraternities found it necessary to legislate heavy fines and possible expulsion for any brother found smoking in the common areas of the house. UJB hearings on student possession of marijuana often engendered sympathy for violators even from conservative student circles.

The formation of Students for Education only crystallized doubts about the relevance and utility of student government. The fact that an ad hoc organization had to be created to raise issues of the nature of the curriculum, the educational process, and other questions that had never gained serious attention within student government encouraged the editorial writers of the *Cornell Daily Sun* to argue that student government was a failure and even to bury it in an editorial entitled "Student Government: RIP." While SFE burgeoned, student government's contribution was limited to a donation of $150 to the new organization. While SFE was studying aspects of campus life and arguing out new educational policies, student government, by functioning as it always had, re-emphasized its own irrelevance.

In April 1965 a number of faculty committees established by the Vice President for Academic Affairs advocated, among other matters, the ending of fraternities' national affiliations and the establishment of a letter-grading system. The grading issue created considerable discussion in SFE. The faculty committee, sympathetic to SFE's critique of the grading system intended to eliminate Cornell's numerical grading system in intervals of five, providing for nine grades between 55 and 100. The shift to letter grading, about which SFE was unenthusiastic, was intended to decrease the number of grade intervals from nine to five—A,B,C,D, and F., After a great amount of faculty debate, the ultimate outcome on May 19 was establishment of a letter-grading system with pluses and minuses, which increased the number of grades from nine to thirteen. This decision both subverted the intent of shifting to the letter grade system and stood in opposition to the SFE approach.

Despite this, the short-lived SFE could point out that it had produced a number of significant effects by the end of the academic year. The campus bookstore was broadened into something more than a repository for curricular texts. Commitments were made to establish a coffee house to facilitate student-faculty contact. A commission on student employment was established, and while only one of its nine members was a student, the student minimum wage was raised from $1.05 to $1.25 an hour. Finally, a high-powered faculty commission was appointed at the end of the academic year to examine undergraduate education at Cornell. This commission was to give rise to a number of changes in Cornell's undergraduate program.

Many student activists who had become involved in off-campus activities during the summer of 1965 translated these into campus actions on their return to Cornell. Some students were particularly active in civil rights work, continuing previous activities in Fayette County, Tennessee, while others took part in a new project in East Harlem, New York. As freshman registration began, the *Sun* set the tone for the new year, carrying articles on the Fayette and East Harlem projects and outlining plans for restructuring student government. There was also a lengthy review of the previous year's protests and of student concern with Vietnam. Meanwhile a Cornell graduate student, returning from a summer with the SDS chapter at the University of Buffalo, planned to vitalize the small group within the *Ad Hoc* Committee that had been calling itself SDS with neither organizational nor ideological contact with the national organization. His efforts awakened an active SDS group that dominated events for the next few years.

As the upperclassmen returned, Cornell was treated to its first protest of the year. Severe overcrowding of off-campus housing had been caused by a significant increase in student admissions. When students established "Perkinsville," a tent city on the Arts quadrangle, they provided a few chuckles and indicated that activism was back on campus.

In terms of demonstrations and confrontations, 1965–1966 was a quieter year than the previous one had been. Organizational consolidation and techniques preoccupied student activists as well as the many faculty members becoming increasingly militant under pressure from the Vietnam war. Student groups, such as the *Ad Hoc* Committee and the newly organized Students for a Democratic Society (SDS), as well as faculty groups, such as the Inter-University Committee (IUC), began to meet regularly. Students returning from civil rights work in the South, especially the Fayette County participants, made good use of the organizing skills they had acquired. As antiwar, student power, and more general leftist groups grew in size, they began to develop their own new, particular organizational styles. Such groups as SDS were practicing running meetings by participatory democracy and learning to develop the battery of arguments by which other students might be reached. This period also saw the establishment of stronger trust between members of the radical community as many activists began to rent apartments with the idea of forming communal living units. All these common experiences, including marijuana smoking, helped, because of their social and quasi-political nature (the latter because of its illegality), to increase group solidarity.

The Vietnam war had clearly emerged as the salient agitational issue during the previous school year; it continued to preoccupy the activists in 1965–1966. In October a small teach-in was held; in mid-November a small crowd of supporters of American policy met in the lobby of the student union. By the end of November, however, pressure for and interest in the national antiwar mobilization in Washington began to build up; 35,000 protestors from all over the country participated. Cornell's contingent consisted of one busload and a fleet of cars. In early December the Young Socialist League (YSL), a far-left group of the old left tradition, began soliciting funds in the student union for the National Liberation Front. Student union officials ordered the solicitation stopped, and several YSLers were put on probation. Although there was much debate about the action, no confrontation developed. As the semester ended, the continuing concern with Vietnam was manifested in a symposium attended by over a thousand people.

During the spring semester the pace of antiwar activities increased. When the South Vietnamese Ambassador to the United States visited Cornell in early March, he was greeted by 200 critical pickets. Picketing at the downtown U.S. Post Office, fasts, and vigils on campus were by this time standard features of the Ithaca scene, but militants were just beginning to be frustrated by the ineffectiveness of these tactics.

In March changes in the Selective Service regulations were established by the national administration. These called for a national examination for those college students who would be available for military service under the new draft regulations. The new regulations gave rise to another teach-in plus a plethora of debates and meetings, as well as informal arguments and the continual use of the *Sun* as a means of communicating views. In anticipation of widespread student protest against the Selective Service exam, a faculty commission was established to consider whether the exam should be given on campus. Its decision, given in May, was to permit the examinations to be given; the commission's decision was adopted by the university faculty.

The situation was far from "cooled," however. To avoid difficulties with the students, the university administration sought to provide draft-status information to students, so that they could forward it to their draft boards instead of placing the university in collusion with the draft by making it responsible for forwarding such information directly. At least some of the students were not deceived by this procedure, and certainly the faculty report did nothing to placate them. On

May 18, after a protest meeting on the Selective Service exam, a sit-in in President Perkins' office was led by the local SDS organizer. Only seven students managed to penetrate this inner sanctum, but another hundred supporters gathered outside, providing vociferous encouragement, although they were precluded by campus police from joining the seven.

This sit-in demonstrated the tactical advantage of spontaneity; the idea was conceived, apparently on the spur of the moment, by Tom Bell, the President of Cornell SDS. Bell, a graduate student who had withdrawn at the beginning of the year to devote himself fulltime to political activities, proposed to sit-himself-in in the President's office when he addressed the 300 students opposing Selective Service exams on campus. The movement from this meeting in front of the student union to the President's office was spontaneous and caught the overwhelming bulk of the audience by surprise. When Bell announced that he was going to sit in, a number of the militants moved along with him, followed by a large number of stragglers, who arrived too late to join those who had penetrated into the President's office. Many of these students provided a supportive audience that pressed against the outside doors for hours. This exterior group also included many onlookers who were not necessarily in sympathy with sitting in but who were increasingly hostile to the war and dismayed by its growing presence on campus and who, at the same time, were curious about the fate of those militants who were willing to engage in strong actions.

The sit-in was followed by the usual citations from the Proctor and meetings before the Undergraduate Judiciary Board and the Faculty Committee on Student Conduct. Again, however, the antiwar impetus built up by this sit-in was dispersed, coming as it did at the tail end of the semester.

The campus was not, however, concerned solely with the war question. On March 14, seventy students, mostly dissociated from the student activists, applied the sit-in technique to the undergraduate library. Their refusal to leave after the library's closing hour was intended to point out the need for better service for undergraduates. On this relatively minor issue no one was cited before the university's judicial machinery. A few days later, for their traditional St. Patrick's Day high jinks—spraying green paint on everything and everybody—forty-five architectural students were called before the Proctor. In May the Society for the Prevention of Cruelty to Animals was picketed by forty students, in opposition to new restrictions on dogs' traditional rights to total freedom on the campus.

By the end of the term the nature of activists' reading matter indicated their intense involvement with internal university matters. The publication of President Perkins' book, *The University in Transition,* led the militants to accuse Perkins of justifying the existence of the multiversity attached to established sectors of society and supporting the nastier qualities of American life. "Must" reading included a powerful attack on Perkins' book by Len Silver, a Cornell mathematics professor, and Hal Draper's attack on Clark Kerr's book, *The Uses of the University.* The Draper pamphlet, published by a small socialist group in Berkeley, was widely circulated among the Cornell student militants.

Although it was a year of very substantial debate and intellectual turmoil, 1965–1966 was not a year of confrontation. But in the summer of 1966 the student movement at Cornell experienced significant growth. Perhaps most important to the movement was the establishment of an off-campus office, which became known as "The Office and the Glad Day Press" and was commonly called The Office. Throughout 1965 most of the movement's leaflets had been printed in the bedroom of Joe and Pat Griffith on a small mimeograph machine. Joe was a lecturer in chemistry, and his wife had helped direct the Fayette County project the year before. In the spring of 1965 so many leaflets were being printed that a second-hand offset printing press had to be purchased. This machine, however, was too noisy for the family's three children, and an office about two blocks from campus was rented.

By the time the students returned to campus in September 1966, The Office had become a hive of organized activity. Besides printing local leaflets, The Office quickly became a national center for reprinting and distributing antiwar and related articles, the mailing address for every left-of-center group on campus, a meeting place for student activities, and a general social center.

Except for one girl, who was paid $30 a week to keep the books straight, volunteers handled all labor. Folding, cutting, stapling, stuffing, and mailing literature was all done by students; two or three students who had the time to serve a two-day "apprenticeship" operated the printing press. Although the sale of literature provided some money, The Office operated at a clear loss and depended on contributions from the Cornell community.

Although there were no formal constitutions, by-laws, or legal agreements, there was a fairly high consensus about the purposes of The Office and the few decisions that had to be made. For instance, the printer, in consultation with others who happened to be in The Office at the time, decided which of two submitted leaflets should be distributed in the morning. At least once an innocuous Conservative Club leaflet was printed; on other occasions the printers simply refused to "give their labor" to a cause they did not support. Considering The Office's anarchist structure and its seemingly chaotic operation, it ran surprisingly well. Work at The Office and summer activities placed Cornell's student movement in contact with groups at other colleges and universities. While no formal linkages were established, the communications network allowed exchanges of ideas on strategy and tactics. More importantly, however, knowledge about activities at other schools gave Cornell's movement a spirit of optimism. Cornellians were not working in isolation to end the war in Vietnam but were part of a burgeoning national movement.

During the summer of 1966, also, the *Ad Hoc* Committee dissolved, and SDS emerged as the key group in Cornell movement politics. SDS was the first strong multi-issue coalition at Cornell. From the outset Cornell's SDS was concerned not only with ending the war in Vietnam, or with transforming the university, but also with establishing the nexus between both these problems and with others with which they believed the society was beset. While SDS and

The Office leaflets dealt with any individual issue that might bring in new support, attempts were always made to place the issue in the broadest possible perspective.

SDS meetings gave equal time to arguing specific tactics and to discussing and analyzing the nature of the broader perspective in which tactics should be placed. Because the distinction between analysis and action was fuzzy (indeed, both opponents and supporters of SDS often argued that SDS analysis *was* action), strategy and tactics became interchangeable concepts, and meetings were very chaotic. It was impossible to plan an agenda, since any topic might seem relevant to discussion. But under a chairmanship that revolved at each meeting, consensus was achieved on many actions, even occasionally on ideology, though enormous numbers of man-hours were required.

The final change in the movement during the summer of 1966 was the appearance of "organizers." At Cornell they have been either recent graduates or dropouts from Cornell who have decided to "work fulltime against the war and the system." Until the spring of 1967 the three Ithaca organizers were ex-graduate students of Cornell. One was supported by his parents; one by a part-time job; and one by the regional SDS. Although the three were in no sense formal or informal leaders of the movement at Cornell, they were instrumental in seeing that necessary work got done and in recruiting new activists.

The academic year 1966–1967 was the beginning of two sucessive years of serious confrontation at Cornell. No sooner had the fall semester begun than a student militant interrupted a university symposium on drugs for being one-sided, since it contained no proponents of drugs but only critics. For this interruption the student was placed on disciplinary probation for two semesters. The tone for the academic year was set.

Early in October campus religious leaders initiated an outdoor "pray-in" in front of Cornell's religious center to protest the war in Vietnam. The Selective Service exam held in the fall semester also reinforced antiwar sentiment on campus.

The Students for a Constructive Foreign Policy (SFCFP) was specifically dedicated to reaching nonactivists in the university dormitories and eliciting their involvement in campus affairs, although many of its members were also in SDS. It was active in dorm organizing from the first week of school.

In November student government shifted markedly to a more militant stance as it began searching for issues to focus student grievances. The natural grievance provided by the quality and price of food enabled student government to organize a boycott of Cornell's public eating facilities and a picket of the administration building in which 300 students were involved. The food boycott lasted for several days and produced an inquiry.

By the middle of the month large buttons began to appear, inscribed, "I am not yet convinced that the proctor is a horse's ass," accompanied by smaller buttons which read, "I am convinced." Student militants quickly picked up the idea of wearing these buttons, and within a few days an incident occurred in which an assistant proctor shoved one of the leading activists, Bruce Dancis, down the steps of the student union. Immediately a crowd of angry students who had witnessed the affair surrounded the assistant proctor and asked him if it would be all right to shove him down the steps if they did not like his tie. Engulfed by scores of students, the assistant proctor was completely flustered. He dared anyone to touch his tie, which he held out in his hand.

The buttons were then worn to the public briefings that had been organized earlier by the administrative leadership of the university to open channels of communications to the students. After a heated exchange, the Vice President for Public Affairs suspended the briefings because the students refused to remove their buttons.

Antiwar activities reached full swing when Bruce Dancis publicly destroyed his draft card on campus on December 14. The following day 120 students marched to the Ithaca draft board to protest the bombing of Hanoi.

No sooner had 1967 begun than a confrontation developed over the right of free speech. On January 19 the head of the Cornell Safety Division (acting on his own initiative) seized copies of the *Trojan Horse*, the campus literary magazine, for alleged obscenity; the same day an injunction against future sale was obtained by the Ithaca District Attorney and served on the *Horse's* editors. The *Sun* carried the story, including the editor's announcement that the magazine intended to defy the ban by selling the *Horse* on the steps of the student union at noon.

The rally at 11:30 was attended by 2,000 students; speakers—including the Vice President for Student Affairs, the *Horse's* editors, the Chairman of the Faculty Committee on Student Affairs, and other professors and students—denounced the injunction. Precisely at noon the magazines went on sale, and the DA and several Ithaca plain-clothes police who were waiting began to make arrests, breaking a hundred year old tradition of campus nonintervention by civil authorities. When the DA put five arrested students in a car, it was quickly surrounded by the bulk of the students. Unable to move, the DA offered to release the students in the car and to leave campus himself if everyone selling magazines would sign an admission of complicity.

By the next day an aroused campus was united in support of the sale of the magazine under the right of free speech. The Scheduling, Coordination, and Activities Review Board (SCARB) voted eight to nothing not to oppose the sale of the *Trojan Horse*; the Interfraternity Council voted to provide bail for anyone arrested; over 1,500 students and faculty members signed a notarized list admitting complicity in the sale of the magazine. The Acting President of the University (the whole top echelon of university administrators was in New York City at a trustees' meeting), although "not encouraging sales," made it clear that Cornell would not prohibit the sale of the *Horse*.

The DA made no further move, and on January 25 the state courts overturned the injunction. After considerable internal discussion in the administration, the head of the Safety Division resigned on February 6 (he was later to become Deputy Chief of Police in Ithaca). The *Horse* incident concluded the fall semester in a blaze of activist glory.

By the opening of the spring semester antiwar activities were ready for takeoff. On February 6 a letter in the *Sun* with 293 faculty signatures urged a halt to the bombing of North

Vietnam. The following week Bruce Dancis and four other
students announced that they were dropping their studies
(but remaining at Cornell) to oppose the war fulltime. Several days later a national student conference held at Cornell
urged a halt to U.S. bombings.

Throughout February and March the activists concentrated
their activities on the Spring Mobilization to End the War in
Vietnam, scheduled to be held in New York City on April 15.
Speakers from the mobilization committee in New York (one
of whom was a Cornell professor who later resigned to work
with the committee fulltime) talked about the mobilization at
fraternities, in the dorms, and at specially called meetings. In
addition to a march, the main activity of the mobilization,
individual groups, it was hoped, would "do their thing" in
New York to demonstrate their opposition to the war.

A small group of Cornell students who had been engaged
in draft counseling for the previous six months decided to
make their contribution a mass draft card burning. Although
individual protesters had already publicly destroyed cards,
no group had yet attempted to do so on a mass scale. The
Cornell students decided to spread their idea nationwide and
to seek pledges to burn their cards publicly during Spring
Mobilization from other students. On March 7 a letter soliciting these pledges was circulated on campus. SDS, supported by a number of auxiliary organizations, began the
process that eventually led Cornell to a major confrontation.
All of March was devoted to issues pertinent to the Spring
Mobilization and, more significantly, to obtaining pledges.
The issue crystallized in Willard Straight Hall, the student
union, when SDS sought routine permission to set up a table
in the lobby to solicit pledges. The student commission rejected the request on the grounds that this was a solicitation
for an illegal act, and it sustained its position through a
number of appeals. The position of the antiwar forces was
that the burning of draft cards was not yet an established
crime; appeals were currently being heard that would ultimately go to the Supreme Court. Furthermore, distinction
should be made between the burning of the draft
card—which might be an illegal act—and solicitation for the
commission of an illegal act. As far as the activists were

concerned, solicitation involved free speech; if some illegal act was being solicited, it was none of the university's business, and the university could not, therefore, impede the process of solicitation.

The Willard Straight controversy about draft card burning solicitation posed the question of the doctrine of in loco parentis on political rather than personal grounds for the first time. The history of objection to the doctrine concerned sex and personal conduct, but the issue in March 1967 was focused on political conduct. The University authorities insisted that the university had a responsibility to protect students from engaging in political crimes on the campus.

The confrontations began on March 16 when a table was manned by supporters of SDS and the open solicitation of pledges began. Shortly after noon the Proctor arrived. His suspension of several demonstrators triggered a sit-in in the administration building in front of the Proctor's office several hours later. During the next week more and more students and faculty members were drawn into the vortex of the issue of the politicalized doctrine of in loco parentis.

Hundreds of students—some supportive, other merely curious—filled the lobby of the Straight to participate in the "teach-in" that resulted. In the debate the central issues were put in direct terms by the student participants themselves. Bruce Dancis, now an ex-student, said in passionate language:

> We're saying that we will no longer go along blindly, or go along without doing anything, while our government is committing what we consider to be mass murder in Vietnam. We are willing to risk five years in jail and a fine of $10,000 to stop this murder. We are saying that the university rules and Proctor George are irrelevant to this killing. We cannot be hung-up here while people are dying in Vietnam. We feel that this war is wrong. We said we will not fight in it, and we are going to destroy our draft cards because we feel it's wrong. And we feel we have the right, and we have the duty. We say we cannot go along with this, and we must appeal to you to feel the same way: to say no to this government, and to destroy your draft card when we're going to do it on April 15th.

David Burak, another of the active militants, dealt with the issue of advocacy:

Let us be tried in a federal court. If we can't have freedom of advocacy in the universities of America, then where can we have it? I'll answer that. No place! We're going to have something else. We're going to have what may be fascism. And you may not like this term, but I'll tell you, Huey Long once remarked cynically, when fascism comes to the United States it's gonna come wrapped in an American flag with a lot of glitter on it. This is what we see now. We see the rules with a lot of glitter on them.

This led, of course, to counterarguments about a lack of form and the student militants' refusal to adhere to the due processes of the university. Art Kaminsky, chairman of the Scheduling, Coordination, and Activities Review Board (SCARB), the student committee that had refused permission for the solicitation, stated:

Why did SCARB decide as it did? SCARB has a constitution, given to it by the Faculty Committee on Student Affairs. Cornell, no matter what you may think of it, is a society, a bit of society unto itself. It lives by rules, and it dies by rules being broken. The rules that govern this university say that SCARB will make decisions about student organizations. . . . As you have a responsibility to yourselves, to your consciences, to fight with all you have against this evil war, as an individual, I tend to think that I've done my part to fight this war. But SCARB and the members of SCARB have a moral responsibility to their position, positions that they took, that they were given, that they swore to uphold, and this meant to follow the rules as prescribed in the constitution. . . . But right now, if you live in a society, and you do, you do not break the rules and then change them, you change them first.

With seven students suspended, the Undergraduate Judiciary Board (UJB) began to meet as daily confrontations continued in Willard Straight Hall. The activists sought to convert every activity into an educational forum, attacking particularly the character of the war but also dwelling on the defects of a society that would sustain such a war and of a university that would permit itself to be implicated in the war. Burton Weiss, who had been disciplined for interrupting the meeting on drugs at the beginning of the semester, spoke eloquently on this subject:

The members of the UJB labored under the belief that they had two roles and each role was more or less important. One was the role of member of UJB and the other was the role of human being. We had already made the decision. We were going to act as human beings. They tried to make a decision, but I think so far they've failed. Because as soon as they decide that the role of human beings is *the* role, the other role disappears and all the language, all the words, that referred to SCARB, that referred to bureaucratic frivolity—all those disappear and you're only left with weighty words. And if you're a member of the UJB and you decide to get rid of the frivolous words, the words that only refer to your secondary role, then you must resign. If you're a member of the Faculty Committee on Student Conduct or the Faculty Committee on Student Affairs and you weigh your words, and are left with the words that refer to human things, to sorrow, compassion, and human outrage, then you must resign and begin to work for peace.

Cornell experienced a frantic week as the energies of hundreds of students, as well as substantial numbers of sympathetic and hostile faculty members, were involved on a twenty-four hour, round-the-clock basis. In addition, thousands of students were drawn into the confrontational dramas staged at noon each day between the student militants and hundreds of supporters, opponents, and curiousity seekers; besides these, other meetings and debates were carried on throughout the campus. On the fourth day of confrontation, after a quiet weekend, the Proctor's activities re-escalated, bringing about the first direct faculty involvement. A group of sympathetic faculty sought to interpose themselves between the Proctor and the students, but the suspensions continued. Ultimately, the situation was eased by the intervention of the President, who established a commision. This group recommended, for the following year, the elimination of the doctrine of in loco parentis concerning all aspects of student conduct except the use of drugs.

Despite the hectic week of confrontation, the student militants never lost sight of their main purpose—obtaining pledges to burn draft cards at the Spring Mobilization— and about thirty students signed up for the mass conflagration. Many other students were unwilling to face the consequences of draft card burning but wanted to take a militant stand against the war. They initiated a "we won't go" pledge, stating that they would not serve in the military as long as the United States remained in Vietnam.

The university's confrontation with itself was no sooner resolved than Secretary of State Dean Rusk appeared on campus on March 24. Cornell's Bailey Hall, site of the various teach-ins, was packed. When Secretary Rusk was introduced by President Perkins, he was greeted by a walkout by part of the audience, while others donned death-head masks or turned their backs to him during his speech.

As April 15 and Spring Mobilization drew near, leaders of the draft-card-burning movement were flown from Cornell to New York City for a last-minute attempt by moderate elements in the Mobilization Committee to postpone the burning to a different day. The students returned to Cornell prepared to carry out the action as planned. Hundreds of students began to sign up for the bus trip to New York. The march ultimately encompassed between 250,000 and 500,000 protesters of the war. The buses and cars left Cornell with 1,200 students, as 75 counterprotesters again attempted to impede them but respectfully responded to the request of the Proctor to clear the way.

After Spring Mobilization activity subsided, although on May 22, 200 Cornell students marched to a downtown park to protest World War III. The statement by over 300 students in the *Sun* that "we won't go" also created a stir on campus. But the central issue during the final part of the semester was that of the Cornell Aeronautical Laboratory (CAL), a research facility donated years before to Cornell and located in Buffalo. CAL, like many such research organizations, chiefly engaged in government sponsored research, and the Cornell students criticized the university's attachment to an organization known to be conducting secret research about the war in Vietnam. Early in May the Cornell University faculty rejected a proposal to sever relationships with CAL. The main defensive viewpoint of the meeting, which was heavily attended by engineers, was that the relationship benefited the university more than it harmed it. The faculty did not know that CAL was already engaged in negotiations to conduct research on counterinsurgency in Thailand; the fact was made known later in the summer.

The most serious event of the academic year 1966–1967 was the March confrontation between the students and the Proctor that had great potential for becoming violent as long as the university authorities insisted on their legal rights. The fact that the university had adhered to established procedures did not enhance its position, since it was seeking to enforce the doctrine of in loco parentis on a political issue. The weak substantive position of the university administration undermined its procedural correctness, and in this case at least, the wisdom of abandonment of procedural forms for substantive goals produced a quieting of the campus atmosphere.

A number of major events occurred during the summer of 1967. The first of these was "Vietnam Summer," a group centered nationally in Boston for the first time made a concerted effort to move the issue of the war off campus into surrounding communities. Ithaca's Vietnam Summer had two paid organizers and a score of part-time workers who printed a newspaper, rang doorbells to talk about the war, talked in churches, and spoke to community organizations. In another attempt to reach into the Ithaca community, graduate student activists began to set up a Neighborhood College and *Dateline,* a newspaper intended to reach the downtown audience. The college, directed by Cornell graduate students and ex-graduate students, was staffed by Cornell and Ithacans with special vocational skills. Courses ranged from remedial reading to social theory and functioned at vocational and college levels. Tuition was free. As extensions to the college, a library, an activities center, an activities-bookmobile, and a special lecture series were established. *Dateline,* one of the few radical papers in the country directed at a nonradical audience, went entirely on subscription after the first year.

The Office was also doing its part in the underground press movement. Aside from two weekly newspapers and two monthly magazines it published for the Ithaca-Upstate New York area, The Office printed newspapers for groups as far away as Boston and Wisconsin. By subscribing to the Liberation News Service (LNS), The Office became part of a nationwide radical communication network.

During the summer, The Office and Glad Day Press moved to larger quarters, where printing facilities and staff were expanded. Backed financially by a new faculty group,

Friends of The Office (FOTO), based largely at Cornell, The Office acquired new photo-offset equipment, paper handling machines, and three full-time workers at $40 per week and two half-time printers at $20 per week. This bureaucratization caused serious unrest when activists started to find The Office "all work and no play." Also, for the first time in Office history, the supply of voluntary labor exceeded the demand. This problem, however, was resolved by the next year, when the number of publications put out by The Office increased greatly. Soon a "cultural revolution" hit, and the quality of layout and color work improved; the changes were in large part responsible for making 1967–1968 the year of the leaflet at Cornell.

The growth and subsequent bureaucratization of The Office was paralleled to a lesser extent in SDS. Throughout the previous spring members had talked of the need for some kind of committee structure in SDS, and during the summer a number of committees were established. Although membership in SDS continued to be loosely defined and people could belong to as many committees as they wished, the change was an important one. The serious work of SDS shifted from the biweekly mass meeting to the committee level. It must be emphasized, however, that SDS at Cornell has been united as much by social interaction as by political ideology. The mass meetings as well as committee discussions continued to last into the early hours of the morning, and by the fall of 1968 the majority of the most active SDS members had shared an apartment with almost all of the other activists at some time during their stay at Cornell.

The academic year 1967–1968 began with the public exposure of CAL's involvement in a Thai counterinsurgency program. This news was apparently too much for President Perkins, who resigned his post on the CAL Board of Directors. The issue of Cornell's relationship to CAL was again discussed by the faculty; aroused this time, they voted to sever relations.

Fall Mobilization was set for October 22 in Washington, D.C. When a request was made that student government provide financial support for Fall Mobilization, a student referendum was called on the issue of financial support as well as on various other issues relating to the war. The referendum, held on October 12, made it clear that students were strongly opposed to the war but equally strongly opposed to providing funds for Fall Mobilization.

One of the groups that had planned the April 15 draft-card burning was dedicated to the tactic of draft-card turn-ins. Known as the Resistance, it was supported by an "adult" group known as Resist. The purpose of both groups was both moral and political. They hoped that by demonstrating personal moral outrage at the war they might galvanize others into action and thereby impede American war efforts. The group also worked in draft counseling and arranged demonstrations for students wanting them at their physical and induction refusals.

On October 16, in the first march of the season to the Ithaca draft board, fourteen students turned in their draft cards. This became a recurring event during the semester. Cornell participation in Fall Mobilization in Washington on October 22 was smaller than it had been in the spring, but the activities in front of the Pentagon drew national attention to the escalation of antiwar protest. In the event, 21 Cornell students and one professor were arrested in Washington.

On November 17 the first confrontation to keep recruiters from access to campus occurred at Cornell; over 200 demonstrators blocked the entry way to Marine recruiters visiting Cornell. The Undergraduate Judiciary Board refused on December 5 to impose any penalties. Two days later the Faculty Committee on Student Conduct reprimanded 19 graduates and provided mostly reprimands for 132 undergraduates for the November 17 blockages. As a result, three members of the UJB resigned in protest.

Early in December the Resistance had another "turn-in" at the Ithaca Draft Board. A small crowd marched down with the eleven students who turned in their cards. During the remainder of the fall semester no major activities developed, although there continued to be a great deal of ferment on campus. Early in the spring 1968 semester it was made public that an assistant registrar of the university had, on official

Cornell stationery, informed the draft board of a Cornell student who had burned his draft card. This action, contrary to university policy, immediately created a major stir.

Late in 1967 students who had been involved in the April 15 draft-card burning either at the confrontation in the Straight or at the mobilization itself, began receiving summonses from a federal grand jury in New York City. These summonses were delivered by agents of the Federal Bureau of Investigation. A favorite game of the activists quickly became "Freak the Feds." FBI agents seeking appointments were invited to meet people on campus and had their pictures taken. Agents never knew when they made a call if they would be invited to dinner or to bed or told to make an appointment with some nonexistent secretary. Students felt more proud than frightened about a visit from the FBI. The light manner in which they treated the possibility of repression was similar to the circus atmosphere at the "Yippie" hearings held by HUAC in early 1969. The Grand Jury, after hearing about fifteen Cornell students and ex-students and an equal number of people from the city, never returned a report.

On February 19 and 20 the School of Business and Public Administration was picketed when representatives of the Dow Chemical Company came to Cornell to recruit. Approximately 800 students participated in the unobstructive picket on the first two days of activity. On March 1, 150 protesters silently faced Marine recruiters in Barton Hall in an unobstructive confrontation. The activities of March 1 represented the last major antiwar activity at Cornell for the year, for in April the scene shifted to a dramatic week in race relations.

Through the previous years black students at Cornell had played no significant role in antiwar activities. The build-up of black students was noticable, though their absolute number was not great. By the academic year 1967–1968 the blacks on campus were beginning to organize and to feel their way toward campus activities. The triggering incident came early in the spring semester, when a black girl was given enforced medical leave from the university for alleged violence in the girls' dorms. Upon her insistence, her case was reviewed, and it was revealed that she had been ordered to return home and that, because of her inability to get along with girls in the dorms, she had been labeled psychologically unadaptive. This news gave rise to black demands for separate housing to allow blacks to develop along their own lines without being subjected to the pressures of the overwhelmingly white dormitories. As the university moved to meet this demand, much of the heat was removed from the situation. Not until April 4 was there another major outburst involving black students. On this occasion sixty blacks sat-in at the Department of Economics, barricading the department chairman in his office. The protest concerned the lectures of a visiting professor whom the blacks regarded as racist. Their demands that a lecturer be invited to present a contrary point of view was refused, and having unsuccessfully sought redress at various agencies of the university, the blacks decided upon a sit-in.

The sit-in for the first time raised the possibility that student demands might stand in fundamental contradiction to that deeply enshrined academic value, academic freedom. The right of a faculty member to state his views in lectures as long as these are relevent to the technical materials being presented is one of the most strongly held values of the university. In this case the student argument that a faculty member was presenting racist views challenged the academic freedom of the faculty member involved, and as a result it gave rise to an enormous amount of discussion. This was immediately cut off by the assasination of Martin Luther King later that day. The King assassination sparked a series of fires on and off campus. The university staggered under the blow, following so rapidly after the Economics Department sit-in. A teach-in was scheduled as a memorial, and the blacks invaded this affair to indicate their unbounding contempt for white American society.

Throughout the spring semester SDS members had been doing research on the financial holdings of Cornell University trustees. They discovered that, through Chase Manhattan and four other banks, as well as through a number of other institutions on whose boards of directors Cornell trustees sit, a part of Cornell's endowment fund was invested in South Africa. Other research revealed the extent of Cornell's responsibility for the housing shortage in Ithaca, Cornell trustees' influence in local banks, and Cornell's influence as a wage-setter in the county. The presence on campus of a dynamic South African visitor who spoke about the situation of blacks in South Africa provided the focus of concern for activists for the remainder of the spring term. For a few weeks an ad hoc coalition of SDS and Afro-Americans engaged in a series of actions directed against Cornell's involvement in South Africa. These included a mill-in against Cornell's trustees on April 18 and picketing of faculty meetings on April 24 and May 1. Even the events at Columbia, although a hot topic of conversation, failed to draw the militants away from their preoccupation with South Africa. However, as a prelude to a 1968–1969 Cornell presidential commission report recommending major overhaul of the ROTC program, the faculty of the Arts College voted on May 8, 1968, to withdraw credit for ROTC courses taken by its students.

The academic year 1967–1968 marked the transition from antiwar activities to problack activities and other more local issues. For the first time the blacks emerged on the Cornell campus as a significant force; in this respect Cornell typified what was occurring on most American campuses.

The summer of 1968 provided the usual period of qualitative change in the movement. Many of the active SDS leaders found financial support that enabled them to stay in Ithaca. Their concern focused particularly on the growing size of SDS membership and the need for a change in organizational structure. Plans were made to institute "study-affinity groups" (cells) to broaden the limited perspective of committee work. Each cell would have members from several committees and would attempt to create a general analysis of society in the manner of earlier SDS meetings. Thus each SDS member would work with both a committee oriented toward a specific issue and a social unit whose main goal was creating solidarity and general analysis. When the fall term opened, a small number of these groups met a few times but never became active. The result of their failure was increased power for the steering committee. SDS still maintained its loose definition of membership, and the group was still open to new ideas, but growing size and the collective experience of the more active members made it difficult for a new person to significantly affect the organization. Such influence had been possible and had often occurred in groups such as the Cornell Liberal Union, Students for Education, the *Ad Hoc* Committee to End the War in Vietnam, and, until now, in SDS. The SDS ideology was becoming more consistent than it had ever been before: the whole American system had to be dismantled, particularly its worst manifestations—racism and imperialism. At the root of the world problems was American capitalism, and the answer was to be found in some form of socialism. SDS shifted its activities toward the Third World in general and at the same time toward the local Ithaca housing problem. The Cornell movement in 1969 was still a long way from the sectarianism of the 1930's, but it had changed considerably from its totally anarchistic beginnings in CLU, SFE, the *Ad Hoc* Committee, and the spontaneous outbursts over sex in the 1950's.

The development of a study program for black students also provided a base for continuing and ongoing discussion by black activists during the summer. Sponsored by the university and paid for their involvement, black students attended classes before moving into industries and factories to study personnel policies and racism. Since the blacks were insulated from the other students on campus largely through their own wishes, the continuous process of contact during the summer probably facilitated their planning future activities.

1968–1969: The Big Confrontation

By the time the academic year 1968–1969 opened, several organized but diffuse student forces and a coherent, crisis-management-oriented administrative leadership had emerged from Cornell's four years of turmoil and confrontation. The faculty, inchoate but worried, unable to

260 The Knowledge Factory

define distinctive tendencies within itself, was largely impotent as new crises arose. But the coherent forces that existed typified, perhaps, the situation that had developed at many major American campuses.

Perhaps it is best to consider the approach to crises developed by the administration through the years of trouble. Under the iron-handed but velvet-gloved leadership of President James Perkins, a team had developed geared to crisis management. Unlike the kinds of leadership at other campuses, the Cornell University leadership had formulated an approach of sufficient breadth to contain—at least until 1969—student activism without unduly offending faculty, trustees, the local community, and the alumni.

The approach of the administrative leadership can be subsumed under nine approaches.

Cooptation describes the process by which elements of the protesting groups are incorporated into the decision-making apparatus in ways that occupy their time, on the one hand, and remove them from their constituencies, on the other. By tying up activists in committees involved in lengthy fact gathering, the energies of militants become diffused; some of the more coherent leaders may become so integrated into the committee structure that they lose credibility and are no longer in a position to mobilize followers.

This is not to say that the cooptative process is necessarily "fake"; students are drawn into the decision-making centers, but always as part of a larger group involving faculty and administration. Faculty decision making is ponderous, at best, because the academic mind insists upon a careful assemblage and weighing of all facts before decisions are approached. Thus activists' participation in the process— cooptation—contains them to a considerable degree.

Another manipulative quality of the cooptative process is that the administration decides the areas within which to coopt students and places them into the least threatening decision-making situations. When SFE was organized in 1965, for example, the variety of issues raised by protesting students included the quality of instruction and the character of books in the bookstore. Student representatives were coopted to the board of the bookstore and placed on some of the preparatory committees investigating the quality of instruction. But no student representation was proposed for the review committees that examine the performance of professors and assess their capacities as researchers and teachers. Because the administration selects the specific areas within which cooptation may take place, it can defuse a confrontation situation to the degree that students believe that the cooptative action represents a significant concession by the university.

Stratification or *differentiation recognition*—the understanding that any confrontation is the result of a variety of interests and points of view—permits the cooptative process to operate successfully. At most universities the administration tends to regard a confrontation group as undifferentiated, homogeneous rabble, and it loses the possibility of cooptation. At Cornell a general orientation by which stratification within the activist group is recognized not only guarantees success in the cooptative process, but also provides the third component of Cornell's managerial strategy:

Divisiveness of the demonstrators. By recognizing that any demonstrating force is heterogeneous, the administration—if it provides some concessions—is able to establish divisions within the demonstration group. The less militant student demonstrators, seeing that they have had some effect, begin to retract from "nonnegotiable" positions. The militants may persist, but the incessant debate that develops internally serves to erode the morale of the total group, and very often, demonstrations simply fade away.

Decrystallization or *defusing* refers to the development of highly sensitive, trouble-oriented organizational antennae to discern the troublespots around which protest may crystallize and to defuse them before disruption begins. The developmental process whereby antennae are "grown" represents a high level of sophistication, not seen on most campuses; at Cornell it has been developed to a considerable art. Once potential troublespots are located, it is necessary to move with dispatch (but without haste, since it can trigger demonstration) to alleviate situations before they become crystallization points for demonstrations.

Continuous demonstration management. When a demonstration begins on campus, the leading administrators carry on a continuous meeting for the duration of the crisis. Thus the leading group within the university is paying total attention to the demonstration as long as it is in process, assembling information, assessing it, projecting alternative possibilities and their consequences for different constituencies of the university, maintaining informal contact with opinion leaders of these constituencies, and sending forth emissaries, mainly informal but sometimes formal.

Insulation of top decision makers is a process whereby the president of the university is only marginally involved publicly with respect to the demonstration. By utilizing emissaries—either from the administration, members of the faculty sympathetic to the students, or students themselves—the top leadership maintains maximum flexibility for movement.

Insulation also permits *personnel substitution* in the actual "front line"; that is, dealing with the students is left to lower-ranking personnel. By successively utilizing various approaches, the university leadership is able to develop continuous feedback on demonstrator responses and to formulate new proposals in ways that will permit cooptation and divisiveness to develop.

Since the abrasive contact of crisis situations is hard on both administrators and students, personnel substitution also allows the administration to replace those with tattered credibility and to gain the advantage of having a fresh person involved in discussions with fatigued students (although students have begun to deal successfully with the fatiguing aspect of crisis).

The technique of *give* permits compromise and concessions when they become necessary. In a number of confrontations at other institutions—Berkeley, Columbia, and San Francisco State are classic examples—the administration finds itself unable to provide much "give." At Columbia the lack of give originated with President Grayson Kirk's rigid conceptualization of presidential prerogatives; in California the lack of give stems from the detailed involvements of the regents and other political forces at the administrative level of the university or college. In contrast, Cornell's trustees serve (except on financial matters) largely as a legal validation group, placing the seal of approval on actions already taken elsewhere. Nor does the faculty function as a coherent unit (except when its prerogatives are at stake) in impeding the freedom of maneuver of the administration. Thus it was possible for President Perkins to make significant compromises when and where necessary until April 1969.

Giving, of course, is facilitated by confrontations in that the demonstrators create pressures to which the administration can yield with grace. With militants pressing for very substantial demands, some lesser concessions become justifiable to faculty, alumni, and other interest groups.

Finally, the technique of *coercion* is always available to the administration, although its effectiveness at Cornell has depended upon its being used as a diffuse threat rather than actually applied. As long as no specific threats are made ("if you do not get out, you will be suspended forthwith"), the administration retains considerable leeway in handling students. Above all, Cornell's administrators have understood that the presence of naked and open coercion (such as is provided by policemen) must be avoided at almost all costs. At most demonstrations and confrontations, campus police are kept away from the scene except when they are in mufti; nothing arouses students more than the sight of a cop-with-gun pushing around a student. The presence of police forces also reduces the control the decision-making leadership has at any given moment, since police forces have their own autonomous command systems. The administrative leadership prefers to use on-campus coercive mechanisms, over whom their control is complete; agents such as the proctor go to the scene of confrontation with highly explicit instructions limiting their options.

The modus operandi of the Cornell administration can best be seen in its attempt at handling events in the academic year 1968–1969. Two major student groups and one minor group absorbed the administration's energies. Both Students

for a Democratic Society (SDS) and the Afro-American
Society (AAS) were active—although independently and in
greatly different ways. In addition, the graduate students on
campus began to organize with relation to bread-and-butter
issues of wages and remission of fees.

Before dealing with the more dramatic events, it would be
well to examine several issues that were defused before any
crystallization of dissatisfaction occurred or grew too rapidly.

Cornell's vulnerability, caused by its employment of mi-
grant workers to pick apples in several of its orchards, became a source of concern. Once the upper echelons of the
university became aware that it employed migrants, steps
were taken to minimize the university vulnerability to criticism. In another example, the closing of a dining room, because of its economic unviability, created a certain amount of
protest. To meet the demands of potential demonstrators, the
dining room was reopened. In these cases (and in others as
well) the university leadership identified problem areas and
defused them before the situation became unmanageable.

Cornell teaching assistants (TAs), who received salaries
ranging from $3,500 in some sciences to nothing in the de-
partment of classics, threatened to strike in the fall of 1968
unless salary parity was established. Sensing the seriousness
of the TA demands and the probability that their strike would
materialize, the university found enough money to meet most
of the demands.

On the other issues, however, the crisis-management approach did not fare so well. Students became increasingly
sensitive to crisis-management and began circumventing
parts of the technique. Black students, for example, began to
use personnel substitution themselves. They were less concerned with avoiding fatigue problems than with counter-
acting the tendency of highly skilled and sophisticated administrators to subvert and coopt their leadership. SDS response lay in conducting its own research, extensively and
for lengthy periods, before confronting the university. The
development of masses of documentable data in advance
served to undermine the cooptative process to a considerable
degree, since students have been and will be presenting

highly documented cases, day after day, to Cornell and to the general community — seeking to involve the community in the debate over facts instead of leaving fact gathering to a small elite committee.

From research done the previous spring and summer SDS had formulated a housing proposal, the main point of which was that Cornell, responsible for one of the worst housing shortages in the state, should directly fund but not control more than 1,000 units of low- and moderate-incoming housing for the Ithaca community and 1,500 units of student housing and should, in addition, pledge to begin financing the housing of 75 per cent of its students. The serious and continuing housing shortage and Cornell's responsibilities were well-documented by SDS; during the fall 1968 term SDS gained wide support from community groups including both low- and middle-income people. A Joint Housing Committee, representing a broad coalition of community groups, and MOVE, a Cornell faculty group formed in response to the murder of Dr. Martin Luther King, endorsed the SDS program. In conjunction with the housing drive, the Ithaca Tenants Union (ITU), composed primarily of students, was formed to deal with specific housing complaints.

Early in 1969 SDS announced that it was prepared to meet on March 1 with representatives of the Board of Trustees to negotiate implementation of the program. On January 15 President Perkins wrote a letter to SDS, pointing out several obstacles to the funding of the program; he proposed that a group of administrators, faculty, and interested students discuss the issues. The SDS reply of January 23, however, noted that the man Perkins had named to head the group was to be out of the country for a month and that the President had failed to respond directly to any of the SDS points. The final paragraph of the SDS letter established the hard-line nature of the SDS-community demands:

> We are certainly willing to clarify our proposals if that should be necessary, but we insist that enough study has been done on the housing situation, and it is time now to talk about implementing solutions. We repeat our desire to negotiate the implementation of our housing proposals on March 1 with a delegation of

University personnel authorized by the Board of Trustees. There will be a group of student and community representatives ready on that date.

Many of the administration's crisis-management techniques were recognized and avoided by the proponents of the housing proposal. Early in 1969 MOVE rejected an administration offer to fund separately one of its smaller projects, which would have divided support for housing. Later SDS refused to participate in the administration's housing group even after, in a clearly cooptative attempt, it was raised in status to a "commission." The commission was considered irrelevant and was picketed. SDS demands included the specific provision that the administration negotiators be "authorized by the Board of Trustees"—an attempt to avoid some of the effects of the insulation of the real decision makers and the techniques of personnel substitution.

During February SDS, the Joint Housing Committee (JHC), MOVE, and other affiliated groups on and off campus focused their attention on the housing issue, and attempts to increase support were intensified. Several demonstrations, including a torchlight parade, indicated that the support existed, and negotiations between the JHC and a trustee group got under way. When the initial response of the trustee negotiators to the housing demands was negative, SDS made it abundantly clear that it intended to take strong action. Two days later, at a meeting called by SDS, 800 students, many of whom were at their first SDS meeting, met with mixed reactions the news that a planned takeover of the administration building scheduled for less than fifteen minutes away was cancelled; the trustee housing committee had acceded to JHC's major demands.

Another issue arose over the impending departure of several noted historians and humanities professors. Humanities has not been strong at Cornell; it is not an area to which the administration has paid any serious attention. The issue was, therefore, one that mobilized many Arts and Sciences students. And in mid-April a popular sociology professor, one of the first winners of a teaching award, was refused tenure because of his weak publication record.

One follow-up of the South African affair of the previous year was that the Center for International Studies began to plan an elaborate conference on South Africa and apartheid. In its planning phases this project involved many of the students who had been active in the earlier South African protests. And its conceptualization—how to come to grips realistically with apartheid, as a matter of American policy considerations—was intended to order feelings about South Africa rather than letting them burst out in demonstrations.

However, the twenty-five speakers at the symposium, of whom only three were black, were not greeted sympathetically by an audience composed for the most part of Afro-Americans, black Africans, and SDS supporters. The latter moved rapidly from verbal hostility to more openly disruptive interventions. At a meeting on the second evening of the conference the blacks turned out en masse to challenge Cornell President James Perkins on university investments in South Africa. As Perkins was speaking, one black student grabbed him by the collar and pulled him from the podium. Perkins, badly shaken, left the room. The campus reaction to this incident was hardly in favor of the blacks, despite the fact that there was an increasing sentiment that Cornell's endowments should be free of the taint of apartheid.

The fall of 1968 also saw a crisis involving black student demands at Cornell.[3] In the spring of 1968, primarily in response to the murder of Dr. King, Cornell began planning an Afro-American Studies Institute, to be structured along the lines of already existing programs, such as one in Asian Studies. By late fall, however, the rate of the program's implementation, as well as its structure, proved to be less than satisfactory to many Cornell blacks. Militant black students gained control of the Afro-American Society (AAS), the only organized black voice on campus, and demanded an autonomous black college, to be run by black students; several lesser demands were also made. Although negotiations on the main demands were carried on privately with the admin-

3. The following discussion of the April 1969 confrontation is based almost entirely on William H. Friedland and Harry Edwards, "Confrontation at Cornell," *Trans-action*, 6, 7 (June 1969), 29–36, 76.

istration (neither party would discuss the issue with the press), black students staged several demonstrations to illustrate their lesser demands. The demonstrations for the most part were nonviolent, but they were wild enough to cause an uproar on campus. In several libraries hundreds of books were moved from shelves to the circulation desk to point out their irrelevance to black students' needs; blacks danced on tables in the student-union cafeteria to demonstrate a need for a "soul room"; the clinic was filled with "fainting" black students to illustrate a need for a black psychologist; and some black students ran through various campus buildings carrying toy guns and knocking over candy machines in a general protest when the administration failed to meet their ultimatum on the autonomous college. The same week six members of the Afro-American Society forced three whites to leave their offices in a university building on Waite Avenue—a building that the administration had promised to the Afro-American studies program—and during the same affair a photographer for the *Cornell Daily Sun* was roughed up when he refused to turn over a film.

Despite their sometimes playful aspects, these demonstrations had an ugly and threatening undercurrent. The administration nevertheless, moved toward implementing a black-studies program. Not all black demands were met, but a black was chosen as acting director, and compromises were worked out to make the program a degree-granting one. Another consequence was that the black students saw their demonstrations as part of a political program necessary to help them gain a meaningful education at Cornell.

Campus reaction at this time varied from those agreeing with black students' goals and tentatively supporting their tactics to those who decried both. Conservative groups made use of the civil rights rhetoric they had so long despised to argue against "reverse segregation." Tension was building to a tremendous pitch when classes ended for the Christmas vacation. By the time the new semester began in February, the moderates seemed to have gained control of AAS. Because the administration at this time wisely avoided penalizing the black demonstrators, things cooled down for a while.

The faculty and administration response to the demonstrations had nevertheless been hostile, and the process of finding scapegoats upon whom retribution might be visited began. In January six students were charged before the Student-Faculty Conduct Board. The decision with respect to these students was one of the important factors leading to the 1969 confrontation. Preliminary to the trial of the six members of the Afro-American Society before the Student-Faculty Conduct Board, the AAS was claiming that the demonstrations of December had been political acts, for which the organization should be held responsible; selection of a few members could be regarded only as victimization. Accordingly, the six refused to appear before the Conduct Board. Then followed a period in which the six students were verbally threatened with suspension if they failed to appear before the Board. When they did not appear, letters were sent. In April, just before the events that brought Cornell into the headlines, an obscure clause was discovered that permitted the Conduct Board to take action without the black students' being present. On April 18 the Conduct Board reprimanded three of the blacks and dismissed charges against two others, while the charge against the last student was dropped because of his departure from the university.

Throughout this period campus groups had been enunciating principles to support their positions on the issues involved. For the Conduct Board (and implicitly for the faculty and much of the student body) the issue raised was: Is the university a single community? If it is *a* community, must all "citizens" adhere to its rules? The blacks not only challenged the idea of *a* community, but put forward the principle that no man should be judged except by a jury of his peers. The blacks also challenged the legitimacy of the Board, contending that it was not a voluntary product of the campus community, but one imposed by the racist apparatus of American society. In partial justification of their statement the Afro-Americans pointed out that there was no black representation on the Board. A second conflict of principle arose over the issue of how personal, in contrast to political, acts could be judged. Some university groups argued that individuals rather than organizations had to be held responsible for their acts; organizations could not be tried before the Conduct Board. The blacks asserted that the reverse was true; their actions were political, and therefore their responsibility was collective. The blacks also argued that the university was not only the aggrieved party, but the judge and jury as well, going counter to principles of Anglo-Saxon justice. The Afro-American Society suggested that "arbitration," as in industrial relations, might be the appropriate model for a resolution of the problem.

In addition to the disciplinary issue, a number of other questions were deeply troubling to numbers of both students and faculty. During their seizure of the Waite Avenue building, the blacks had insisted that their demands for an Afro-American studies program were "nonnegotiable." This assertion was pure rhetoric; negotiations were going on through intermediaries, and most people knew it. Nevertheless, many faculty members interpreted the position of the blacks as needlessly intransigent. The black separatism issue had not been well received by many in the university community either—especially the incident involving those tables in the student union that had been claimed as black territory. Blacks moved around the campus in groups and were never found fraternizing with whites. This occurrence was upsetting to most faculty and students.

These issues, and others, created an atmosphere of tension that threatened to come to a crisis on Wednesday, March 12, when the university faculty was scheduled to meet. But when the day came, the faculty adopted a resolution supporting the integrity of the adjudicatory machinery of the Conduct Board, and the situation continued to seethe, with neither confrontation nor resolution.

At three A.M. on the morning of Friday, April 18, persons still unknown threw a burning cross on the porch of the black girls' cooperative. Responding to a call, the campus safety patrol reached the coop, where the fire was stamped out. What exactly the campus safety patrol did at the scene of the cross burning is not clear, but apparently all officers covering the incident withdrew, ostensibly on other business, leaving no protection at the coop. Much later, a guard was established, but by that time the blacks had lost whatever confidence they may have had in campus protection. This feeling was to be exacerbated as campus officials, while strongly deploring the incident, referred to it as a "thoughtless prank." To the blacks the symbolism of the event was as powerful as if someone had burned a Mogen David in front of a Jewish fraternity. Had such an event occurred, the blacks reasoned, all the powers of the university would have been brought to bear, and the cries of outrage would have been mighty indeed. As it was, the somewhat cavalier attitudes of the university seemed still another reflection of institutional racism, less open, perhaps, than in the occasional group of white boys who had shouted "nigger" at black girls, but racism nevertheless.

As word of the cross burning spread among the blacks, they assembled at the coop to decide on action to protect their women. The defense of their own kind: this was to become a central symbol for the blacks during the events that followed. As for their choice of target—the student union at Willard Straight Hall—this was in part dictated by the dramatic possibilities implicit in the fact that Parents' Weekend had begun and the opportunity to demonstrate before thousands of parents was tactically so tempting that rumors had been circulating that some group would seize some building somewhere regardless of the issue. How significant a role the rumors played in the deliberations of the blacks is not known, but the tactical impact of the seizure was clear. But it is clear that in deciding to take over the student union, the blacks were intent only on giving an emphatic warning to the campus to "get off our backs"; they were not concerned with specific demands. Indeed, the original intent was to seize the building for one day only before surrendering it peaceably.

At six A.M. on Saturday, April 19, the blacks marched into Willard Straight Hall, ordered service personnel preparing for the day's activities to remove themselves, expelled from guest rooms in the loft a number of visiting parents, and locked up the building.

News of the seizure soon spread throughout the campus; by eight A.M. everyone knew that the university was in another confrontation. For many of the students, particularly those at either end of the political spectrum, having an audience of parents probably served as a stimulus to action. The conservative students tend to be concentrated in a small number of "lily-white" fraternities. One of these, Delta Upsilon, is known as the "jock house" because of its unusual number of athletes. It is also one of the most WASPish houses and at that time included no Negro members. Around nine in the morning, about fifteen to twenty DU members attempted to break into Willard Straight Hall, and some eight or nine succeeded in getting in before a group of SDS people prevented the rest from entering. While a good deal of pushing, shoving, and arguing was going on outside, inside there was a brief but violent battle between the blacks and the DU men. Three whites and one black were injured but not seriously. The battle ended with the expulsion of the fraternity boys, but the blacks, badly shaken, announced that any other attack would be met by mounting escalation of force. SDS members, standing outside in sympathy with the blacks, rejected a proposal to seize another building and maintained a picket around the entire Straight to show their support.

The DU attack can be, and was, interpreted in various ways. From the viewpoint of the blacks, it represented a university attempt to oust them from the building. The campus patrol was supposed to have been guarding the building to prevent entry. Therefore the fact that the DU people had gotten in was all too easily understood by the blacks as administrative complicity, rather than what it probably was—a spontaneous, self-organized attempt by fraternity boys. For their part, the DU men insisted that they had entered the building to engage in discussion with black athletes inside and that there was no intent to recapture the building. (There is no evidence, however, that any black athletes were ever involved in the seizure.) The DU men claimed that they went in empty-handed; the blacks insisted that the athletes came in with clubs.

Following this incident, the campus gave itself up to an orgy of rumors. Throughout the day the tale was circulated that armed vigilante groups were preparing to mount an attack on the Straight. Inside the union the blacks received continuous telephone messages about these vigilantes. By Saturday afternoon—according to the testimony of the blacks and the administrators in telephone contact with them—the occupiers were in a state of terrible tension. It was then that they decided to bring in guns to protect themselves. In the end, they were to have thirteen rifles and two shotguns.

Saturday night passed quietly, but the tension throughout the campus was approaching a critical point. By Sunday morning Cornell administrators had decided that it would be necessary to end the occupation of the Straight at almost any cost.

That the occupation of the Straight was a precipitous act, probably triggered by the cross burning, is attested to, first, by the length of time it took the blacks to formulate demands; and, second, by the relatively flimsy nature of the demands. By Saturday afternoon three had emerged from Willard Straight, of which one was subsequently withdrawn. The first demand called for a nullification of the three reprimands handed down by the Conduct Committee after the demonstrations of December; the second called for a full investigation and report to the Afro-American Society of the cross-burning incident. That the blacks would take such serious steps for such modest demands indicates their state of fear and tension. But this was never communicated to the campus, except to those in the administration, Dean Robert Miller especially, who were in direct contact with them. With the latter, the blacks entered into a six-point agreement to end the Straight occupation. It included a commitment to call a full faculty meeting and recommend that the reprimands be declared null and void.

However, the occupiers of the Straight were still determined to demonstrate to Cornell whites that they were no longer sitting ducks. So it was that, despite pressure from administrators for a decorous exit, the blacks proceeded to make a dramatic exit, brandishing their weapons. It soon became convenient for the shocked white majority of the university to look upon this flourish as a new escalation in student activism; while campus after campus had experienced confrontation, it was argued, this was the first time that students had taken up guns. It was within this context that Cornell arrived at a new level of internal tension on Monday, April 21.

The sight of armed students marching across their campus was too much for the overwhelming majority of the faculty. Unable to understand, or ignorant of, the black students' side of the story, their immediate reaction on Monday was one of bitter hostility to any compromise or accommodation of black demands. Their antagonism focused on the six-point agreement reached between the administration and the blacks. Some forty members of the faculty, largely in the government and history departments, signed a statement declaring that they would resign if the reprimands were nullified at the faculty meeting called for Monday afternoon.

Tension increased during the day as opposition to nullification crystallized in the faculty. What the reaction of the blacks would be to a refusal to nullify was unclear, but there was an unspoken and widespread fear that Cornell might be headed toward a shootout. In these circumstances President Perkins called a convocation in Barton Hall just before the university faculty meeting. Some 10,000 students, faculty, and staff assembled to hear an innocuous twenty minute statement by the President that left issues more undefined than before.

There had been an expectation that presidential leadership was to be asserted. Instead, in an atmosphere of diffuse fear and anger in which the focused hostility of the government and history departments stood out, the faculty assembled at four P.M. in unprecedented numbers. The meeting began with a report by Dean of the Faculty Robert Miller, who introduced a formal motion calling for nullification of the reprimands. The Dean's assessment was that the danger to human life at Cornell was real and had to be avoided, even at the cost of failing to sustain the authority of the adjudicatory machinery, the Conduct Board. His approach was rejected by the faculty. Instead, a substitute motion was voted that upheld the legitimacy of the adjudicatory machinery and took no action on the nullification of the reprimands. Continuing for over four hours of intricate parliamentary maneuvers, the faculty meeting showed that the majority was adamantly opposed to nullification, but there was also an obdurate, vocal minority supporting the blacks or concerned with the consequences of refusal to nullify. President Perkins had little political capital at this meeting, despite his earlier proclamation of limited emergency—a statement that anyone carrying guns on university property would be suspended summarily, and that disruptive demonstrations would lead to immediate suspensions. Nevertheless, he was able to achieve minimal consensus with a resolution calling for the initiation of discussions between the Faculty Council and the Afro-American Society and calling for another full faculty meeting.

Dean Miller now tendered his resignation, stating that by refusing to vote on his motion, the faculty was repudiating his estimate of the situation. He was promptly given a standing ovation, which neatly illustrated the faculty's dilemma. The members respected him and wanted peace, but they felt it necessary to refuse to make concessions under what they saw as the threat of armed coercion. As the meeting ended at 8:15 and the faculty departed for long-delayed dinners, there was the sense that no solution had been found and that the campus was entering a new and more dangerous situation.

On Monday evening an SDS meeting was attended by 2,500, but it ended inconclusively. SDS was waiting for the blacks.

By Tuesday morning the campus was in chaos. Many classes did not meet, and in those that did, the only topic of discussion was the confrontation. The university leadership, seeking desperately to remedy a deteriorating situation, consulted the deans of the colleges and proposed meetings of college faculties and the beginning of a broadly based discussion at all levels. The intent was to structure free-floating campus anxieties into organized meetings geared to a search for solutions. In the leadership vacuum created by the conflict between the administration's willingness to make concessions and an obdurate faculty, the administration sought only to keep a dialogue going. The fear of bloodshed was everywhere.

At noon an ephemeral organization named "The Con-cerned Faculty," consisting largely of elements supporting the blacks, convened for several hours. Urged on by mem-bers of the Afro-American Society, "The Concerned Faculty" was unable to decide on anything more than gestures of solidarity. Twenty-six of those attending agreed to seize a building if necessary, while some 60-odd announced their willingness to strike.

Meanwhile, at meetings of the faculties of the various colleges, change in campus opinion began to be felt. The colleges of Arts and Sciences and Home Economics voted to recommend nullification of the Conduct Board's reprimands, and at its 7 P.M. meeting, the Faculty Council did the same, while calling for another meeting of the faculty for Wednes-day noon. But several other faculties were still determined to maintain business as usual.

That same Tuesday student opinion on campus began crys-tallizing around a call by SDS and the Inter-Fraternity Coun-cil for a teach-in at Barton Hall, the largest building on campus. By early evening thousands of students had moved to the hall. Like the faculty, they too seemed intent on avoid-ing violence between the blacks and other forces. Some-where between 8,000 and 10,000 people gathered, and as the evening went on, a consensus emerged that it was vital for Cornell students to remain in the building and act as a pres-sure group on the Cornell faculty, which was scheduled to meet the next day, Wednesday, April 23. SDS speakers pro-posed that the students declare they had seized the building, thereby defying President Perkins' new regulation prohibit-ing such actions. Only a handful objected, and later in the evening Perkins condoned the occupation of Barton Hall, though he persisted in defining it as a teach-in rather than as the seizure the students had declared it to be. This "legal" anomaly continued through the night. Thousands made prep-arations for the all-night meeting; a collection was taken, and soon sandwiches and drinks were being passed out among the teeming mass of students.

As the evening wore on, students organized according to their colleges to lobby faculty members for their vote on

Wednesday. Around the edges of the hall there were dozens of meetings involving tens and hundreds of students. At 3 A.M. meetings were still continuing; they included not only groups from different colleges, but also various ad hoc committees on the press, particularly the *Cornell Daily Sun.* One large group of biology students was attempting to deal with the problem of a professor who refused to cancel a quiz scheduled for the next day. The mood in Barton Hall was tensely hopeful; that such an incredible outpouring of students could take place showed that student sentiment had shifted to the blacks, although it was less clear whether the shift had occurred for substantive reasons or because of the fear of violence.

On Wednesday, April 23, the students were wakened by a banjo ensemble, and the speech making began again in Barton Hall. Elsewhere on the campus hundreds of meetings were taking place as faculty members were visited by student lobbyists.

Soon after the faculty meeting was gaveled into session by Provost Dale Cornson, it became evident that a shift had occurred among the members. Despite hardline speeches by government and history faculty members, a motion to nullify was replaced by a second motion that not only called for nullification but also for restructuring the controversial judicial system in cooperation "with the Afro-American Society and other appropriate groups." The substitute was introduced by Professor Clinton Rossiter, who had only two days earlier signed the statement threatening resignation if the reprimands were nullified. The considerable discussion within the faculty showed that the government and history departments remained the main opponents to nullification, while the remainder of the faculty had shifted under pressure of the presence of the thousands of students in Barton Hall. In this respect Nobel physicist Hans Bethe expressed most clearly the sentiments of the faculty. Pointing out that, as the moderates had moved to the SDS left, it was necessary to win back the moderates by reversing the decision, thereby — it was to be hoped — isolating the radicals.

The resolution calling for nullification and restructuring

the judicial system was carried by a voice vote of something on the order of three or four to one. The faculty then accepted a resolution intended to express their solidarity with the students. This resolution read:

> This Faculty declares to the student body: "We hear you, we care, we are trying to understand you, and we want, together with you, to do something."

The Faculty Council was thereupon instructed to meet with a representative group of students to create a "broadly based body designed to recommend to the whole community our future course of action at Cornell." It was the combination of these two resolutions that laid the basis for the proposed restructuring of the university.

A thousand faculty members then moved to Barton Hall, where they received a standing ovation. The faculty action demonstrated to the students the latter's influence on the decision-making process; from this point emphasis shifted to the second resolution on restructuring the university.

As the faculty arrived, Eric Evans, vice president of the Afro-American Society, was talking. President Perkins came to the podium where, according to Evans, he put his arm around him, smiled in fatherly fashion, and said, "Sit down, I want to talk." Evans refused to surrender the microphone. Nothing better demonstrated the students' new mood than the hilarious cheering that broke out when Evans informed them of this exchange. While Perkins fidgeted uncomfortably on the floor with the students and faculty, Evans continued a leisurely review of events leading up to the Willard Straight seizure. When he finished, Perkins spoke and was followed by a succession of others. Slowly the Barton Hall meeting achieved a catharsis from the tensions of the past five days. By 5 P.M. the teach-in had ended. Cornell now entered a new phase ostensibly dedicated to a restructuring of the university.

A series of meetings and discussions in the next few days centered around how best to effect this restructuring. At a large meeting in Barton Hall the idea was conceived of forming a constituent assembly as the restructuring body of the university. It was hoped that this body would provide the core for a new and more "meaningful" university community—a community which would be relevant to all the diverse interests and needs of its various members.

The faculty met and endorsed the formation of a constituent assembly, the function of which would be to make recommendations concerning the governance of the university rather than to become its governing body. The constituent assembly was to be composed of representatives from the administration, faculty, students, nonacademic staff, and individual "interest groups," with the faculty and student components based proportionally on department membership. Thus the constituent assembly—the hope for a new crisis-free order—which met during the summer of 1969, was a body with no power of its own, with no designated channel for its recommendations, and with representation based on the department—the most conservative structure in the university, which the assembly was intended to reform.

General campus reaction to the formation of the constituent assembly was optimistic (which may have been more the result of wishful thinking than of rational analysis). However, campus activists, who were well accustomed to having their recommendations ignored because they were not backed by power, were skeptical about the efficacy of the assembly in bringing about significant changes in the university. Accordingly, Students for a Democratic Society and the Afro-American Society, now renamed the Black Liberation Front (BLF), decided to ignore the assembly and did not elect representatives to it.

An Assessment of Five Years of Student Activism

When all is said and done about Cornell—or, indeed, most other American universities—the history of accomplishment with respect to structural change has remained negligible. After dozens of minor skirmishes with the students and several major ones, including one that placed the university on the brink of total disruption, no fundamental issues with respect to the distribution of powers within the university have been resolved. A few students have been placed on lesser committees; students are listened to somewhat more seriously than they were before Berkeley; but no change in the distribution of power or in the involvement of students in the determination of the inner life of the institution has been obtained.

Even the "new experiment" much vaunted by the campus liberals, the constituent assembly, hardly represents a startling innovation. Essentially a consultative talkfest, its deliberate structuring upon representation from the existing departments of the university has meant that whatever power it does contain flows from existing structures. Rather than innovating with new bases of representation — for example, representation based upon competitive programs for the restructuring of the university — representatives come from existing structures with vested interests. The prospects for reform were indeed small.

Thus, unless something else changes in the system, it is highly unlikely that the constituent assembly or any of the other minor changes can possibly satisfy the student radicals, *since the preconditions for student disaffection remain untouched.* Under these circumstances, continued and probably increased levels of student activism can be expected. Cornell entered its second century of existence in conflict, and it appears that the major portion of the first decade of its second century will have to be devoted to dealing with student activism. And until more substantive changes can occur, the likelihood is that high levels of student activism can be expected to continue.

Sit-In at Stanford

On Thursday, May 9, 1968, the Associated Press wire service released a story that was picked up by newspapers from Boston to Los Angeles.

Topless dancer Vicki Drake has won a preliminary election for presidency of the Stanford University student body. In an unprecedented turnout Wednesday, the students voted 1,575 for Miss Drake and 1,252 for runner-up Dennis Hayes.... The photos of her unclad, 38–22–36 figure, which Miss Drake and a number of her supporters tacked up early in her campaign, disappeared in less than an hour and reportedly now are lodged on the walls in and around the campus. Vicki declared after the victory that she had run for office only because of her interest in Stanford.

This news could easily have led the American public to believe that the only change taking place on university campuses across the country was an escalation from panty raids to topless coeds. In contrast to the violence and sit-ins at Columbia University, taking place at the same time, the news must have relieved many people who had begun to wonder what had turned the "silent" student generation of the previous decade into political and moral militants. A less reasuring response to the wire service release appeared in the *Stanford Daily* of the same day. The campus newspaper presented a different conception of what was newsworthy at Stanford that week.

281

Fifty-six and one-half hours after they walked into the Old Union with only themselves for support, over 650 student demonstrators peacefully departed last night with an unprecedented vote of support for their demands by the Stanford faculty.

The Academic Council, assistant professors and above, met yesterday afternoon and early evening for three and a half hours, and recommended after heated and emotional debate, that the proposed suspension of seven Central Intelligence Agency demonstrators be set aside by President Wallace Sterling. The Council also asked, in a vote of 284 to 245, that no students be penalized as a result of the current demonstrations in the Old Union. The Council strongly urged the demonstrators to leave the building.

The Council recommendations, which passed largely with votes from the humanities, sciences, and medical school faculties, supported a comprehensive plan for reformed judicial structures which the Committee of 15 created early Wednesday morning.

Affluent campuses such as Stanford are large enough to support both the absurd dramatics of topless dancers and the confrontational politics of militant demonstrators. Although the wire service release tells a great deal about the media's idea of what interests the American public, the fact was that at Stanford Miss Drake provided only the frosting on the cake; center stage was occupied by a much more serious drama.

Causes—Legal and Symbolic

The issue at Stanford was not the invasion of the Old Union, the destruction of campus property, or freedom run rampant. The strategy was not violent insurrection or arson. No attempts were made to fashion goals for a new society. The broad and underlying issue, as all concerned knew, was the measure of student power on campus. The discipline of the student activists, no less than the results of the sit-in, demonstrated the social realities of student power better and more dramatically than could any administrative actions or faculty resolutions.

In this sense Provost Richard Lyman was correct when he stated that the struggle had become symbolic and that it concerned not only setting aside the conviction of seven anti-CIA demonstrators, but also the structure of university relations per se. In the rush to politeness that followed the faculty resolution essentially supporting the students' demands, this aspect of Provost Lyman's assessment was minimized by formal proposals asserting faculty respect for Stanford's administrative authorities. Yet the fact remains that the settlement, which involved faculty support and administrative acquiescence, increased legitimation and recognition of students' real power. The demonstration offered justification for the belief that students have the right to participate in university decision making.

Perhaps the most accurate assessment of symbolic and long-range goals involved in the sit-in was given voice by Professor of Religion Michael Novak. In response to the administrative officials' pleas to students to meet and reason together, Professor Novak replied during the height of the demonstration on Tuesday:

> I commend both the wisdom and the courage of the students who are sitting-in at the Old Union. They show political wisdom, because they rightly understand that the issue is one of power: the power of students to determine their own affairs. Where one group has almost all the power in an institution, one must be suspicious of appeals to "reason." For "reason" in such contexts usually means docility to the way those in power perceive things. Students have very little power in the university; hence their views are not often taken to "be realistic." Realism is defined by those who exercise or defend present power. By sitting-in, however, the students create a new factor in the situation, which the "realistic" must take seriously. In this way—and often in this way alone—do human beings make progress in genuine communication. The old "realism" must be altered. The new realism must take into account a new consciousness and a new power. The students, sitting-in today, by their courage are creating this new consciousness and this new power. Many of us are grateful for their creative act.
>
> I would like to call attention to the fact that the substantive issue amid all this debate is not legal or procedural. It concerns the university's ties to the CIA and to other government agencies. What do we students, faculty, and administration wish our university's qualities to be? The seven convicted students

should not be penalized, they should be commended, for awakening us to Stanford's moral responsibilities when no one else cared. That is what education is all about.

The fifty-six-hour confrontation had various causes and occurred against a background of events that contributed to the specific forms that developed. Long-range and immediate problems, played against a series of on-campus and off-campus issues, created tactical considerations that uniquely contributed to the unfolding of the Stanford demonstration.

The immediate cause of the Stanford demonstration was a legal one, having to do with the issue of double jeopardy — whether students, having charges dismissed against them after due process, can be retried on the same grounds. This legalistic "injustice" provided the basis for the student cause and broadened support within the student body even when the tactics of the radical students were not endorsed. Grievances concerning local issues rather than community or national political problems triggered the Stanford sit-in.

Underlying the immediate issue was the more general question of the nature of justice and of student equities in the university. Like many other high-quality universities, Stanford placed responsibility for student conduct with faculty committees while reserving ultimate decisions to the administration. In challenging a specific legal decision involving the retrial of students, the Stanford demonstrators came to grips, albeit inchoately, with the generic relationship existing between different units of the university — a triad composed of the faculty, the administration, and the student body as a collective entity.

At the source of the dispute were broader issues related to the university's position in the larger social structure, a system with which many students have become disenchanted. The Stanford demonstration illustrates the process whereby national political issues — which cannot be effectively confronted by student militants — become translated into local issues. Without conscious intent or forethought, the Stanford demonstration revealed how an issue of breadth and distance such as the Vietnam war is made a meaningful local issue. Despite demonstrations, silent vigils, teach-ins, mobilizations, and other activities that have involved the energies of many college students, the Vietnam war has always been difficult to confront within the university. Proposals, for example, to suspend normal instruction and devote classes to discussions of the Vietnam war have always been combated on the grounds that such action will not resolve the war. The implicit point is that the formal academic program of the university is as irrelevant to the war as the war is to the university's academic program.

Even picketing the campus recruiters of the Central Intelligence Agency or Dow Chemical is a distant event for most students. However, when the forms of justice are violated in a normative sense in response to such picketing (through what is considered to be "double jeopardy"), then the issue of an unpopular war is translated into a basis for student demonstration and obtains wide support in the student body even if many disagree with specific tactics.

Before discussing the sit-in itself, consideration must be given the background and peripheral causal phenomena that helped determine the degree of militance of the demonstration and the social solidarity that was exhibited.

First, it should be noted that the Black Student Union (BSU) won a victory several weeks earlier. The BSU, demanding increased admission of and participation by black students, used threats to achieve its demands—which included hiring more Negro faculty and administrators as well as black supervision over entering Negro students. The resolution of these demands in favor of the black students provided an example of the possibilities inherent in other student actions. However, the demonstrators failed to consider the limited nature of the black students' demands. These demands, after all, were for separatism rather than for domination. What they also left out of the reckoning was that the Black Student Union had a base of support in the Negro community, particularly in the East Palo Alto ghetto area. As one of the demonstrators observed during one sit-in meeting, the action of the black students bore an implicit threat that "a group of East Palo Alto studs would invade the campus" much as had been done at San Francisco State. The absence of such community support has become noticeable in recent struggles, not only at Stanford, but on other campuses as well. In any event, the tactics and the demands of the Black Student Union provided a model for the Stanford demonstrators as the black-power movement has provided a model for student activists in general.

Second, a general politicalization of the student body had taken place in 1968. In California widespread hostility to the Vietnam war had given birth to the Peace and Freedom Party, which provided an outlet for left-oriented students. The campaign to support Senator Eugene McCarthy for the presidency had "turned on" other students for whom the politics of the Peace and Freedom Party were either too militant or too marginal. The McCarthy campaign provided a legitimate outlet for students disaffected with the war and searching for a critical stance in keeping with their moderate inclinations. Although the momentum of student participation in presidential politics declined slightly with President Johnson's self-removal from the campaign (as on other campuses, there were widespread spontaneous manifestations of collective delight on the Stanford campus when the president made his announcement), that momentum was not completely lost. Since the Stanford demonstration was triggered by the suspension of students for picketing CIA recruiters, the relationship between national political questions and campus issues is clear. Throughout the sit-in many "McCarthy for President" buttons and some Kennedy buttons were worn. For a number of students the sit-in seemed a natural extension of the national campaign to either end the war in Vietnam or limit that war by eliminating the most conservative candidates from office.

A third cause of the demonstration was the phenomenon of in loco parentis — that set of informal norms that absolves the college student in America from the usual responsibilities to law and authority. Students respond in a highly ambiguous way to in loco parentis. On the one hand they fully realize the advantages of differential treatment at the hands of police and university officials; but on the other hand they resent this special paternalism as precisely what must be eliminated if students are to receive equal treatment in university affairs.

More than one Stanford student, both in writing and in speaking, alluded to in loco parentis and insisted upon equal treatment before the law even if such treatment resulted in fewer "superficial" advantages. The President of the Associated Students of Stanford University (ASSU), Cesare Massarenti, in the Monday noon rally which sparked the initial burst of protest, flatly opposed in loco parentis. However, even if the students did not particularly relish their protected position, the administration felt responsible for them as quasilegitimate offspring. In a university comprised of upper-middle-class young people, combined parental influence is sizable, particularly in the state of California. Parents would hardly take kindly to the administration's sending police to beat the skulls of their children. The administration had to manipulate a rapidly maturing student process of politicalization while serving its inherited legacy, both financial and ideological, as the guardians of errant as well as aberrant youth. As a result of this contradiction, the administration was unable to call upon the public law to the fullest degree. It had to grant privileges and prerogatives – including the forcible entrance and take-over of one of their own buildings as the headquarters for a student sit-in.

The students, for their part, although they resented the system of in loco parentis and the concept of obedience before the abstract paternal rule of the university president or provost, were shrewd enough and capable enough to make use of the contradictions of in loco parentis. Their attempt to gain equal treatment for students as members of an adult citizen population made use of the special privileges and prerogatives enjoyed by students since medieval Europe. A basic cause of the sit-in, in loco parentis also served as a protective covering for the students during the sit-in.

Currents and Cross-Currents

On November 1, 1967, fifty to a hundred students participated in a demonstration against a recruiting agent of the Central Intelligence Agency. The demonstration was prototypical of hundreds of confrontations on campuses throughout the nation between antiwar students on one side and recruiters for the CIA, Dow Chemical, and military programs on the other. In these demonstrations students usually attempted to impede the recruitment process and inevitably came into conflict with the university's administrators. This is what happened at Stanford.

At first the students attempted to occupy the west wing of Encina Hall to prevent the potential interviewees for the day from reaching the CIA recruiter. However, after Dean of Students Joel Smith informed them that they were violating university policy on demonstrations, they withdrew to the surrounding grassy area to continue their protest without disrupting any of the interviewing going on within. Ten days later Dean Smith brought charges against ten participants. The case was first heard by the judicial council of the Associated Students of Stanford University (ASSU). After a considerable length of time the council found all ten students not guilty on the grounds that the university policy on demonstrations was too general and therefore unenforceable.

This decision did not go unchallenged. The not-guilty decision rendered on February 19, 1968, was followed by a letter on February 21 from Dean Joel Smith to Professor Howard R. Williams, the chairman of the Interim Judicial Body (IJB), in which exception was taken to the decision of the ASSU judicial council. A copy of the notice of appeal was sent to the student respondents, and a hearing was granted by the IJB. Disciplinary action against three of the students was withdrawn, but a hearing was scheduled for the remaining seven for April 30, 1968. This faculty board hearing was held de novo—that is, entirely anew, without reference to the previous ASSU hearing. The grounds for so doing were the refusal of the student judicial council to surrender possession of the tapes of the previous hearing. As a consequence the seven students were again tried on exactly the same charges. The IJB ruled the university policy on campus demonstrations to be entirely enforceable and therefore the decision rendered by the ASSU judicial council to have been an erroneous one.

Professor Howard R. Williams outlined the IJB's decision.

Each respondent registered at Stanford University was suspended. The extension of the previously scheduled hearing by the IJB prevented final disposition of the matter until after registration for and substantial completion of the current quarter; therefore the suspension was not to take effect until the end of the current quarter. The suspended students would then be deprived of the privileges of registering for course credit, of attending classes or working in university laboratories, or of receiving financial aid. The period of suspension was to terminate on September 1, 1968, for five respondents; for the other two, because of earlier violation of university policy on campus demonstrations, suspension would terminate on January 1, 1969. Each student was placed on disciplinary probation for the balance of the second quarter of 1968 and would remain on probation for the first two quarters for which he registered after his suspension period expired.

The IJB decision set the stage for the student demonstration. On Friday, May 3, Stanford President Wallace Sterling and other officials of the university met with Cesare Massarenti, President of ASSU, and other student leaders. Student leaders did not think this meeting productive and called a rally at White Plaza, the center of most student demonstrations and political gatherings at Stanford.

Only about 150 students attended the Friday noon meeting, but it quickly moved toward action when a proposal to shift to Building 10, where President Sterling's office was located, was made by Marc Sapir, one of the students proposed for suspension by the IJB. The students temporarily sat down in protest in front of President Sterling's office but decided to plan an action on a larger scale for the following week.

The tone of the coming demonstration could be sensed in the words of some student speakers. ASSU President Massarenti, who had been active in the 1962 student protests in Italy, called for construction of a mass movement around the issue of the suspension. A veteran of Berkeley's Free Speech Movement, Steve Weissman, foreshadowed a key element of the confrontation about to take place. Emphasizing that a demonstration had to be sufficiently militant "so that students have to choose sides," Weissman argued that "the best thing Stanford students do is to be concerned." Thus, "veterans" of past student struggles provided ideological support for events to come.

The student protest was given its first definitive form in front of President Sterling's office. Four basic demands were formulated in the give-and-take discussion that characterized student-protest decision making during the entire course of the demonstration. The four demands, which were iterated and reiterated during the subsequent few days, were:

1. The IJB decision calling for suspension of the seven students should be set aside.

2. The IJB must be disbanded immediately.

3. In its place, an appeals board should be created, composed of four faculty members and four student members, with a law student—selected by the eight—as chairman.

4. The appeals board should consider appeals only from defendants.

What is striking about these demands is that only the first was concerned with the suspended students; and that tacked on to this demand were proposals for reshaping the judicial procedures of Stanford with respect to student behavior. Implicit in the third demand was the issue of student power—the relative weight to be given to students and faculty in disciplinary procedures. Also entailed was the termination of the president's power of review of these decisions. The students wanted decisions to be final and residual in the proposed new appeals body.

The students demanded that President Sterling meet them at a noon demonstration at White Plaza on Monday, May 6, to respond to their four-point program. Having made these decisions, the students adjourned their brief sit-down and moved into preparatory actions for the Monday rally.

The IJB action and the Friday meeting warned the campus community that action was forthcoming. In an attempt to head off potential student action, different parts of the campus establishment began to firm up attitudes and positions, most of which appeared in the Monday morning issue of the *Stanford Daily*.

Perhaps the most serious statement issued from the President, J. E. Wallace Sterling. He pointed out: "Issues this complex are not going to be resolved in White Memorial Plaza, this noon or any other noon. Issues this ambiguous are not going to be resolved in answer to an ultimatum." Indicating that the orderly process of judicial review would be worked out by the campus community to the satisfaction of all but a few "zealots" of the "far Left" and "far Right," the President made a shrewd observation, the implication of which he was apparently unable to follow through. He pointed out that the issues themselves had changed a good deal. "When the problem first arose and until fairly recently, it was viewed as a controversy about the judicial system. It has become clear in the last few months, as the result of hard work by the members of the Committee of 15, that we must simultaneously resolve closely linked issues of rule-making and judging. Two different kinds of bodies, one to make rules and another to pass on alleged violations of the rules, are now being discussed in the Committee of 15. Both kinds of bodies are intended to include students."

This is as close as any member of the administration came to acknowledging that the major issue was, in fact, student power and not simply judicial reform, but the President negated his own observation by concentrating the remainder of his statement on juridical aspects with no further mention of the judgmental features of the crisis. Perhaps the most significant feature of the statement was his conclusion when he had to face the question of the anti-CIA demonstrators directly. On these specifics he reserved both rule making and judging as a prerogative of presidential office. President Sterling excluded not only the students from a decision-making role on this sensitive issue, but the faculty as well. He frankly stated that "the Interim Judicial Body's recommendations in the CIA demonstration case are now before me. Accordingly, I am inviting each of the defendants in that case individually to present any facts he may wish to bring to my attention before I decide to accept, modify, or reject the recommendations of the Interim Judicial Body."

As if anticipating that his position would not be accepted, and that he would need the support or at least the legitimation of the rest of the community, Sterling closed by stating that "a meeting of the Academic Council will be convened for 4:15 P.M. on Wednesday, May 8th." Sterling also used his open letter to invite the ASSU president and one other student officer to appear at the faculty meeting on Wednesday to present their claims.

The student body's attitude toward the need for overtly militant actions was undoubtedly reinforced by the agreement on the question of procedure of spokesmen for the faculty with the administration. For the involved faculty seemed satisfied, if not enthusiastic, about the performance of IJB. The quasi-official campus faculty spokesmen also seemed even less informed than the administration about the collision course the school had embarked upon. Law faculty response only hardened student attitudes. Typical statements appearing in the *Stanford Daily* were those of William F. Baxter, Professor of Law, speaking for the "conservative" faculty, and Kenneth J. Arrow and Leonard I. Schiff, speaking for the "liberals." Professor Baxter pointed out that, in his opinion, "on the afternoon of Monday, May 6th, serious damage may be done to the generally successful pattern of student-faculty-administration negotiations, over university government that has prevailed at Stanford for several years." While he expressed his hope that the damage could be averted, he did not indicate what the successful pattern of negotiations had been in the past or what was wrong in the present. Indeed, he went on to indicate a rather wide permanent divergence of opinion among these three bodies — administration, faculty, and students.

Professor Baxter felt that the demands of the students — to set aside the conviction of the anti-CIA demonstrators and establishing a new judicial body containing a large number of student representatives — were threats to the community and that even the students were not really convinced or even hoped that they would be accepted. He concluded by saying: "In any sizable community one must expect and cope with some member or persons who seek trouble, and even violence, for its own sake or for their own personal aggrandizement. Demonstrating in support of demands known to be unacceptable is a tactic of such persons. If they are very few in number, the processes of negotiation and accommodation can continue. If their number is large, such processes fail, and the community must accept its destruction or government by dictation and force." In this way a key member of the faculty indicated his disbelief in the sincerity of student demands and his corresponding belief that any mass action would somehow entail anarchy and destroy law and order.

The attitudes of the liberal faculty also did little to encourage students to believe that a genuine assessment of their demands would be made. The statement by Kenneth J. Arrow and Leonard I. Schiff, both with national academic reputations, read: "Great issues are at stake that can be settled to the satisfaction of students, faculty, and administration. To accomplish what is possible, time is required and reasonable discussion must be continued. Open discussions in White Plaza and meetings like that between representatives of students, faculty, and administration on Friday afternoon have their parts to play in arriving at settlements. Demands accompanied by deadlines, sit-ins, and forcible destruction of academic activities do not; they are destructive of the good will that exists in the overwhelming majority of the three constituencies." The statement by these two influential figures concluded by pointing out that, although they spoke for themselves, "we are confident that we represent nearly all of our faculty colleagues in urging patience, and abstention from the use of force. We believe that any other course will merely delay the institution of the changes in student-faculty-administration relationships that all agree are needed and toward which all are working."

Since no part of the administration or the faculty would accept the idea of setting aside a judicial decision made by faculty members, a hardening of student attitudes over the weekend was inevitable.

The Committee of 15 (more commonly called the C-15), which had been organized almost three years earlier to deal with a variety of questions involving issues of student participation in decision making at Stanford, was composed of five administrators, five faculty members, and five students. The

C-15 had performed some useful work, but if its production were to be judged by normal faculty standards, it would have been refused tenure. While most of the reasons given for its lack of action were reasonable, the fact remained that student judicial procedures had remained unresolved. The IJB decision therefore focused attention and criticism on the Committee of 15.

Tom Forestenzer, a student member of the Committee of 15 for two and a half years, represented the dominant student view of the situation—or at least the viewpoint of enough students to bring about a demonstration. His statement is of particular interest because in the name of the students he gave vent to the sort of attitudes that made a confrontation inevitable, whatever the ideological bases of those who came to be the sit-in leaders. Mr. Forestenzer espoused vigorous combat with the existing system and support for the potential student action, whatever such action might involve—"not as a result of the recent outrageous IJB decision, but because the IJB itself is a perfectly accurate representation of how the administration has systematically excluded students from any positions of power and responsibility over student affairs." He noted that the "I" in IJB stood for "interim"—"a useful word for those in the administration who hope that student demands for such radical innovations as trial by jury of one's peers are temporary and sporadic outbursts of fickle youth. The IJB has been interim for no less than three years. During those three years I was personally involved in several efforts to establish a plain old JB, with half student-faculty representation."

After accusing the C-15, particularly the administration delegation to that committee, of procrastination, Mr. Forestenzer went on to the core of the issue, the exploitation of students per se, and not simply the suspension of seven of their number.

> Behind this intricate quadrille are harsh realities which I now enjoy expressing. The sentence passed on the CIA demonstrators is vicious, but it is no more brutal than the year-to-year, day-to-day treatment of students at Stanford whenever they rock

the boat. Every time an interim solution is adopted (which is the same as saying that students are barred from choosing their own representatives to such vital panels as the IJB or the SES or any presidential advisory board), that patronizing Dean or Provost says: "Golly gee, I wish we could do this because I'm really on your side, but we're in a bind." What he is really saying is, "Go to hell."

The weekend at Stanford was a busy one for a small number of administrators and campus militants; both groups were preparing for action. Since several of the students proposed for suspension were graduate assistants belonging to the local chapter of the American Federation of Teachers, AFT officers were busy conducting a telephone poll of its members on Saturday, May 4. It was decided to support those AFT members who were to be suspended, but there was less agreement as to what should be done in the case of a sit-in. This decision was left to the individual members of the union.

On Sunday evening a meeting of the students was organized to plan for the Monday demonstration. This meeting, itself the product of a mounting wave of agitation following the Friday meeting, attracted over 200 students. A number of key decisions shaped subsequent events. The four demands formulated on Friday were re-endorsed, and students agreed that the demonstration would hold firmly to all four demands and not be satisfied with only the first. A Tactics Committee was elected, composed of eight graduate students and one junior; it included students in general studies (the one undergraduate), political science, mathematics, law, sociology, communications, medicine, and Latin American studies. The weighting of the Tactics Committee toward the graduate students, although the electors present were predominantly undergraduates, indicated a shared deference toward the greater experience of the graduates.

A curious note of the Sunday meeting was the presence of Willard Wyman, Associate Dean of Students. Wyman was recognized by the students present, and discussion centered on whether he should be permitted to remain. Ultimately no action was taken to remove him from the meeting—a decision that served as a prededent for student attitudes in future meetings and actions. These meetings displayed strikingly democratic characteristics during the entire period of the demonstration.

Monday, May 6, found the campus girding its loins for battle. Students arriving on campus were greeted by news of the Friday sit-down in front of President Sterling's office, by headlines in the *Stanford Daily* that President Sterling had rejected student demands, by statements and letters on the *Daily's* inside pages, and by the mimeographed leaflets of student militants calling for attendance at the noon rally at White Plaza.

A major characteristic of any significant political event is the development of some symbolic focus around which action can unfold. In this respect, the demonstrators were aided by an unwitting administration. Forewarned that the Old Union, presently a second-echelon administration building, would be the target for a potential takeover, the administration decided on a course of action. On Monday, at the very time that the students gathered in White Plaza to hear the complaints of their colleagues, the administration locked the building. Not only were the students locked out, but the premises were emptied of all staff; in effect, everyone including administrators, was locked out. The lockout was performed with chains and a master padlock on each of the doors. This visible representation of administration intransigence to student demands provided the students with a further opportunity to take over the building and to remove the symbols of the administration lockout, in this case the chain and locks. The campus police timidly stood guard while the campus went mad.

When the administration refused to address itself to or be addressed by the constituency it serves, its ability to retain campus management became minimal. Thus the focus as well as the problem shifted from the administration until the very end of the strike itself; once the administration locked itself out of its own building, its initiative evaporated quickly. The issue of the seizure was minimized only by the play of major forces within the administration or faculty. As one graduate student of economics, Frederick D. Berger, put it: "Refusing to negotiate under pressure will lead only to greater pressure, that is, violence."

While the Stanford events were certainly far less violent than similar student outbursts elsewhere, it would be a mistake to think that no violence occurred. The administration building was broken into; there was a considerable amount of scuffling between campus police and student strikers. And while no one was hurt, great potential for violence remained during the rest of the sit-in period. Violence was minimized by the administration's decision not to battle with the demonstrators and to keep the Old Union building locked. This decision, taken under the pressure of the student invasion, was the most moderate course of action open. Free access to a "liberated" building guaranteed a forum for the expression of militant students' demands and provided a key channel of communication among all sectors during the period.

Attended by well over a thousand persons, many of them curiousity-seekers, the Monday noon rally on White Plaza was relatively brief. It was soon clear that no administration spokesmen would appear to discuss the students' four demands. After some brief talks by student leaders—including one by Massarenti, informing the students that the Tactics Committee had not recommended strong action—there was a general movement from the Plaza to the Old Union, located adjacent to the Plaza. This movement was not a spontaneous one; the militants had agreed to shift the meeting to the Old Union to confront representatives of the administration if none presented himself at the White Plaza meeting. However, the speakers urged the students not to break or destroy property; the memory of Columbia was sharp in the minds of the students.

What was to become a major characteristic of the Stanford demonstration was announced policy from the start. The students were disciplined and restrained. This restraint was evident even in the way in which the Old Union was penetrated. Surrounding the building at a variety of key points, they made a number of attempts to get into the building. Several students attacked the molding of one of the windows on the ground floor and attempted to pry it open. A slight tap on the glass with the tool that one of them was using would have broken the window; the care being exercised showed that they would avoid destruction of property even at a minor level. Several students formed a human pyramid to raise another student to a tile roof, from which he climbed in through an open window on the second floor. At a third doorway students lined up to loudly negotiate with the campus police captain who stood guard. At this point a minor scuffle between police guards and students broke out; the willingness on both sides to negotiate student entrance to the building enabled nonviolence to prevail.

At roughly 1 P.M., or one hour after the meeting at White Plaza, the building was opened. A student sawed the chain off the door handles and removed the symbol of administration intransigence. The students filed in; many sat down and others stood milling around discussing tactics. Outside the building, on the grass and in the graceful fountained court, an amplifier system was mounted. At the original rally the lack of amplification had made the students advocating the strike appear weak. Setting up an amplifier made it possible to attract and deal with large numbers of students who were unwilling to enter the building but who somehow felt involved—particularly those who supported the demands but were unprepared to occupy university property.

That the demonstration was not merely a political act but a new form of good times became clear with a performance of the Stanford Guerrilla Theater immediately after the occupation. The Theater offered an allegory in which Irving Impotence, the prototypical Stanford student, was unable to "make it" with Sally Stanford until she was attacked by President Sterling, acting on behalf of the CIA. Once Irving perceived what was going on and rescued Sally, he was able to "make it," not unlike the way Clyde Barrow finally succeeded with Bonnie Parker in the movie. The scene then shifted to the President's and the Dean's discussing the need to castrate Irving; having grabbed and made off with him, they raised their knives, only to be interrupted by the narrator for the Guerrilla Theater, who asked the soap opera question: "Will Irving be castrated? Or will he find his manhood again? Tune in tomorrow." This bit of ad hoc fluff ended with a brief but inconclusive meeting, after which many students left the premises.

The atmosphere of carnival that pervaded the Old Union and its court should not be minimized. Throughout the action a tone of theatricality, of the entertainment value of the political act, was felt. In a romantic revolutionary sense the demonstration represented politics as poetry; the sit-in represented mass psychodrama as much as it did mass politics, an operational way of providing 1,000 characters in search of a drama with a good time and a good part. It might almost be said that the theatrical aspects were prearranged, since administration, Establishment faculty members, and radical students, all seemed at the outset, at any rate, to be creating a drama that would lead to confrontation rather than seeking a pragmatic solution to the problems at hand.

But all was not fun. As the afternoon wore on, meetings began in which the demonstrators started living out a new kind of politics. Confrontation involves approaches different from those found in standard American political life. Thinking in formal political terms has led all too often to terminated communication between demonstrating students and their elders in the administration and faculty. Nor is communication facilitated when administrators see Bolshevik menaces or other conspirators in the deepest recesses of the student revolt. When student rebels meet openly and reach tactical decisions on questions of enormous import while associate deans are present, charges of conspiracy make them question the motives of the accusers.

The key element in the Monday afternoon meetings was the political socialization of many individuals who had joined the demonstration. Emphasis was placed on spontaneity rather than on planning. The inevitable confrontation with university officials became defined as involving the entire group of student demonstrators. Because, in fact, administrators are unwilling to negotiate with several hundred students, smaller groups were chosen. The members were defined as messengers rather than representatives, however. In this way the antirepresentational bias was kept intact.

Even the familiar processes of political socialization had

special twists. Cooptation, political recruitment, socialization, and concern for tactics and the role of leadership were handled by student leaders more in terms of what they had learned from Harold Lasswell than from Vladimir Lenin. Sit-in leaders seemed to be menaced by the experience of the old left as well as by the intellectual confrontation with political theorists who, if they had not necessarily convinced students of the role of pluralism in American politics, at least had convinced them of the necessity for maintaining democracy within their organizational ranks.

The students introduced to the sit-in several new approaches that represent changes in political tactics. These tactics are perhaps restricted to student use; they would probably work poorly with a more heterogeneous class grouping. But the common experience of undergraduates in large classes taught mainly in sections by graduate students, and of graduate students as the donkeys of day-to-day instruction, has in fact created great homogeneity of opinion within the students' ranks. Many students who have not previously experienced sit-ins seemed to grasp intuitively the need to deal with the peculiar exigencies of such situations quickly and effectively.

Student speeches tended to be relatively short; when the concept of brevity was violated, stony silence or gestures of physical discomfort (such as wriggling) indicated that the audience was bored. Sentence structure used in debate was simple; the usual convoluted expressions that faculty members find characteristic of many students were absent in this situation. Finally, many students who rarely spoke in a classroom situation found themselves speaking to the other demonstrators, even addressing large numbers of students and urging them to a specific course of action.

Several key elements in consensual-action[1] politics became evident at the outset. Not only is the physical shape of

---

1. We will be referring to the pattern of decision making followed by the students through most of the demonstration as "consensual action." Our choice of the term is deliberate and, perhaps, unfortunate. We feel the need

argument different from addresses by elites to masses, but the audience response is vocal and clear. It does not usually take place unless a speaker says something outrageous or is outrageously boring; rather, reaction comes after the completion of the remarks by the speaker. The norm of free speech is strong among the student activists and, indeed, became a crucial aspect in the gathering storm. Throughout the meetings of the demonstrators, expression of dissenting views was strongly encouraged. The demonstrators' microphones were used not only to denounce them, but also to call the opponents to meetings.

As the meetings continued, the norms of the rebellion began to be worked out. With the foyer of the Old Union crowded with students, it soon became uncomfortably warm. Tins of soda and bottles of fruit punch began freely circulating among the demonstrators. Although it was hot and people were thirsty, each person took a small drink and passed the container on. The shared excitement of risk as well as shared minor travails and tiring hours of sitting on hard floors through endless hours of tactical discussions soon were a key element of the "new ethic."

As the afternoon wore on, the question of confrontation with the university administration was foremost. A committee of students was rapidly chosen to talk to Provost Richard Lyman. The shape of the evening's activities became clear when students learned that the Provost was willing to meet and discuss issues with them, but that he was concerned with the choice of location. He was unwilling to meet within or near the confines of the Old Union. Some of the students on the committee were impressed by the "reasonableness" of the Provost's willingness to talk, but others

to distinguish the kind of politics engaged in by the students from the "politics of consensus" defined by elitist politicians. The consensual action of the students was closer to the kind of search for consensus that occurs in small-scale societies and collegial social groups where the norms of social cohesion are strong. If anything, the consensual action of the students was closer to the decision making of African tribes than to that of modern American political parties.

wanted the administration to meet with them in or near the demonstration site.

Anxious to broaden their base and to bring larger numbers of students into the sit-in, the demonstrators decided upon a meeting of the campus student body for 7:30 P.M. Messengers were sent to various living units to alert students. At the same time the Provost's meeting was scheduled for 8:30 P.M. at Stanford's Memorial Auditorium, a five-minute walk from the Old Union. A clash between the two meeting times was therefore averted and the drama was scheduled for two different physical sites.

By 7:30 P.M. several thousand students had gathered in the courtyard of the Old Union and had distributed themselves on the porticoes and roofs of the surrounding buildings. The meeting included a number of fraternity men and athletes, who had responded to the call by organizing a heavy turnout. The list of speakers was smaller, but the presentation of conflicting views continued.

The group's size and heterogeneity made consensual action impossible, and the "normal" style of American politics—the presentation of and voting on motions—prevailed. Where majority-minority decisions have to be made, it becomes possible for skilled organizers to manipulate decisions. At the evening meeting, however, the organizational tactics of old left politics were noticeably absent. There was no discreet placement of speakers in the audience. There was no attempt to continue the meeting indefinitely until only hard-core radicals remained. There were no efforts at parliamentary tampering. Rather, a simple statement was offered that a variety of interest groups was involved and that core principles were at stake.

At this critical meeting of the campus student community a series of votes was taken in rapid-fire succession. First, a motion to separate the demands to the university administration and vote on them one by one was defeated. Second, a motion supporting the four demands en bloc was accepted. Third, a bitterly contested motion endorsing the tactics of the militants in seizing the administration building was voted down by a ratio of roughly sixty to forty. And fourth, a motion demanding protection against prosecution of the students who had participated in the building seizure was accepted. As the meeting concluded at 8:25 P.M., the militants found that although their key tactic had been repudiated by a constituency that they themselves had assembled, their demands had been sustained.

The student militants thus had campus support for their demands but not for their tactical handling of those demands. While one group of militants immediately pointed out that matters of conscience cannot be voted, the fact remained that the entire voting procedure had involved matters of conscience. It was also on this basis that the militants decided to attend the meeting in the Memorial Hall Auditorium.

The older generation's inability to deal with consensual action was clear at that meeting. Stanford's Memorial Auditorium was packed to its capacity of 3,000. On the stage with Provost Lyman were two faculty members and the Dean of Students, a key figure in the events leading up to the protest. The discourse was academic: restrained and polite. The proceedings were dominated from the stage; members of the audience were informed that they could ask questions after remarks by the panel. The presentations were made calmly, as if to emphasize the rational framework within which the administration was operating, in contrast to the implicit irrationality, haste, and ill-considered judgment of the students.

Provost Richard Lyman chaired the meeting and was its first speaker. An overwhelmingly sympathetic audience applauded him as he rose. His position was eroded, however, from that point on. Addressing himself to the four demands, Lyman rejected the first demand—that the IJB decision for suspension be rejected—by stating that President Sterling did not want to act until he had consulted individually with the "defendants." He went on to reject the demand that the IJB be disbanded, pointing out its thorough legitimacy as a body. "To grant its demolition under the kind of pressure we now have would be a sad commentary on our times," he added. The third demand, for an appellate board composed of four faculty members and five students, would be met "in

spirit" when the Committee of 15 presented its recommendation—which at that Monday meeting Provost Lyman thought
would be six weeks in the future. Finally, Lyman noted that
the fourth demand could only be heard on appeal from the
defendants to the appellate board; and further, that it could
not be met because the ASSU council was the creature of the
legislature and that as a consequence the student legislature
would have undue power over all other sectors of the community. The Provost thus would not yield even on minor
points, much less on the major issues at stake.

Lyman was followed by Professor of Law William Baxter,
who emphasized his presence as an individual faculty member rather than as chairman of the IJB. Professor Baxter
pointed out the need for the rule of law, unless "we were to
accept the premise of coming home to find someone else
occupying our bed"—an untenable position, "at least not
without our permission." Calculated to amuse the students
with its sexual connotations, the remark fell flat. Baxter's
reasoned argumentation avoided the accusations that had
been made against legal procedures followed for nearly three
years with no significant success. For his part, Professor Hubert Marshall of the Political Science Department and Chairman of the Committee of 15 argued that the C-15 could be
expected to make an announcement of new judicial procedures almost immediately.

While the meeting in Memorial Auditorium was starting,
the student demonstrators in the Old Union assessed the
votes just taken and debated whether they should be bound
by the decision condemning their tactics in seizing the Old
Union. After considerable debate, the majority concluded
that the vote required them to abandon the Old Union. The
fact that the scene of action had shifted to Memorial Auditorium probably also contributed to the decision; whatever the
reason, the bulk of the demonstrators left the Old Union for
the Provost's meeting.

The arrival of several hundred students changed the character of the Provost's meeting. While the audience had previously been dominated by conservative students, faculty
members, and a heavy representation of visibly older people,

the demonstrators' arrival gave courage to elements in the audience that had been sympathetic to the demonstrators but had so far remained silent. Increasingly the Provost lost the support of the audience as the demonstrators demanded greater participation in the Memorial Auditorium meeting. Why, the Provost was asked, were student representatives not present on the platform? The Provost responded that he hardly had any procedure to select representatives, considering the many factions of students. But this answer was not satisfactory. Nor did some of the Provost's acerbic comments (for which he is justifiably well-known at Stanford) on student demeanor sit well with the audience.

As momentum against the Provost built up, reasoned but impassioned statements were heard from the student members of the Committee of 15. These students, representing varying political persuasions, called upon the Committee to meet on a continuous basis until revision of conduct procedures could be completed. They threatened to resign unless their proposal was accepted by faculty and administration members of the Committee. The student members' action served two notable ends: it rebuked the Provost's slow and easy approach; and it provided the coalition of administration and faculty with a face-saving device whereby the "results" of the Committee of 15 could be meshed with the demands of the students for amnesty.

The academicians and administrators on the platform were prepared neither intellectually nor ideologically to deal with a continuous and sustained barrage of student criticism. In a situation pregnant with opportunity for conversion into a familiar give-and-take — the teach-in — members of the panel were unable to shift to a different mode of discourse. The teach-in format would have had definite advantages from the point of view of the administration; it could have served as a significant substitute for the occupation of the Old Union. There would have been disadvantages to a teach-in, of course. At any rate, the Provost was unable to gear himself to the possibilities of change and took refuge in a statement about the 'different diurnal schedules" of his generation — confirming student prejudice about the differences between the generations. Thus, at 10:15 the panel, led by the Provost, decamped and abandoned the platform to the students.

At the conclusion of the Memorial Auditorium meeting students spontaneously drifted back to their fortress in the Old Union. The building had never been completely abandoned by the demonstrators; a group had held it pending the outcome of the meeting at the Memorial Auditorium. The administration thus lost its last opportunity to resolve the strike on its terms. If student legitimacy demanded that the demonstrators listen to the administration position, confrontation politics demanded that they return to the building they had captured during the day since the administration was refusing to talk on equal terms.

The late-evening sessions following the fiasco at Memorial Auditorium mainly concerned formal arrangements for the maintenance of the building. Groups were established to police the grounds; to maintain a certain amount of rigor in sleeping arrangements, to arrange for seminars, classes, and discussion groups. At this point realization that a long-range stay in the building was possible took hold; with this realization, the social consequences also became apparent.

The logistics of the Old Union made possible some easy solutions to problems that had plagued the Columbia revolt; the Old Union directly faces Tresider Memorial Union, whose student union cafeterias minimized problems of provision of food. Students could easily be rotated in and out of the Old Union; there was no crush to bring food to the demonstrators. In fact, the movement to and from the building was remarkably uncontrolled and unsupervised.

By the end of the evening the students had begun to live their revolution. Unlike rebels of the past, this generation is *not* alienated from its peer group—they swing almost as a strategy. While serious discussions on the focus and tactics of power have their place, the students see little virtue in suffering for its own sake. They do not mind being identified with millennialism or with early Christianity, but they repudiate the protestantization of American culture typified by their elders of all religions. While many were deciding matters of tactics, and others were working out arrangements for living quarters, a dance began to round out the evening. The earth-shaking rock groups now standard on American campuses provided a kind of relaxation previously unheard of in the crucible of revolution. The first evening ended as it had begun, with the practice of politics as poetry instead of the traditional politics of poverty; the students were true to the affluence of their class backgrounds.

As the sound and fury of the rock band died away, signs of intensive organization became manifest. Education committees, press committees, food-and-drink committees, and a host of other essential operations were set up, all stemming out of the Tactics Committee. By making the Tactics Committee the key coordinating group, all questions of principle, all matters of ultimate ends were left open to debate—ideology joined organization as a "happening." Naïveté became a reasonable "style," not just a low degree of political consciousness.

The following morning was largely devoted to arranging for a second noon rally. This time it would not be held in White Plaza but in front of the Old Union. This time the acoustics were good, the loudspeakers were working, and the audience could hear from any part of the lawn or the interior of the Old Union building. Patterns of internal organization established on Monday evening had crystallized to such a point that certain students had specialized jobs, such as policing the ashtrays, or cleaning the floors, while others picked up junk strewn about the court. No "status" demotion was involved, since no system of status promotion was tolerated.

The paramount fact was that the Old Union had become a center of gravity that could be ignored no more by the opponents than by the participants. Leaflets pro and con were in abundance.

One leaflet, "Moderation or Occupation"—which was widely distributed without molestation of any sort—read:

> Last evening in response to Cesare Massarenti's call for a mass meeting, over 1,200 students gathered at the Old Union for a discussion of issues and tactics. They overwhelmingly rejected the occupation of the building as a tactic to settle the IJB dispute.

Today this tactic continues to hinder the normal function of university business and threatens to silence the forces of moderation. We must pledge our support for rational negotiated settlement with the university in a spirit of good faith. Let us, the silent majority, express our confidence in the negotiation process by wearing a white armband until the occupation ends.

The demonstrators circulated a leaflet giving the program of "Seminars: Relevant Here and Now." Some of the courses were: Latin American Student Movements; University Administration and Corporate Power; On Doing Good Overseas; The Spanish Student Movement; The Sociology of Lenny Bruce; Sergeant Musgrave's Dance as Political Drama; Black Panthers (Tapes and Discussion); Stanford Imperialism; Malcolm X; Radical Community Living; and Leninism Today. Everything from the final speeches of Martin Luther King and Malcolm X to the social satire of Lenny Bruce could be heard in a cacophony of sound, live and recorded, in the Old Union. These activities served not only to pass the time, but also to create a climate of relevant education that existed, as students wanted the whole Stanford plant to be aware.

The second noon meeting was attended by over 500 students, most of them favoring the sit-in, but a smattering consisting of opponents. The session began by flogging of the press for its coverage of Monday's events. An announcement was made that the press committee, set up the previous night, would be available, and that to straighten out the record a press conference would be held later in the day.

Next a leader of the sit-in, Steve Weissman — a former leader of the Free Speech Movement at Berkeley and hence a veteran "professional student," endowed with a mystique of action — provided the rationale for the reoccupation of the building. He pointed out that, had the vote gone to continue the sit-in at the rally on Monday evening, students would not have felt compelled to sit in; by the same token, he felt that the vote against the occupation tactic was not binding on the demonstrators. Weissman commented on the personal remarks directed at him by Provost Lyman at Memorial Auditorium the previous evening and went on to talk about that meeting. It was Weissman's opinion that the meeting had indeed been a communication mechanism — one which the administration had not expected to work out as it did, for it had demonstrated anew the paternalism being protested by the student sit-in. It had also illustrated the depth of student hostility for the administration and, in so doing, had informed the members of the administration of the seriousness of the situation. Weissman went on to advise the administration on how to save face. The essence of his position was that, either through the Committee of 15 or the Academic Council meeting scheduled for the following Wednesday, the administration could extricate itself from its untenable position. He pointed out that mechanisms for solving the problems were available; that the students simply wanted their demands to be met—others could claim victories. His speech ended with a demand for amnesty for the demonstrators.

The amnesty demand was the product of the experiences of the students who in the aftermath of other demonstrations had seen select students singled for prosecution and disciplinary action. At Columbia University amnesty had represented a key issue dividing the students and the administration. The demand for amnesty illustrates some of the terminological inexactitude that can develop with relatively inexperienced student leaders. Even for some of the students themselves, the term had a negative meaning, connoting an admission of guilt. What was intended by the demand was that no single student should be prosecuted, that all should be held equally responsible for the sit-in. The more accurate and classic demand—"no victimization"—did begin to replace the amnesty bid, and the latter phrase tended to remain in use only among those who opposed the demonstration. At the final stage of the sit-in the "no victimization" slogan was legitimated by a statement of complicity signed by many students acknowledging their participation in the sit-in. The move from amnesty to nonprosecution reflected the demonstrators' growing assurance and was also a move away from the inherited campus struggles that had taken place earlier at the University of California in Berkeley or three thousand miles away at Columbia.

The next speaker, Marc Sapir, one of the expelled students, announced that Provost Lyman was in the audience and that he could now talk to at least four of the students proposed for suspension in front of the audience if he so wished. The statement triggered the first enthusiastic response of the meeting. People began clapping in cadence and standing up until most of the audience was clapping rhythmically and demandingly. This demonstration continued for two minutes. The chairman then announced that in response Provost Lyman had walked out. Sapir continued by pointing out that he, Sapir, would be glad to explain his participation in the CIA protest movement and also what had been going on during the past twenty-four hours of demonstrations and, finally, what would happen if the demonstrators did not win their demands. Although Sapir never made this threat more explicit, escalation was a thought of many other students.

The following speaker was Tim Haight. Mr. Haight, who had the good fortune of combining hip language with a radical rhetoric, was listened to attentively. His key point was that nothing prevented the administration from using the Old Union for its bureaucratic purposes; the students, while they intended to continue the occupation, did not intend to prevent the administration from carrying out its work. All the student demonstrators wanted were discussions with the administration.

What gave particular poignancy to Haight's remarks was that, on the same Tuesday morning, two of his letters appeared in the *Stanford Daily* under the title, "Two Letters of Conscience." Both were remarkable for their universal expression of the quality of mind and conscience of student opposition that led to the sit-in. The first, addressed to the Selective Service System, Local Board No. 95 in Los Angeles, read in part:

> I can no longer cling to the sanctuary of the university while the people I most respect are turning in their cards. To me the Selective Service System is an embodiment of the coercive forces our materialistic, racist, sexless, and soulless society has used to push people of basic decency and dignity into molds unfit for human beings. You want us to be killers, or workers, or technological innovators, so that America can lead the way in changing a beautiful planet into man's progeny and his products. Worse than that, you wage senseless wars, exploit people, and discriminate in savage ways.

The second letter was addressed to Professor Edwin D. Barker of the Scholarship Committee at Stanford, notifying Mr. Barker that Haight had returned his draft card to the local board and that he was forthwith announcing his rejection of his grant money. This letter, too, is worth citing:

> Although the pursuit of truth is a noble venture in itself, it cannot be carried out in isolation. You are in the madhouse with the rest of the crazy people, and withdrawing to a corner to do good work will not change that. If you and professors like you would tell this society and its government that you would do nothing for it unless it made immediate, genuine, and lasting commitments to wipe out the blots on America, change would come. Society needs you.

The letter then concluded with a critique of faculty performance that summed up the feelings of the majority of the protesters.

> But if you won't accept that, you will discuss the fine points, and check the methodology, and run it through the computer. By that time the extensions of your system will have murdered and degraded millions more and perhaps have destroyed the world. How do you do it? How do you segment your life so that you can be the good professor in the corner of the arena, while the emperors direct their games? I hope one day to come back to work with you again, but there are more important things right now.

After a few more speakers discussed the "more important things" (tactics for future struggles) and announcements were made of afternoon seminars, Eckhard Schulz—a graduate student in engineering from Wiesbaden, Germany—stood up to announce another meeting for Wednesday in Bishop Auditorium, in the Graduate School of Business. Its purpose would be "to unite those groups who oppose the tactic of the sit-in." Schulz referred to the meeting on the previous Monday night and to the vote of the students disapproving of the occupation of the Old Union. He objected to "demands" being made on the administration, leaving implicit the notion that he agreed with their content but not with their style. He proposed that those disagreeing with the sit-in should convey their feelings to the administration by an act of their own. Schulz was followed by Fred Cohen, a demonstrator, who urged the students opposed to the tactics but in favor of the

demands of the anti-CIA demonstrators to organize their own
protest. His point was that the demands should be met irrespective of the tactics of different student groupings. Students
who feel like Mr. Schulz should protest and take action in
their own way, he pointed out.

The next speaker, James Forester of the Medical School,
introduced a new factor which was to be expremely important in the final settlement. He emphasized the existing unity
concerning the demands for setting aside the suspensions
and for amnesty. He announced that the Medical School
faculty would put strong pressures on President Sterling to
ease the penalties, if not to remove them. As it turned out,
even Mr. Forester underestimated the consensus prevailing
among the Medical School faculty, which rested not only on
righteous indignation but on the feeling that disciplinary
action against a Medical School student should be taken by
the Medical School, and not by the president. Forester concluded that the sit-in on Monday had been justifiable because it had brought the issues into focus and to the attention
of the university community. While he was uncertain as to
the correctness of the reoccupation, he felt that the issue was
not of great moment in the light of Provost Lyman's Memorial Auditorium performance.

That the Stanford protest was not an isolated event but one
of many protests at campuses across the United States became clear when the chairman of the meeting read a telegram of support from the Northwestern University students
who had successfully concluded their own sit-in the previous
week. This telegram was received with cheers, after which a
proposal was introduced to hold an open house for the faculty on Wednesday, between two and four in the afternoon, just
prior to the Academic Council meeting. As it turned out,
many of the faculty availed themselves of the opportunity to
speak with demonstrators directly.

The next student, Richard Arnold, reported that the Santa
Clara Central Labor Council had sent a night letter to President Sterling asking him to meet with the American Federation of Teachers' local chapter. Arnold expressed the need
for external pressure-group techniques to produce greater

community action, such as had been achieved by the Black Student Union earlier. The dilemma was that such external groups were largely mythical in character; community consensus did not form to back the students; on the other hand, it remained amorphous and was not directed against them. In some measure the reason for this circumstance locally lies in the Palo Alto *Times'* sensitivity to the general community spirit and its desire to respond positively to university community needs, including many of its student readers on campus. The local newspaper took a position not unlike that of conservative faculty members — namely, leaving open the claim for judicial review of the anti-CIA demonstrators while deploring the tactics. If the community was not alerted to the exact nature of the struggles, it at least was defused in terms of possible action against the demonstrators. The absence of a hostile local press relieved pressures on the administration to take precipitous police action, which they were clearly loath to commence, at least in the opening stages of the sit-in.

The final speaker of this meeting was Assistant Professor Robert Polhemus of the English Department, who read a letter being circulated among the faculty. It declared the Monday evening meeting in the Memorial Auditorium a communication failure and asked that another be held in which: (1) the platform would be shared among a wide spectrum of views; (2) the audience would participate and not be formally limited to asking questions; (3) the meeting would not be suspended arbitrarily but would be of sufficient length to permit a full airing of all issues; (4) the moderator would be nonpartisan; (5) and an attempt would be made to achieve some agreement and solution. He noted that the failure of the faculty to support the demonstrators would indeed mean a black day for the university, and he concluded by urging students to contact faculty members in their offices or homes to explain their position. Polhemus' letter made a noteworthy thrust at Provost Lyman. For the first time a faculty member connected, if only tenuously, student struggles with the nature of the administrative handling of the university bureaucracy as a whole.

Professor Polhemus was one of a small number of faculty

members willing to speak in favor of the student demands. But even his statement had an aura of legalism and neutrality rather than expressing the kind of partisanship that the students had felt they could expect from at least a portion of their faculty. Unexpected support for the students did come from a mild and gentle member of the mathematics department, Professor Robert Finn, whose statement was one of the more unusual events of the day.

It seems to many students a world of futility and of terror. It is a world which the students neither created nor chose. Yet it is they who will have to bear its burdens. It will be for them a kind of taxation without representation, in which the taxes are paid in blood — the blood in the veins of those who must fight, and the blood on the hands of those who devise and operate the machines to produce the bombs and missiles and jelly gasoline, and the gases and chemicals and germs. Our college youth have been exposed since birth to the unsavory spectacle of their elders busily preparing the annihilation of the universe for private profit. And they are now constrained to witness the complicity and silence of their university on this central moral issue of our time. They are right if they feel that a university which is unable or unwilling to disassociate itself from the development of instruments of torture, murder, and mass destruction or with the loathsome activities of the CIA is a university whose highest officials should be called to account. In this situation it is the militant students whose actions reflect the real best interest of all of us and it is those who are content to let matters slide who betray us. It is love for their university as distinguished from its buildings that motivated the CIA demonstrators and which motivates these students now. Their actions will not destroy the university; they may instead rejuvenate it.

The noon meeting came to an end when the chairman announced that those who had to go to class should do so, while those who had no classes ought to move back into the Old Union. One curiosity of the entire demonstration was that classes went on; students continued to meet in White Plaza and at Tresider Memorial Union. The normal routines of the university were, in fact, only slightly disrupted, for the action was limited to the sit-in at a single building, and no attempt was made to generate either a strike of students or a disruption of normal academic activities. The noon meeting and subsequent afternoon events took place against a background of the meeting convened in response to the demands of the student members of the Committee of 15.

The tactics sessions contributed significantly to the development of social solidarity and political socialization. In the afternoon hours of Tuesday, the second day of the sit-in, a new articulate group of rank-and-filers began to emerge, able to express themselves from the floor on tactical and strategic issues without hesitation. Indeed, unlike the faculty, students had a remarkable ability to accept criticism generally rather than personally and without malice. The contrast between student sobriety and faculty pique was remarkable enough to discomfit students who were shocked to realize that even in their manners they were not necessarily inferior to the faculty.

Typical was a discussion on Tuesday afternoon that concerned itself with whether students should leave the Old Union prior to the Wednesday faculty meeting. The attending faculty members were unable to indicate what students' attitudes should be if the faculty vote went contrary to their demands; further, when students plied their professors, some of them wearing "McCarthy for President" buttons, many indicated a lack of faith in faculty sentiments or in the faculty's ability to function as an autonomous body apart from administrative needs. The faculty participation on the IJB and its virtual absence from strike activities reinforced student hostility toward and alienation from professors. When faculty members did come to the Old Union, they usually advised the students to leave or made a five-minute Cook's tour of the premises and then departed, having satisfied themselves either of the curiosity of the event or of its hopelessness.

In response to criticism, one of those recommended for suspension, Marc Sapir, backed up by David Pugh, a student "radicalized" by the struggle, tried to speak on behalf of the students and to note that the sit-in was representative rather than coercive; not violent, but nonviolent; not intended to cajole, but to protect the interests of both the students and the community as a whole. Sapir pointed out that "to leave the building and seek re-entry at a later date would mean real violence, real confrontation. It would also alienate the affections of student support more thoroughly than anything before that."

The sentiment for continuing the sit-in, no matter what the Committee of 15 reported or what the Academic Council decided, was overwhelming. The lines hardened by the second day; the tactics meetings emphasized the gulf between the demands for law and order and demands for setting aside the penalties inflicted by law and order.

The highlight of Tuesday's events was the attendance at the sit-in of David Packard, a Stanford trustee and President of Hewlett-Packard Corporation of Palo Alto. Mr. Packard, listed as one of the wealthiest men in America in the May 1968 issue of *Fortune* magazine, was clearly the coup of the student evening. He pointed out: "If you get into these confrontations, you may lose everything you have gained. Keep working with us, and you will find a good solution to this. . . . We are willing in principle to allow you to have a larger voice, but not at this point to decide everything." Packard called for a partnership approach. He stated, "We don't want the type of thing we had at Columbia University. I came here to gain a better understanding in case the trustees have to decide anything in this matter—and I hope we don't."

Mr. Packard expressed fear, not so much of student power to win its demands, but of its power to disrupt the operations of a major university. The collective conscience inspired by the shutdown of Columbia also provided a sense of solidarity in the hall that evening. As liberal faculty members—such as Professors Favin Langmuir (History), Walter Meierhoff (Physics), Lucil Ruotolo (English), and Lorie Tarshis (Economics)—all echoed Mr. Packard's call for harmony and partnership, students' resolve stiffened. Even many of those who had earlier argued for a more moderate and legalistic approach had become convinced that the sit-in tactic was the key to future success.

The second day of the strike ended with a statement from an important member of the Board of Trustees that ostensibly called to the students to abandon their sit-in; it could just as easily have been read as a warning to the administration not to allow the situation to become another Columbia. The reference to involvement by the Board of Trustees was not easily ignored by the administration. A final resolution was also submitted by the Committee of 15, recommending a judicial overhaul, but this resolution more properly belongs to the events of Wednesday, since those who were still awake were not notified of what had transpired at the Committee of 15 meetings until 3 A.M. By that time the 200-odd children, grown into young men and women, were sleeping with a grim discipline that belied the activities of their waking hours.

Wednesday, May 8, the final day of the sit-in, saw the important decision making shift from students and administrators to the faculty. The recommendations of the Committee of 15 were based on faculty ideology and orientation. Wednesday was also the day of the Academic Council meeting. Indeed, as the events unfolded, support for the Committee of 15 resolution became contrasted with support of the resolution to the Academic Council submitted on behalf of the faculty of the Medical School by Professor Halstead Holman. These two documents were, in effect, statements that pitted the "ethics" of the Medical School against the "rules" of the Law School.

The Committee of 15 proposal avoided the key issue that had precipitated the crisis—the proposed suspension of the CIA demonstrators; it urged the President to "make his decision . . . independently of previous decisions." The bulk of the Committee's proposal, however, was taken up with spelling out in detail a revised judicial procedure. In contrast, the Holman resolution focused upon the immediate demands of the demonstrators and called for setting aside suspensions and penalties against the orginal seven students. In a sense the statements were really two ships in the night, passing each other untouched. In part this was because the Committee of 15 represented long-range as well as legal interests, whereas the Medical School resolution was concerned with resolving the problem that had polarized the Stanford campus.

The students pointed out the peculiar dilemma that had

arisen when they stated that, despite their support for the Committee of 15's final statement, "the Committee failed tragically to meet the specific grievances which the current demonstration protests." The Medical School resolution to the Academic Council addressed itself to precisely these specific grievances. Its similarities to student demands for amnesty were clear. In fact, the Provost recited the student demands later in the afternoon and matched them up against the Medical School resolution to show their proximity.

But as these faculty activities began to take shape and to dominate the events of the day, they did so at least symbolically behind the backs of the students, since the students were pressing on with the sit-in and other actions. The main work of the demonstrators on Wednesday was oriented toward convincing the faculty to support their demands. Students were delegated to visit with the 900-odd members of the Stanford faculty, while faculty members were invited to "open house" at the Old Union.

The students opposed to the sit-in, who had simply reacted to the sit-in demands for the previous forty-eight hours, began to mobilize organized action on mid-Wednesday. The demonstration had kicked off a number of individual actions, but not until Wednesday did the students opposed to the demonstrators coordinate their activities. The relative impotence of the student supporters of the administration (or opponents to the demonstration) is worth noting. It is often stated that demonstrators represent a minority of the campus, without appreciation of the degree to which administration supporters represent a smaller and less coherent faction of the campus. In point of fact, one real victory of the demonstrators was their ability to mobilize a "middle" sector of the campus community that had never before participated in the political life of Stanford. In a sense the organization of a meeting in support of the administration represented an alternative to and a test of student sit-in organizational styles.

The meeting of the administration supporters was held, appropriately, at the Graduate School of Business. Although fire marshalls patrolled the aisles as if the meeting were of the same scope and magnitude as the one held on the Monday evening at Memorial Auditorium, it was quite different. Attendance was sparse; a head count taken midway through the meeting revealed that there were not more than 212 people in the auditorium, including adults, photographers, and perhaps a third of the audience who were either demonstrators or supporters of the sit-ins.

The purpose of the meeting was to obtain a mandate, a seal of legitimacy, for a five-man group to speak to the community in the name of the people present, plus the 2,000 students who, the audience was informed, had signed the anti-sit-in petitions.

The master dilemma of those students supporting the administration was, of course, the absence of an articulated position. The leaders of this meeting were unable to agree on very much aside from their opposition to the continued occupation of the Old Union. Equally significant was their failure to prepare for what might have been a significant meeting by obtaining a parliamentarian or, even better, having a chairman with some experience in parliamentary decision making. The chairman of the meeting, Eckhard Schulz, announced that the modus operandi for the counterdemonstrators' meeting would be parliamentary procedure. It rapidly transpired that the chairman had far less grasp of the niceties of *Roberts' Rules of Order* than many others present.

Chairman Schulz announcement that the meeting was "closed" except to participants who deplored the tactics of the demonstrators stood in sharp contrast to the open quality of the demonstrators' meetings, where Schulz himself had spoken several times. The lack of any grass-roots feeling was made plain by the fact that the seal of legitimacy was intended to be endowed on Schulz himself and on four other students. The leaders showed no agreement on any points other than their deploring the tactics of the demonstrators. They requested that a vote of confidence be given their leadership, which would be limited to a two-week period, after which they would reconvene and have another meeting.

Schulz revealed the hopes which the administration was placing on this meeting when he attempted to show the importance of the session for students. Contacts with the administration, he said, had shown that the students selected by this group would be given representation in the various transactions that would take place. Shades of the notorious strike-breaking formulas of the 1930's were implicit in Schulz's recital. By obtaining a vote of confidence, it slowly became clear, the five "leaders" (the term continually used by Schulz) would be able to provide support for the administration from an ostensibly organized and constituted body of students.

The awkwardness of student participation on terms set forth by the administration became manifest as organizational inexperience when a full five minutes of discussion was required before one person in the audience had the sense to move a vote of confidence in the five proposed student leaders.

When the discussion from the floor opened, however, no sentiment jelled. The meeting floundered for several minutes, until a Mr. Shanahan rose to repeat what Shulz had stated more concisely. He sat down to some applause, the first and about the last to be heard at the meeting. Shanahan was followed by a motion to close debate, which was put to a voice vote and adopted, with about twenty in agreement and fifteen opposed. At this point, several of the pro-sit-in demonstrators tried to get the floor and began to tie the chairman into parliamentary knots. A student opponent of the demonstrators finally proposed that Mr. Shanahan become the chairman of the meeting; but since Shanahan did not wish to accept and Mr. Schulz did not want to relinquish the chair, the meeting limped on. A vote of confidence in the leadership was finally adopted amid confusion as to whether the vote was one of confidence in the five leaders or a vote to close the debate.

After finally obtaining a vote to close debate, a series of confusing votes on the main motion—the vote of confidence—followed. Finally a hand vote was taken, resulting in ninety-six in favor and eighteen opposed. From this point on, the strategy of the sit-in supporters was to demand a record of the size of the actual voted. Mr. Shanahan spoke angrily, to the effect that no claim was made that the majority of the student body was present. A British student proposed that the number voting on the resolutions be incorporated into any report. His proposal, strangely enough, was adopted by a voice vote. The countering response came from the floor when one of the audience pointed out that the chosen leaders represented, not just the people present, but all the 2,000 signatories to the various antidemonstration petitions.

The next resolution—that the anti-CIA demonstrators not be excused from punishment—revealed the weakness of the opponents of the sit-in. This resolution brought a severe response from a student member of the Study of Education at Stanford, a committee organized to investigate educational innovation—a man who had been in the sit-in himself. He departed from the meeting. Mr. Shanahan then dealt with some of the moral issues this student had raised, pointing out that students could have moral discussions anywhere they liked but not in university buildings. The general applause given this remark was touched with some derision. As the time for termination of the meeting drew near (the hall had to be vacated by 1:00 P.M.), votes were taken amid increasing chaos. The resolution to punish the CIA demonstrators failed. The meeting was dismissed with a motion to adjourn amid shouts to the effect that the meeting should be declared a farce.

Back at the Old Union demonstrators had decided to use both the outside court area and the interior portions of the building. The contrast with the meetings of the antidemonstrators was staggering. The demonstrators had already received preliminary reports about the meeting of the antidemonstrators and had shrewdly decided to ignore the meeting as having been totally ineffective. The demonstrators' meeting was casual, relaxed, unhurried. Its members were aware that the crucial faculty meeting was about to take place, but the relaxed tone reflected their feeling that they had done their work; now it was up to the faculty. There was considerable speculation about what the faculty would do. The demonstrators did not exactly have a noble impression of faculty sentiments, but they did have a keen appreciation of how a faculty could carry out decision making roles even against its own will.

In a leaflet distributed to the faculty as the professors

entered the meeting hall the students reiterated their four demands. The statement emphasized the faculty's duty to decide whether to pay attention to the Committee of 15 proposals or to the main issue of the suspension of the demonstrators. The leaflet read in part:

> We have overwhelmingly rejected the Committee of 15 proposals as humiliating, obscurantist, and antithetical to the substance of our demands and demonstrations, because the proposed student conduct legislative council and the proposed Stanford judicial council are designed to be stacked against the students, with all power still residing in the President. He would control this judicial council by a simple 5-4 majority. He has a clear advantage in the proposed legislative council. The sections on interim regulations for student conduct, the judicial aid defendant cooperation, and alternative student procedures help to expose this proposed court as kangaroo-like in nature. Your meeting was called to take action concerning the suspension of seven demonstrators. This, and not the C-15 recommendations, remains the central issue.

Interestingly, this particular document was not authoritative. Signed "Students Against Political Suspensions," it represented the work of a few of the most radical of the demonstrators. Yet it must be said in all fairness that, as the meeting of the faculty began, the choice was indeed between the Committee of 15 approach and that taken by the Medical School. The extreme radical posture had, in fact, accurately estimated the situation as it obtained at 4:15 P.M. – when the faculty convened.

The faculty seemed an unwilling power elite being compelled to make a decision that would be binding on both the administration and the students. The impotence of the powerful was never better demonstrated than that afternoon. Inadvertently rather than through design the meeting became the major watershed in the struggle. It marked a decisive victory for the students by giving them a voice in the tripartite university as the faculty members were compelled to face the issues of faculty power as decisively as the students were confronting the problems of student power.

The specific format of the faculty meeting initially called for consideration of a motion proposed by the Executive

Committee of the Academic Council. The motion endorsed in effect the decisions rendered earlier that day by the Committee of 15, urging the Committee to put its proposals for judicial revision into final form as quickly as possible. This resolution also called upon the students to vacate the Old Union. Thus the Executive Committee focused faculty attention, as expected, on the Committee of 15's work. In contrast, a resolution introduced by Professor Halstead Holman called for setting aside the CIA suspensions and for taking no action against the demonstrators. The discussion was lengthy and acrimonious; the faculty's decision was one in which great stakes were manifest.

Although it took five hours for the meeting to run its course and for the resolution favoring the students to be adopted, the central conclusions of this meeting were clear. First, the faculty in the main perceived student demands as a loss rather than as a gain to its own power. This feeling was certainly present in those 245 members who voted against the Medical School resolution. It was also felt by many of those voting in favor of Holman's resolution, since the vote was not so much prostudent as antitrouble. This became especially clear in the constant reiteration that the vote did not represent criticism of the administration. In fact, the following day a group of the more distinguished liberal faculty — including Gabriel Almond, Robert McAfee Brown, William A. Clepsch, Philip Dawson, Halstead Holman, Donald Kennedy, David Levin, Mark Mancall, Davie Napier, Louis W. Spitz, and Lorie Tarshis — in a letter to the Stanford community explained that, while they had voted affirmatively on the resolution, they were disturbed by two inferences:

> At no point did we intend our actions as a vote of no confidence in the administration. We expressed a difference of opinion — a very deep difference — but we believe it to be the essence of the democratic process that reasonable men may disagree on future measures. Consequently, we reaffirm our full confidence in President Sterling, Provost Lyman, Vice Provost Packer, and other administration officials with whom on this occasion we may have differed. And we look forward to working under their leadership in building Stanford's future.

At no point did we intend our action as an encouragement for sit-ins or civil disobediences. These do not seem to us the appropriate methods for determining university policy. Nor do they create the kind of atmosphere conducive to fruitful dialogue and real learning and they should not be contemplated except in the most extreme circumstances, when all other means of communication have clearly broken down.

It is clear that faculty members perceived this vote to be crucial. An informal sample of those who did not attend or those who attended and chose not to participate showed that reasons were not related to apathy or to lack of concern. Rather, there was profound fear among faculty members that going on record either for or against the proposal would cut them off from the university community as a whole. The vote represented an end to the politics of ambiguity—an end brought on by external and unwanted pressure.

If the votes of individual faculty members had been revealed, the consequences could have been profoundly negative. Faculty members cherishing their credit with students might have found it rendered into bankruptcy; or colleagues might have taken issue with one another's vote. It is all too easy to accuse faculty members of lacking courage. While such a charge may be true of some, the more central point is that this kind of a vote forces decision making roles upon men who prefer dialogue to resolution.

The vote did have a bitterness reminiscent of a deadlocked party convention. Yeas and nays were often spoken emphatically and belligerently, while at the other end of the spectrum some whispered their votes in the vain hope that no one would pay attention. This was hardly possible, since the vote was taken on roll call, and each member of the faculty was polled separately and individually.

To a great degree the genuine issue became transformed into a symbolic one. The Provost in particular chose to transform the issue of student amnesty into one of confidence in administration policy. If this transformation of values did not shake the vote loose from its moorings, it did embitter administration with faculty and, even more, faculty with each other.

There seemed to be a last-minute administration ploy to break up a faculty intent on avoiding "trouble" (defined as either a prolonged student disruption or an invitation to the police to solve the strike through armed force). The three arguments used were: the faculty was ill-informed on the issues; the faculty should have considered the resolutions of the Executive Committee of the Academic Council as a first order of business; and the faculty was not equipped to act as a committee representing the whole on delicate matters of law. When this approach had no apparent effect, the Provost then indicated in the strongest terms that a vote to set aside the IJB convictions would amount to a "repudiation" of his own position. This only accentuated divisions in the faculty rather than alleviating them. Indeed, it seemed as if the moral backs of the faculty stiffened as a result of the Provost's insistence on a roll-call vote. Any vote switching after the preliminary results had been anounced would have resulted in a severe loss of prestige for the faculty.

The Provost failed to take into account that, by making the vote on the demonstrating students a vote of confidence by the faculty in the administration, he was shifting the burden of the issue from student power to faculty power. And a faculty possessing the relative autonomy of Stanford's faculty could not be coerced (an often used and abused word during the sit-in period) by such a heavy-handed tactic. Thus the roll-call vote proved to be an exercise in futility. It merely guaranteed that the faculty would seize upon this issue to register its own claims to university-wide power — however tenuous those claims might be either in fact or in expectation.

The faculty meeting of Wednesday afternoon had a precision and formal elegance that was as unexpected as it was unintended. The insistence of Provost Lyman on a roll-call vote, "given the extremely serious nature of the vote, and how it reflects directly on the confidence this faculty has in the administration," made it possible to connect professional lines of endeavor with political attitudes in a way most unusual for "men of knowledge."

Only 515 of the roughly 930 faculty members eligible to vote exercised this option. An estimated additional 100 either decided to abstain or left the auditorium prior to the vote. In any event, no more than 60 percent of those eligible actually participated in the voting. Those absent or abstaining were randomly distributed; that is, no one school seemed disproportionately overrepresented or underrepresented. The final tally was 281 in favor of the "Holman Resolution" and 233 against it.[2]

A second fact to be noted is that the vote of the Academic Council was by various "faculties"; thus it was possible, however crudely, to gauge the differential response to student demands. There was a remarkable degree of bloc voting (which will herein be defined as a minimum of two-thirds voting either for or against the Holman Resolution). The strong "yea" vote was given by the Faculty of Humanities and Sciences and by the Faculty of the Medical School. The strong "nay" vote was supplied by the faculties of the Business School, the Engineering School, and the Law School. The one faculty conspicuously divided on an almost equal basis was the Faculty of the School of Education. Since a majority of the faculty is contained in the schools voting approval for the Holman Resolution, with the marginal "deviant" ballots cast somewhat canceling each other, the student petition was acted upon favorably, although the tallies were close.

Academic Council Vote on the "Holman Resolution"

University Division or School	Vote		Percentage	
	Yes	No	Yes	No
Graduate School of Business	0	18	0.0	100.0
Earth Sciences	3	16	15.8	84.2
School of Education	11	10	52.4	47.6
School of Engineering	29	56	34.1	65.9
Humanities and Sciences	149	74	66.8	33.2
School of Law	2	18	10.0	90.0
School of Medicine	80	24	76.9	23.1
Food Research Institute	2	4	33.3	66.6
Computer Services	5	5	50.0	50.0
Miscellaneous Officials	0	8	0.0	100.0
Totals	281	233	54.3	45.7

2. Our own tally showed 285 in favor, and 245 against. However, we will use the "official" figures, since they form the basis of the breakdown by school on the final vote.

Any explanation of the faculty voting pattern should take into account several "local" factors: Stanford's high status as a relatively recent member in the elite of American universities; the school involvement in those university activities that may be called "service-oriented," in contrast to conventional "intellectual-oriented" roles; the school's upper-class student population, as measured by values and attitudes and as reflected in the departmental affiliation of those students who participated in the sit-in.

Most of the impetus for Stanford's meteoric rise into the elite of American universities has come from its professional schools.

The Engineering School has utilized the largesse of federal project research funds and the accessibility of technologically oriented industry in the Stanford Industrial Park and at the Stanford Research Institute to develop a first-rate faculty and a renowned graduate education program. Many of the faculty in the School of Engineering are intimately involved with the corporate activities of the area, in advisory capacities and/or in entrepreneurial roles. Lockheed, Philco, and Ampex corporations are just three of the major firms utilizing the engineering output of Stanford—both of its faculty and its graduating students. However, the wealth and relative independence that reflects itself in the fact that over one-third of its faculty did in fact vote *for* the Holman Resolution.

The Business School, capitalizing on Stanford's unique position as the only quality private university on the West Coast, has developed programs heavily funded by the corporate structure of the area, particularly the California industrial base. On the other hand, lacking either the status or the expertise of the engineers, the degree of its commitment to the general ideology of the Board of Trustees is more complete than that exhibited by the engineers.

The Law School, for its part, had always been strong enough not only to segregate itself from other parts of the university system, but also to reinforce that segregation by remaining on the semester system while the rest of the campus went on the quarter system. In this way lawyers-to-be as well as law professors are as effectively isolated as the Medical School is innovative. Thus the structural and organizational parameters of the Law School are clearly distinct from the rest of the campus, and its conservatism is in part a function of its organizational separatism.

To this must be added that traditionally the Law School at Stanford meted out justice and punishment to students and performed a parliamentary and adjudicative role on the campus for the administration. A student victory would not only immediately threaten its own decision making powers, but would further represent a long-range threat to a system whereby the School of Law has had special access to the administration. For these reasons the Law School became as profoundly the pole of conservative opinion as the Medical School became the pole for liberal opinion.

Factors systematically built into the growth of the Medical School render it more radical than other parts of the University. First, the Medical School was moved from San Fransisco to a new physical plant on the Stanford campus in 1962. This move was widely criticized as "Wally's Folly" (in reference to President Wallace Sterling). The School was given little chance of surviving in a non-urban setting, apart from massive, centralized hospital, laboratory, and medical facilities. To counter this criticism, the faculty and staff of the Medical School, from the first day of operation in Palo Alto, sought to institutionalize innovation as a means of raising quality and quieting criticism. This effort has resulted in a highly flexible and unorthodox curriculum, a fifth year of study that allows students to work in other areas of the university, and a faculty that is vitally concerned with the political and social life of the nation as it relates to the health and welfare of individual citizens.

The Medical School at Stanford is therefore known as an innovating institution in its graduate program as well as in the areas of medicine. Faculty and students of the School of Medicine participate in a culture far closer to the social science and humanities orientations of most graduate students than is found in other medical schools. Instead of conventional antihumanistic, antibehavirial science biases found elsewhere, the Stanford community exhibits reverse biases.

An additional factor may have been that the most "famous" student suspended was a Medical School product, and there was a strong belief within the School of Medicine that if punitive measures such as suspension were to be taken, the school should either make the decision or at least be consulted by the university administration. The anti-CIA case thus became a test case for the autonomy of the School of Medicine.

The School of Education is considered one of the finest in the country, but the fact that it still suffers from academic snobbery within the Stanford community means that its identification with university affairs is tenuous and diffuse. This situation is reflected in an absence of any consensus in the School of Education's vote. The tension between student support for the demonstrators and administrative opposition reinforced status anxiety, reflected in the fact that the School of Education had the poorest proportional attendance at the meeting.

The influence of the School of Humanities and Sciences with administration, faculty, and students has waned as that of the professional schools has risen to national eminence. Suffering from reduced levels of importance and holding firm to its traditional role as guardian of learning, the Faculty of Humanities and Sciences tended to identify with the students against the professional schools' faculty and the university administration and cast a largely positive vote on the resolution.

If part of the vote can be explained in terms of organizational and innovative patterns and special relations within the university system, the vote of the faculty also tended to be very much along classic lines of rich and poor, with the wealthy faculty—in the areas of engineering—opposing student demands, while the less well-paid but equally distinguished faculty in the humanities voted heavily on behalf of the students. Social scientists tended to cleave along department lines and exhibited little patterning. This structure may simply represent the differential positions occupied by

the social and behavioral sciences within the university hierarchy, with high-range, high-status social scientists tending
to oppose student demands and social scientists in less en-
viable positions tending to support such demands.

An alternative mode of analysis of the voting behavior of
the various faculties is possible by examining the task performance of the different schools. Here the Medical School
and the School of Education must be treated as deviant cases.
As noted before, innovation and performance have more
closely allied the Medical School with the School of Humanities and Sciences than with traditional medical schools and
professional schools in general.

Generally the professional schools are directed more toward service. Stanford's strength in this area coincides with
the recent acceptance of this dimension as a valid measure-
ment of over-all university quality. The work of the professional schools may be seen as more instrumental than that of
Humanities and Sciences; it has greater "use" or "market-
ability" for nonuniversity interests. This is where the
wage-differential model is most applicable: the work of the
professional schools — as opposed to that of Humanities and
Sciences — is more "valued" by the nonuniversity society.
There is a clearly defined reward system in society for individuals in these professions, which is monetarily greater
than that for Humanities and Sciences people. Further, the
university is only one institution among many where the
professional school faculty member can work. The Humanities and Sciences faculty member is usually more limited
in finding an institution that can utilize his skills without
demanding a radical reformation in the nature of his task.

These considerations suggest that the loyalties and values
of professional school faculty are substantially different from
those of Humanities and Sciences faculty. Professional-
school faculty, because of their service orientation, are less
concerned about ideology or the value of the university per
se. For them, the university is only an employer, and their
purpose there is completion of tasks. Thus, these persons
could be expected to respond to the sit-in as a dangerous

violation of law and order and to consider all issues and questions in terms of their consequences for the restoration of peace. If the price of this peace is such that the university is unable to function or that they are unable to work there without further disruption, if the nature of the university is radically altered by the means used to restore order, they know they can leave it. Humanities and Sciences faculty do not have this option; they have to live with the university. And because these persons are also concerned about the nature of education and other such "abstracts," they are vitally concerned with preserving harmony as well as order and are more liable to engage in critical thought that might suggest other ends or more basic issues and questions.

The overriding fact in the Stanford situation was that the suspension of the students were unequivocally set aside by the vote of the Academic Council; however this decision was read by the administration and faculty, the students perceived the results as a victory for their militants. It not only legitimated student power; it also provided semilegitimation for the tactics of the radical students—which is precisely what administration spokesmen recoiled from in horror.

In the immediate aftermath of the faculty meeting, the demonstrators in the Old Union had to make a decision. While the faculty had voted for the essence of their demands, they had no assurance that President Sterling would accept recommendations from the faculty. The students seemed unaware of how implausible the administration position had been made by the faculty vote. Not all of them were willing to acknowledge the vote as sufficient victory for them to withdraw from the building. Interestingly, H. Bruce Franklin, the most trusted faculty supporter, seemed uniquely appreciative of the magnitude of the student victory.

The discussion was spirited before the decision to leave was made by an overwhelming majority. In keeping with the tone of the faculty decision, students reached the decision quickly; by 10 P.M. Wednesday night the students had policed the Old Union and departed, bringing an end to their demonstration.

The conclusion of the sit-in did not mean that everything had been said. The stance toward the recommendations of the Committee of 15 concerning the structure of a judicial system was still a subject of debate. To continue discussion, it was agreed to hold another noon rally—this time in White Plaza—on Thursday, May 10.

The Thursday noon meeting might be considered a means by which students cooled out their demonstration and phased out their ad hoc political organization. The focus was on the Committee of 15 proposal, which met with a mixed reaction from the demonstrators but which was later endorsed by the student legislature.

In essence the Committee of 15 established a new basis of legal equity that gave both students and faculty a larger voice in the administration of student affairs than they had commanded in the past. To be sure, the administration itself may prefer this turn of events, since it often performs caretaker services in the area of student control by default rather than by desire. Among the essential points in the statement of reform of the student judicial system, the following seem most important.

First, greater equity was established between faculty and students in handling cases of student discipline, with the faculty having six members to the five of the students. Second, the Committee's proposals were not to be construed as limiting in any way the power of the Board of Trustees or the authority delegated by it to the President of the University. Third, the powers of the Dean of Students in handling cases was limited, since he would no longer be in charge of presenting evidence nor responsible for the conduct of cross-examination; thus the Dean was no longer in the position that exacerbated conditions and could lead to difficulties such as those with the anti-CIA demonstrators. Fourth, the pontifical significance of the Law faculty was limited, as was indicated by the provision that the chairman of the Stanford Judicial Council—though chosen by the President from the faculty of the Law School— would have a vote only in case of a tie. Given the degree to which the Law School is an important segment of the Stanford conservative tradition, the Committee of 15 resolution had made a major decision on this point.

The position of the students was best summed up by Eric Triesman, who pointed out, "What we have got now is nothing, but by the passage of the C-15 plan we at least have the possibility of getting what we want. Giving power to the faculty is better than leaving it in the hands of the administration."

If the Thursday student rally was ostensibly called to discuss the Committee of 15 proposals, it rapidly broadened into more generic discussions. Steve Weissman, one of the sit-in leaders, called for an escalation of confrontation politics to gain two new goals — student involvement in faculty tenure appointments and in presidential selection. "We have to take the power away from the trustees. We must demand not only that students sit in on the committee for presidential selection but that students vote in referendum on any choice of that committee." It was not clear whether Weissman's statement was intended as an immediate demand to be acted upon or whether it was an attempt to develop an organizational foothold for future struggles. He concluded by noting, "Students need confrontation politics so they will not be coopted into the consensus of decision making."

The faculty representatives at this meeting vigorously defended the Committee of 15's resolution. Professor Sanford Dornbush of the Sociology Department reviewed the state of the demands with more optimistic conclusions than did the students. He felt that it was inconceivable that President Sterling would override the Academic Council's recommendation and indicated that he doubted seriously that the President would take the CIA demonstration case back through the new procedures when and if they were established. He maintained that everybody had misread the propositions in the Committee of 15 report and then went into a discussion and a defense of the report. He argued, among other things, that the faculty wanted a faculty member to have the casting vote because they wanted decision making to remain in the hands of the faculty in case of a basic split. When questioned as to why the faculty opposed student-originating jurisdiction, he responded that students could then decide against the interests of other segments of the community and unbalance the system from their point of view.

This statement was followed by Professor Marshall's summation of the decision making process in the Committee of 15. Hubert Marshall, perhaps influenced by the general metaphysical tone of student statements, went into an analysis of three types of power that existed at Stanford: legal power, which resides in the trustees; real power, which is shared by the faculty and the administration; and residual power, which the students used when they staged the sit-in. He went on to note that, when employed, residual power can work, but that it cannot be put to use very often. He concluded pungently by noting, "You can't have the reality of power, but you can share it with the faculty." Professor Marshall never quite stated whether the power of the faculty either corresponds to or supersedes the legal power of the Board of Trustees. It is therefore not certain whether he meant to say, as his statement suggested, that the students can perhaps at best share a sense of powerlessness with the faculty.

The sharpest attack on the proposed new legal structure came, appropriately enough, from Tim Haight; having resigned both from the Armed Forces and the university the previous day, he was not about to accept any palliatives. "We're still not equal, just like the black people. The C-15 plans maintain the status quo and we will not get our kind of power unless rational discussion allows us to be equal. It is either this or the streets." The final speaker, H. Bruce Franklin, in effect abandoned the theme of the Committee of 15 recommendations entirely and sought to refocus the issue as one of relating the university to the broader masses in the outside world. Franklin put the issue most directly: the struggle of the students was only a part of larger struggles in society; it was the job of the students to take up those larger issues and to come to grips with them.

At the end of the Thursday meeting the campus returned to normal except for a brief shock wave created by a semi-public speech by Herbert Packer, Vice-Provost of the University. Professor Packer, who is Professor of Law, had been invited to address the annual meeting of the Stanford chapter of the American Association of University Professors on May 13. This invitation had preceded the Stanford events, but Packer's address focused exclusively on the demonstration, with a bitter attack upon the faculty members who supported the Holman Resolution. Coming as it did, as the campus began to settle into the end-of-semester routine, his address opened a number of wounds. Vice-Provost Packer hurriedly appended a letter to his address suggesting that he had perhaps been carried away by events. The issue simmered heatedly but quietly for several days and then faded away.

The aftermath of the letter revealed, however, that while the niceties of everyday functioning called for faculty and administration to recreate the the status quo ante, serious damage had been done to the normative climate of the university by the demonstration, the administration's handling of events, and the faculty meeting. As the term drew to a close, the predictions of members of the faculty that President Sterling would not indeed sustain the suspensions of the original seven students came true. This victory for the militants could only serve as an object lesson: "reason" and "discussion" had not won the day. The regrettable fact was that confrontation had demonstrated the moral position of the students with respect not only to the original issue but, more significantly, to the involvement of students in university decision making.

The Trade Unionization of the Student Seventies*

Consider, first, this press report, datelined Madison, Wisconsin:

"A wholly new chapter in the annals of American university politics was formally inscribed here . . . After a year of negotiations and a 24-day strike, the University of Wisconsin's Madison campus signed a labour contract with the Teaching Assistants' Association (TAA), a local labor union of graduate students who are paid for part-time teaching and research assistance at the university. The contract not only covered various bread-and-butter issues traditional in labor-management bargaining but also granted, in a fuzzy fashion, the right of students and teaching assistants to participate in planning the educational courses in which they are involved.

"The Wisconsin strike was fundamentally different from other student manifestations of recent years. The organizers, as teaching assistants, were not only students but workers as well, with an economic weapon. By staying out of the class-

*Reprinted with permission of the author, Irving Louis Horowitz, and the publisher. This article first appeared in *New Society*, Vol. 16, No. 406, 9 July, 1970.

room they were able to prevent instruction in many courses. As workers, they availed themselves of the traditional collective bargaining process to present their demands to the university. But their demands went beyond the traditional economic aims of American trade unionism to embrace policy and power issues that have motivated other student strikes across the country. The strike leaders claimed, in effect, the right to speak for undergraduate students as well as for their own constituency in bargaining on such issues.

"Although neither side could claim a smashing victory in the settlement, the contract clearly altered the university's power structure by acknowledging the TAA as a force to be reckoned with in the formulation of educational policy at Wisconsin. And the potential exists for a similar movement at every university across the country that relies on graduate students to help teach courses and grade papers. One of the TAA's leaders in bargaining with the university, James Marketti (a graduate student in industrial relations) said shortly before settlement that his union had been contacted by teaching assistant organizations or by individuals from '50 to 60' campuses during the course of the strike."

This press report, along with other developments, shows that phase one of the American student revolution has been completed. The right of students to be treated as human beings (or equivalents thereof), their right to citizen participation, and their participation in the legal definition of the structure and substance of university life, have all been won in hard-fought and sometimes tragic battles from California to Columbia. But it is clear that active student protest has entered a new phase, or at least that the old phase is over, leaving many student leaders and organizations in something of a quandary as to what to do next.

In the interim, there has been intensified interest in environment—air and water pollution and overpopulation. This is a perfect hiatus issue. Like cleanliness and godliness, the ecological issue is one that both excites personal passions (momentarily) and unites the different publics. It also provides the perfect format for liberals without becoming as "political" as the polarised extremisms we have all passed

through in the United States between 1960 and 1969. But as
the environment/ecology movement passes into the province
of civics—with a declining political pay-off—the issue is
bound to leave the student and youth populations somewhat
indifferent, if not entirely cold.

Phase two of the American student revolution is now beginning. The stage is set for economics and administration.
This takes place in two aspects of college and university life:
the academic and the administrative.

The political and social legitimation of student power has
translated itself, more by accident than by design, into the
right of students to determine the contents and even the
types of courses they are offered. The impulse towards independent study and student-designed courses—from the
history of the women's rights movement to sensitivity training classes—has taken on large proportions. At the moment,
such courses are being treated as cream-puff offerings that are
supposed to pacify student rebels.

Sometimes student participants in such courses are given
standard college credits. Their student leaders are, by implication, granted academic accreditation and legitimation.
There is also a nominal faculty representative who ostensibly
supervises—but really rubber-stamps—such student-taught
and student-directed courses. Whatever the arguments for or
against the quality of such course offerings, it can hardly be
denied that they are rapidly being institutionalised on American campuses.

Similarly, phase one of the student revolution transformed
the legal relations that obtained on American campuses. And
this has had large-scale administrative consequences. Students participate in everything from the board of trustees at
Princeton to key financial committees and alumni fund-
raising groups on other campuses. Students also now
participate extensively in setting up degree requirements for
graduate and undergraduate schools; they help design curriculum programs, select faculty promotion and tenure, and
even serve on search committees for new university presidents and provosts.

So far so good. But while everyone has been con-
gratulating themselves and each other on "cooling out" the

rebellion of the sixties, a whole cluster of new issues and problems have been created that have thus far strangely not received public attention.

A situation could evolve in which professors and instructors have sharply depleted course enrollments while student courses absorb most of the potential enrollment (with student-designed "independent reading courses" absorbing the remainder). The teacher hired as such receives a stipend for his role rather than his performance. He is paid *as if* he were teaching, not *for* teaching. Students, in the meantime, are given credits as if they were students, rather than being paid for what they are in fact doing—teaching.

This embarrassment could be exacerbated by the fact that "teaching assistants"—who are usually working on Ph.D. theses—do receive a modest stipend for their teaching activities. As students themselves, they serve as a model for the new pattern of student-run courses. But there is an equally finite limit on the amount of money available for teaching activities. An active student struggle over payment for teaching courses could produce a struggle between student and faculty representatives that would produce a far graver crisis than that of the previous decade of struggle between students and administrators.

But lest the administrative wing of the university breathe a premature sigh of relief, it is likely that the struggle will remain in force at this level. For example, the definition of research contracts and grants between Massachusetts Institute of Technology and the Department of Defence was made by students in conjunction with university officials. Thus, even if students are not especially keen about being paid for their administrative duties (at present at any rate), they are very much involved in university finances.

I am not suggesting that we should, or even could, go back to a more pristine period in educational history, when administrators, professors and students all knew their respective places, and functioned within the recognized limits of their roles. I am suggesting that this new situation is creating the groundwork for an educated proletariat that has many of the characteristics of the working class and yet many of the ambitions of higher classes.

It is a problem all the way around. After all, it is far easier for university officials to grant students the right to participate in tenure hearings and the design of courses than it would be to pay students for engaging in such "extra-curricular" activities. Yet it seems hard to imagine that the political victories of the sixties won't be translated into the economic struggles of the seventies. For, beyond the redefinition of legitimation, must come a redivision of campus wealth. It is at this level that phase two of the campus revolution will become transformed into a higher stage of confrontation as such.

It comes down to a simple fact; students are the only members of the American academic community who are not paid for the work that they perform.

This is precisely what must change in the seventies. Students who prepare and teach courses will want wages and salaries; students who serve in administrative review boards will not be content with anything less than a negotiated payment for work performed. And this will lead to the creation of a new type of student consciousness, much closer to the trade union consciousness of the "proletarian thirties" than to the radical marginality of the "generalizational sixties." A form of economism will arise in the student movement that will give students a class orientation thus far foreign to them.

A major structural reinforcement for this bread-and-butter phase of the student movement is the growing influx of blue-collar and black youths who have a major stake in vocational orientation, and who see their "liberation" as taking place not within, but outside university life (and after graduation). These youngsters, infused as they are with the American Dream of upward mobility through education, are hardly likely to accept the middle class rebellion against middle class value and affluent parents. On the other hand, they are hardly likely to ignore the key lessons of the past: the confrontation with authorities brings results. Thus, economism is not exclusively a consequence of political legitimation but, equally important, of continued class mobility within American society.

This will entail a conservatizing factor not now realized by the forces that will be called on to yield to student economic demands. For students whose *salaries* depend on "soft money" federal grants, might prove less intransigent about their opposition to federally sponsored research activities. Already the credit crunch has spilled over into an educational crunch. While federal support levels for science and education are markedly decreasing (interestingly, more in the "hard" sciences than in the behavioral "soft" sciences), the number of American graduate students who complete their degree requirements is increasing. There are strong signs that a proletarianized Ph.D. is being created for the first time since the depression years. And this, too, can't help but focus attention on the economic requirements of being a student.

Another positive payoff is for the faculty. Students who teach courses and are responsible for designing them can be expected to have a greater appreciation and better understanding of the role of the beleaguered faculty member.

Canons of scholarship will emerge that will change the nature of classroom performance and participation. And this situation in turn will alter traditional alignments and animosities between students and faculty. They will function together, rather than antithetically, at the key levels of organizing information and gaining financial rewards, for work done in common, or at least on common problems.

The trade union ideology may well be expected to act to conservatize the student revolution. But it will do much more than that. It will serve to restore the university to its original purpose with greater force than any previous student activity. The university will become much more of a community of scholars than ever before in United States educational history, because the critical barrier of who pays and who gets paid at a university will finally be resolved.

With so much of American higher education state and federally controlled, the struggles for higher wages and joint professional identity will require a solid phalanx of university community support. Faculty and administrators will have many tactical reasons to form common fronts with students in the struggle against higher bureaucratic and political chieftains opposed to expanding higher education.

In short, the legacy of the American campus revolts of the sixties, will be the re-definition of the campus in the seventies in much greater trade union and strict economic terms. The rainbow in this cloud is that such redefinition, far from adding to the destruction of the university, will in fact restore it to its original purpose—a search for equity through wisdom, rather than distinction through degrees.

Bibliography

Ariès, P. Centuries of Childhood. New York: Random House, 1962.

Avorn, Jerry L., et. al. Up Against the Ivy Wall: A History of the Columbia Crisis. New York: Atheneum, 1969.

Becker, Howard S. "Student Culture as an Element in the Progress of University Change," in R. J. Ingram (ed.) Institutional Background of Adult Education. Boston: Center for the Study of Liberal Education for Adults, Boston University, 1966, pp. 59–80.

Becker, Howard S., Blanche Geer, Everett Hughes. Making The Grade: The Academic Side of College Life. New York: John Wiley, 1968.

Brookover, W. B., et. al. The College Student. New York: The Center for Applied Research in Education, 1965.

Brownmiller, Susan. "Up From Silence: Cornell Then and Now—Pantie Raids to Guerilla Theatre," Esquire, No. 424 (March 1969), pp. 100–101, 104, 141–150.

Center for the Study of Democratic Institutions. "Students and Society," A Center Occasional Paper, Vol. 1, No. 1, 1967.

Cohn-Bendit, Daniel. et. al. The French Student Revolt. New York: Hill and Wang, 1968.

Cox, Archibald, et. al. Crisis at Columbia: Report of the Fact-Finding Commission Appointed to Investigate the Disturbances at Columbia University in April and May 1968. New York: Vintage, 1968.

343

Davis, Kingsley. "The Sociology of Parent-Youth Conflict," *American Sociological Review*, Vol. 5, August 1940, pp. 523–535.

————. "Adolescence and the Social Structure," *Annals of the American Academy of Political and Social Sciences*, November 1944, pp. 8–16.

Doebler, Charles H. *Who Gets Into College—And Why*. New York: McFadden, 1963.

Draper, Hal. *Berkeley: The New Student Revolt*. New York: Grove, 1965.

Eisen, Jonathan. "Coming of Age: The Legacy of Protest," in Cohn & Hale (eds.), *The New Student Left*. Boston: Beacon Press, 1966, pp. 27–33.

Eisenstadt, S. N. *From Generation to Generation*. New York: The Free Press, 1956.

Erikson, E. *Identity: Youth and Crisis*. New York: Norton, 1968.

Etzioni, Amitai. "Mobilization as a Macro-sociological Conception," *British Journal of Sociology*, Vol. 19, No. 3 (September 1968), pp. 243–253.

Evans, M. S. *Revolt on Campus*. Chicago: Henry Regnery, 1961.

Feuer, Lewis. *The Conflict of Generations*. New York: Basic Books, 1969.

Flacks, Richard. "The Liberated Generation: An Exploration of the Roots of Student Protest," *Journal of Social Issues*, Vol. 23, No. 3, 1967, pp. 52–75.

Friedland, William H., and Harry Edwards. "Confrontation at Cornell," *Trans-action*, Vol. 6, No. 7 (June 1969), pp. 29–36, 76.

Gottlieb, D., and C. E. Ramsey. *The American Adolescent*. Homewood, Illinois: Dorsey Press, 1964.

Gottlieb, D., and J. Reeves. *Adolescent Behavior in Urban Areas*. East Lansing: Michigan State University, College of Education, 1962.

Gottlieb, D., J. Reeves, W. D. Ten Houten. *The Emergence of Youth Societies*. New York: Free Press, 1966.

Hayden, Thomas, and C. Reinier. "A Letter to the New (Young) Left," in Mitchell Cohen (ed.), *The New Student*.

Boston: Beacon Press, 1966, pp. 2–8.

_____. "Port Huron Statement (Students for a Democratic Society)," *Ibid.*, pp. 9–16.

Heist, Paul. "Intellect and Commitment: The Faces of Discontent." Berkeley, Center for the Study of Higher Education, 1965, cited by Christian Bay, "Political and Apolitical Students: Facts in Search of a Theory," *Journal of Social Issues*, Vol. 23, No. 3 (July 1967), pp. 76–91.

Horowitz, Irving Louis. "Young Radicals and Their Professional Critics," *Commonweal*, Vol. 89, No. 17 (January 31, 1969), pp. 552–556.

_____. "Radical Irrationalism: Then and Now," *Radicalism and the Revolt Against Reason.* Carbondale, Illinois: Southern Illinois University Press, 1968.

_____. "The Student Proletariat," *New Society*, Vol. 16, No. 406 (July 8, 1970), pp. 70–73.

Horowitz, Irving Louis, and Martin Liebowitz. "Social Deviance and Political Marginality," *Social Problems*, Vol. 15, No. 3 (Winter 1968), pp. 280–296.

Jacobs, P., and S. Landau. *The New Radicals.* New York: Vintage Books, 1966.

Jenks, Christopher, and David Reisman. *The Academic Revolution.* Garden City, New York: Doubleday, 1968.

Katope, C.G., and P.G. Zolbrod (eds.), *Beyond Berkeley.* Cleveland: World, 1966.

Katz, Joseph, and Nevitt Sanford. "The Student Revolution," *Current*, February 1966, pp. 6–10.

Kenniston, Kenneth. *Young Radicals: Notes on Committed Youth.* New York: Harcourt, Brace and World, 1968.

Kissinger, C. Clark. "The Bruns Strike: A Case Study in Student Participation in Labor," in Cohn & Hale (eds.), *The New Student Left.* Boston: Beacon Press, 1966, pp. 114–120.

Landis, Paul. *Adolescence and Youth.* New York: McGraw-Hill, 1952, 2nd Edition.

Lipset, Seymour Martin. "The Activists: A Profile," *The Public Interest*, No. 13 (Fall 1968), pp. 39–52.

_____. "Students and Politics in Comparative Perspective," *Daedalus*, Vol. 97, No. 1 (Winter 1968), pp. 1–20.

————. "Student Opposition in the United States," *Government and Opposition,* Vol. 1, No. 3 (April 1966), pp. 351–374.

————. *Student Politics.* New York: Basic Books, 1967.

Lipset, Seymour Martin, and Sheldon Wolin. *The Berkeley Student Rebellion.* New York: Doubleday, 1965.

Lorber, R., and E. Fladell. *The Gap.* New York: McGraw-Hill, 1968.

Lubell, Samuel. "That Generation Gap," *The Public Interest.* No. 13 (Fall 1968), pp. 52–60.

Luce, Phillip A. *The New Left.* New York: McKay Publishers, 1966.

————. "Red Diaper Babies," *The New Guard,* September 1965, pp. 6–12.

Lyonns, Glen. "The Police Car Demonstration: A Survey of Participants," in Lipset & Wolin (eds.), *The Berkeley Student Revolt.* Garden City, New York: Anchor-Doubleday, 1965, pp. 519–530.

Mannheim, Karl. "Conservative Thought," in *Essays on Sociology and Social Psychology* New York: Oxford University Press, 1953.

————. "The Problem of Generations," *Essays on the Sociology of Knowledge.* New York: Oxford University Press, 1952.

————. "The Problem of Youth in Modern Society," in *Diagnosis of Our Time.* New York: Oxford University Press, 1944.

Newfield, Jack. *A Prophetic Minority.* New York: Signet Books, 1967.

Payne, Bruce. "Quiet War," in Cohen & Mitchell (eds.), *The New Student Left,* pp. 50–58.

Report of the National Advisory Commission on Civil Disorders. New York: Bantam Books, 1968.

Rogers, D. *The Psychology of Adolescence.* New York: Appleton-Century-Crofts, 1962.

Rudd, Mark. "Symbols of the Revolution," in J. L. Avorn *et. al., Up Against the Ivy Wall.* New York: Atheneum, 1968.

Sebald, H. *Adolescence.* New York: Appleton-Century-Crofts, 1968.

Seligman, Daniel. "A Special Kind of Rebellion," *Fortune*, Vol. 74, No. 1 (January 1969), pp. 66–69, 172–175.

Somers, Robert H. "The Mainsprings of the Rebellion" in Lipset & Wolin (eds.), *The Berkeley Student Revolt*. New York: Doubleday, 1965, pp. 530–557.

Solomon, Fredric, and Jacob R. Fishman. "Youth and Peace: A Psychological Study of Student Peace Demonstrators in Washington, D. C.," *Journal of Social Issues*, Vol. 20, No. 4. (October 1964), pp. 54–74.

Sorokin, Pitirim. "Social Differentiation," *International Encylopedia of the Social Sciences*, Vol. 14. New York: MacMillan, 1968, pp. 406–409.

"Student Protests: A Phenomenon for Behavioral Sciences Research," *Science*. July 5, 1968, pp. 20–23.

Tarcov, Nathan. "The Last Four Years at Cornell," *The Public Interest*, No. 13 (Fall 1968), pp. 122–139.

U.S. Bureau of Census. *Statistical Abstracts of the U.S.: 1968 (89th edition)*, p. 216.

Name Index

Subject Index

DATE DUE

GAYLORD			PRINTED IN U.S.A.